Krishna's Song

Krishna's Song

A New Look at the Bhagavad Gita

Steven J. Rosen

Westport, Connecticut
London

Library of Congress Cataloging-in-Publication Data

Rosen, Steven, 1955–
Krishna's Song : a new look at the Bhagavad Gita / Steven J. Rosen.
    p. cm.
   Includes bibliographical references and index.
   ISBN 978–0–313–34553–1 (alk. paper)
   1. Bhagavadgita–Criticism, interpretation, etc.   I. Title.
 BL1138.66.R68   2007
 294.5′624–dc22   2007027871

British Library Cataloguing in Publication Data is available.

Library of Congress Catalog Card Number: 2007027871
ISBN: 978–0–313–34553–1

First published in 2007

Praeger Publishers, 88 Post Road West, Westport, CT 06881
An imprint of Greenwood Publishing Group, Inc.
www.praeger.com

Printed in the United States of America

The paper used in this book complies with the
Permanent Paper Standard issued by the National
Information Standards Organization (Z39.48–1984).

10 9 8 7 6 5 4 3 2 1

Cover Image: Taken from an illuminated manuscript of the seventeenth century, a rajput king is here
offering obeisance to Krishna. Though not a scene from the Bhagavad Gita, the king's presence evokes
Krishna's four-armed Vishnu manifestation, including the mood of awe and reverence found in the
Gita's pages. Still, the presence of the cows and the gopis, or cowherd maidens, suggest the philosophical
conclusions of the Gaudiya Vaishnavas, which is indeed the emphasis of the current work and harkens
to the real inner meaning of the text.

To Sri Guru Parampara,
without whom the Bhagavad Gita would be lost forever

Contents

CONTENTS

Introduction

Of the sacred books of the Hindus, the Bhagavad Gita is the most widely read and probably the most important text for the understanding of Eastern mysticism.
—R. C. Zaehner (University of Oxford)

As the twenty-first century forges ahead, Bhagavad Gita translations are many. This year alone, several new editions will seize the market, each with its own particular slant and emphasis. Recent breakthroughs in the scholarly study of Sanskrit will allow these works to offer something unique, no doubt, and our bookshelves will support yet more attractive editions of this classic work.

But will our understanding of the Gita be enhanced in a commensurate way? The words of the text might be illuminated in previously unexplored fashion, and commentary and footnotes might make our foray into its ancient pages a bit more enlightening, which is certainly valuable on numerous levels. But what about our overall understanding of the Gita?

What *Krishna's Song: A New Look at the Bhagavad Gita* seeks to do—perhaps in contrast to the above-mentioned endeavors—is to make the Gita more comfortable, more approachable. Rather than merely reiterating what the Gita itself has to say—although this book will certainly do much of that—my primary task, as I see it, is to "culturally translate" the text, to render it in a language that makes it understandable to a contemporary Western audience. I use concepts and categories with which my audience is accustomed.

By engaging familiar motifs—issues of modernity, pop culture icons, and well-known philosophers in the West—I hope to bring the Gita into focus for non-specialists, especially. To accomplish this end, I refer to the likes of Plato, Gandhi, Kierkegaard, Dante, and Jesus, along with Robert Redford, Allen Ginsberg, George Lucas, Star Wars, the Beatles, the Brooklyn Botanical Garden, a contemporary golf novel, and other easily identifiable people and phenomena from modern times. Although I begin with a few introductory articles that might seem like ordinary summaries—just to give the reader some background, some preliminary information on the text—I quickly adopt this strategy of explaining the Gita in a user-friendly way.

To further accomplish this end of accessibility, the present book is a compilation of informal talks, short essays, and elaborate analyses I've written over the years. They are stand-alone pieces of prose, and while this makes for easy reading, it might also at times lead to redundancy: brief synopses of the Gita, its main characters and its essential philosophy, will be repeated in a number of these articles. Still, with nuances of difference, the repetition itself starts to act as an aid, affording readers increased familiarity with the facts and personalities that make up the Gita.

Some of the articles are necessarily scholarly and in-depth, giving background on the text and exploring philosophical and historical details that one might not find in the average Gita translation. The other essays are short, layman oriented, and easily accessible. Overall, the book seeks to explain key concepts of the Gita—such as *karma* (action and reaction), reincarnation, violence and religion, social stratification, psychological empowerment, and the nature of God—almost inadvertently, by engaging aspects of everyday life. The net result should be a broad understanding of the text and its context, as well as its practical relevance for people today.

WHAT IS THE BHAGAVAD GITA?

The words Bhagavad Gita mean "The Song of the Beloved Lord." As a philosophical poem, the Gita is indeed a song—it is Krishna's song. And it is sung first for the benefit of Arjuna, the archer-warrior who is Krishna's devotee on the ancient battlefield of Kurukshetra, and then for all living beings who might follow in Arjuna's footsteps.

There are more such people than one might think. After all, in a sense, Arjuna is not unlike you or I, for the archer's dilemma—in one way or another—haunts us all. We must be spiritual warriors on the battlefield of life. Arjuna faces his demons on an actual battlefield, where he must choose between giving in to temptation and doing the right thing, between running away and doing his duty. In a larger sense, we must all make such decisions. We must choose between selfishness and generosity, dishonesty and integrity.

Like Arjuna, our outer conflict is necessarily accompanied by inner conflict. The Gita is thus replete with depth psychology and advice on ideal social behavior, with strategies involving conflict resolution and the agenda of transformation. In short, the Gita shows us how Arjuna resolves his problem by employing certain methods of practice, which lead him to inner peace. We, too, can find such peace, and that by engaging these same techniques, for, again, Arjuna's problems are very much like our own.

As Krishna—God Incarnate, who is acting as Arjuna's charioteer—pulls the mighty bowman's two-wheeled vehicle in between both armies, ready for battle, they are witness to legions of generals, statesmen, armed battalions, and the paraphernalia of war. And there, Arjuna sees it: Teachers, friends, and even relatives are among the opposing troops. He is overcome with grief, his body giving way to despair. What is he to do?

He is committed to two kinds of duties, or *dharma*. He is a Kshatriya, or a warrior, sworn to protect the innocent. So he must uphold Kshatriya-*dharma*. But he is also a principled man of his day, and so Kula-*dharma*, or duty to family, is also held in high esteem. Here, it seems, is his dilemma: He must choose between one or the other. With family in the rival armies, ready to take his life, he is put in an impossible situation. He is in the ultimate bind.

In this state of confusion, he asks Krishna what he should do. The Gita, of course, is Krishna's answer to this question. In the pages that follow, we learn the details of this answer, as well as Krishna's identity as God Incarnate. In the process, we discover who we really are and how to navigate life's mysterious journey.

SOME BACKGROUND ON THE GITA

Although widely published and read as a separate text, the Bhagavad Gita originally appears as an episode in the Sixth Book of the *Mahabharata* (*Bhishma-parva*, chapters 23–40), one of India's great epics and the longest poem in world literature, consisting, as it does, of 110,000 Sanskrit couplets. The Gita itself consists of 700 verses in eighteen chapters and is often referred to as the "*Gitopanishad*," in that it follows the style and philosophical conclusions of the Upanishads.

The connection to the Upanishads is not insignificant. Traditionally, the Gita is identified with *smriti* ("that which is remembered"), a category of sacred texts that is considered secondary to the *Vedas*, which are known as *shruti* ("that which is heard"). However, the Upanishads are part of the Vedic canon, and so the Gita is often considered *shruti* as well, giving it Vedic status. The Gita's traditional colophons, too, affirm its Upanishadic identity. Moreover, in India, even today, certain classes of society are often barred from hearing sections of the *Mahabharata*, including the Gita, a phenomenon that is peculiar to Vedic studies.[1] All of this serves to underline the Gita's high standing among India's sacred literature.

But the *smriti* component is important as well. Though most Sanskritists would say that *smriti* refers to truths "remembered" by the sages and then passed down to modern students, the seers themselves understood the word in yet another way: The sounds and mantras found in *smriti* literature touch something deep in the soul—*they awaken memory*, igniting realizations that are already encoded in the very fabric of our being. They spark distant recollections of our original life in the spiritual realm. Whether or not one chooses to believe this, the study of the Gita seems to have just such an effect on many souls who read it. They recite its verses—as countless people have done for millennia—and feel deep inspiration, as though they are being reminded of something they have long forgotten.

That being said, there are numerous questions concerning the text's authorship, date, and provenance. To cite the tradition: the divinely inspired bard Veda Vyasa wrote it as part of the *Mahabharata* some 5,000 years ago while in his hermitage in the Himalayas. But it is a bit more complicated than that, especially for modern scholars. First, they question whether Vyasa was one person or numerous authors, editors, and redactors. Second, they wonder whether it started as a smaller text in the pre-Christian Era and was added to over time, beginning, say, in 300 BCE and finishing in 300 CE. One can find any number of variations on these dates. Third, scholars tend to question whether the Gita was originally part of the *Mahabharata* at all, or was simply inserted at a later date. While such concerns occupy the minds of specialists in Hindu studies and Indology, they are more or less nonquestions for believers, who have their own internal evidences for the traditional view, as cited above.

However one chooses to answer these questions, the Gita's depth of wisdom is indisputable and it has inspired numerous commentaries throughout the centuries; the book is said to be the most commented upon scripture in the religious history of man. In India, practically every major teacher, dating back to antiquity, has contributed his or her own commentary on it. And the *Mahabharata* has its own built-in explanation of the text as well, since Book Fourteen includes a summarization of the Gita's contents (called the *Anugita*).

Long-established Vaishnava texts, such as the *Varaha Purana* and the *Padma Purana*, include *Gitamahatmyas* ("verses glorifying the Gita"), which are used by all schools of Indian thought. Vaishnavism is a monotheistic religion—often considered a branch of Hinduism—that focuses on Vishnu, or Krishna, as Supreme Lord, and it bases its teachings on the Bhagavad Gita.

In the seventh and eighth centuries CE, teachers of the non-Vaishnava impersonalist school, too, contributed to the storehouse of Gita exposition. Stalwarts such as Bhaskara and Shankara, for example, wrote what are now considered classic Gita commentaries, though such works lack the personalistic insights of the Vaishnavas. Most important, in this respect, are the many highly theistic commentaries that followed, particularly that of His Divine Grace A. C. Bhaktivedanta Swami Prabhupada (1896–1977), the founder and spiritual preceptor of the International Society for Krishna Consciousness, whose English edition was first released just over forty years ago.

And while we're on the subject of English translations, the Gita's journey to Western shores is covered in this book with some detail. In fact, after the Gita was translated into English for the first time—by Charles Wilkins in 1785—its popularity began to soar outside India. Intellectuals among the Germans (Schlegel, Deussen, and Schopenhauer), Americans (Emerson and Thoreau), Englishmen (Max Mueller, who was English by adoption, and Aldous Huxley), Frenchmen (Romain Rolland), and Russians (Tolstoy) were greatly intrigued by the Gita's message. This message continues to be expounded upon even today, in many ways due to Prabhupada's efforts.

But there are other notable English renditions of the Gita, too, and as 2007 moves into 2008, three of them stand out as particularly significant: I speak of the work of Laurie Patton (Penguin), Graham Schweig (Harper), and Steven Tsoukalas (Edwin Mellon Press). Patton looks for Vedic resonances in her beautifully flowing poetic translation; Schweig digs deeply into the original Sanskrit to reveal hitherto unknown truths of the Gita's inner message; and Tsoukalas's multivolume version draws on traditional commentators as well as more popular contemporary editions. The book of essays you now hold in your hands will go well with each of these translations, and with many others as well. In short, it can serve as a companion volume to any Gita translation or stand on its own as a book that summarizes this sacred text's many teachings.

HOW I DISCOVERED THE GITA

My personal interaction with the Gita might be of interest here. As you will see, my relationship to the text is not only academic but also as a practitioner.

In 1969, my first year at New York's High School of Art and Design, I happened upon a copy of a battered Penguin paperback—it was the Bhagavad Gita. As I eagerly entered its pages, I found its colorful, exotic language extremely alluring, even if I was unable to fully penetrate its cryptic meaning. Somehow, I appreciated that it espoused some sort of spiritual philosophy and that it presented a mystical worldview.

I decided to look up "Bhagavad Gita" in *Webster's Unabridged Dictionary*: "A philosophical poem relating a discourse between Krishna (God) and a warrior, Arjuna; it is a sacred Hindu text." Soon, my fascination transformed into obsession, and I started to collect various editions of the Gita, anxious to see how its many translations differed from one another.

Throughout my high school years I rummaged through old bookstores, looking for direct translations, related publications, and obscure adaptations. Some emphasized the text's poetic nature, while others conveyed the message in straight prose. Most offered something special, and others did not. In any case, the Gita, for me, was a book of inscrutable wisdom, of contradictory truths. Was it, for instance, a glorification of war, or a treatise on nonviolence? Was it allegory, or was it to be taken literally? And what, overall, was it trying to say?

Although my friends and I were reading Hesse, Castaneda, Buber, Tillich, Watts, Suzuki, and many other popular thinkers of the time, I maintained a special interest in the Gita that lasted all through high school.

Then, during my senior year, I picked up a copy of *Bhagavad Gita As It Is*, by His Divine Grace A. C. Bhaktivedanta Swami Prabhupada, mentioned above. Here was a refreshing change. Prabhupada did not explain the Gita in a metaphorical or analogical way. His approach was literal, giving the essential message of each text according to the ancient Vaishnava tradition.

This altered not only my approach to the Gita but also the way in which I lived.

Although, to me, it sometimes feels like I was introduced to Prabhupada's Gita only yesterday, it was almost forty years ago. I was on the train—the New York subway system—on my way home from school. Struggling for comfort in my cold seat, I was surrounded by the conductor's door, which was marked by grotesque graffiti, and a bewildered looking immigrant couple, staring at me as though fearing for their lives. There I sat, reading a popular translation of the Bhagavad Gita, trying to make sense of life. Just then, a Hare Krishna devotee—resplendent in dayglow orange—approached, standing right next to me. He was asking for donations, and he was selling, of all things, the Bhagavad Gita.

I'll remember that devotee's opening words for the rest of my life: "You're reading poison!" He had my attention.

"The Gita is as pure as milk," he continued, "but even milk becomes poisonous when touched by the lips of a serpent." I could understand that he was criticizing the particular translation I was reading. In fact, I had misgivings about this edition myself, as only the first six chapters were translated. Why would the translator leave out the remaining twelve? Agreeing with the devotee that something was amiss, I accepted a copy of *Bhagavad Gita As It Is*, which he gave me without charge.

Prabhupada's Gita was a revelation. Unlike other editions, it provided me with a clear understanding of the book's essential message, along with an unabashed appraisal of Krishna's identity as the "Supreme Personality of Godhead." Remember, I had read numerous editions of the Gita by this point, but I still couldn't figure out what it was trying to say. Now, with Prabhupada's help, the Gita's clear and almost simple message became apparent: surrender unto Krishna, God, with love and devotion. Other translators and commentators seemed to miss this fundamental point.

I am not suggesting that there aren't many good editions out there. In terms of Sanskrit or literal accuracy—there are dozens of valuable renditions worldwide. In some ways, depending on what a person wants to get out of the text, these editions might even be more valuable than Prabhupada's. And yet, Prabhupada seemed to capture something essential—he gives the devotional component of the Gita, which, of course, is its very heart. In fact, years later, Robert Minor, who is renowned throughout the world as a prominent Gita expert, told me in a personal conversation that, "Prabhupada's Gita probably comes closest to the intent of the original author." High praise from someone who has really studied the subject.

But back then, I wanted to be certain. And after I enrolled in Queens College that fall to take a course in Sanskrit, I would be able to compare translations for myself, which I did. I walked away with new appreciation for Prabhupada's accomplishments.

I learned that while some scholars view his Gita as idiosyncratic, in the sense that it emphasizes *bhakti*, or devotion to Krishna, as the ultimate goal of life, most nonetheless admit that it accurately represents the Vaishnava point of view, which speaks for the majority of Hindus today. Some scholars even praised his work as a definitive edition, for it is read and accepted by practitioners as a legitimate reading of the text. His books, I learned, were in 75 percent of America's college and university libraries and were sometimes used as course material and supplementary reading in philosophy, religion, literature, and Asian Studies courses.

Dr. Rasik Vihari Joshi, then chairman of the Department of Sanskrit at the University of Delhi, said, "Indian religion and Indology will both forever remain indebted to Srila Prabhupada for making Vaishnava thought and philosophy available around the world through his translations of and commentaries on *Bhagavad Gita* and *Srimad-Bhagavatam*. Words fail to express my joy and appreciation for these excellent editions." Similarly, Dr. Samuel D. Atkins, Professor of Sanskrit at Princeton University, wrote, "I am most impressed with A. C. Bhaktivedanta Swami Prabhupada's scholarly and authoritative edition of *Bhagavad Gita*. It is a most valuable work for the scholar as well as the layman and of great utility as a reference book as well as a textbook."

Why Prabhupada entitled his edition *Bhagavad Gita As It Is* becomes clear when one reads Lord Krishna's statement in the beginning of the Fourth Chapter. Regarding Arjuna's qualification for receiving the teachings of the Gita, Krishna explains that it is not because Arjuna is a great *yogi,* ascetic, or scholar. Rather, Krishna said, it is "because you are My devotee and My friend; therefore you can understand the transcendental mystery of this science" (4.3). In the prior verse, Krishna says that the Gita can be understood only by those who adhere to one of several authorized lineages; such adherence is known as *parampara,* or disciplic succession. Of the four well-known successions recognized by the Vaishnava tradition, the line associated with Lord Brahma and Chaitanya Mahaprabhu (1486–1533) is flourishing, with Prabhupada as the thirty-second teacher in that line; his students are carrying on the message even today.

This hearkens back to the devotee's rather dramatic statement, "You're reading poison!" Though apparently provincial, he was simply referring to this idea of disciplic succession. According to the Bhagavad Gita, spiritual truths reach the most sincere students by a descending process, from the scriptures themselves, the great sages, and through a genuine and qualified spiritual teacher, who acts as a guide on the path of devotion. Thus, the real import of the text is not to be had through learning Sanskrit, or realized by incessant philosophical wrangling. Nor is it to be captured by a dazzling display of sophisticated hermeneutics. Rather, its mysteries are revealed by offering a loving heart to Krishna and His purest representatives in disciplic succession. This is implicit in the Gita itself and in Prabhupada's reading of the text.

Interestingly, before the release of Prabhupada's edition, few Westerners had become devotees of Krishna. And this is quite strange, since Krishna makes it completely clear in the Gita that becoming His devotee is the goal to which the text hopes to bring its readers: "Always think of Me and become My devotee. Worship Me and offer your homage unto Me. Thus you will come to Me without fail. I promise you this because you are My very dear friend" (18.65).

In this way, by 1973, I had found what, for me, was to become the definitive Bhagavad Gita, and I was convinced that Srila Prabhupada, both personally and through his books, would guide me to unravel the mystery of the text once and for all. Along the way, I found many other important editions as well, and numerous studies, such as those mentioned by Jagdish Chander Kapoor,[2] inform my understanding and appreciation of Lord Krishna's sacred words. But Prabhupada's version will always remain my guiding light, and it stands at the basis of what you'll find in the following pages.

NOTES

1. For an interesting discussion of the Gita's "Vedic status," see Catherine A. Robinson, *Interpretations of the Bhagavad Gita and Images of the Hindu Tradition* (London: Routledge, 2006), p. 4.

2. Jagdish Chander Kapoor, *Bhagavad Gita: An International Bibliography of 1785–1979 Imprints* (New York: Garland Publishing, 1983).

—1—

A Preamble to the Bhagavad Gita: Man Is Meant to Be Thoughtful*

Underlying the Bhagavad Gita's many teachings is one overarching truth: Man is meant to be thoughtful. Human life is meant for more than merely eating, sleeping, mating, and defending—the basic animalistic propensies with which we are all too familiar. Most people will admit that. We, as humans, are distinguished from other species—animals, birds, aquatics, insects, and so on—by our intellect, by our ability to reason. Actually, in Sanskrit, the ancient language of the Vedas, there are two words that make the distinction between animal and human quite clear.

First, the Sanskrit word for animal is *pashu*, which is derived from the concept, *pashyati iti pashuh*, indicating the limited ability to see only superficially, to see externally, and to only be aware of face value. And this is, in fact, how animals view the world; for them, if it is not edible, they are not interested.

The English word "man," on the other hand, is derived from the Sanskrit word *manushya*, from the root *mana*, which means, "mind," or, actually, "to think." The implication of the word *manushya* is that man was not created for superficiality, or to view things from a flat, one-dimensional point of view, but, rather, to think deeply about things, and to contemplate reality—to see what, for animals, remains unseen.

According to the Gita, human beings should realize that life is not meant for petty enjoyments, for brief distractions. The human form is meant for getting to the root of what existence is all about. We should not be content to just see an object on the physical platform, but we should know the truth behind it. The purpose of human life, therefore, is not for enjoyment alone; it is for knowing the Truth. Why? Because, as the Bhagavad Gita (2.44) tells us: "In the minds of those who are too attached to sense enjoyment and material opulence, and who are naturally bewildered by such things, the resolute determination of service to

---

*A lecture at the Open Center, New York City.

the divine does not take place." That is to say, materialists do not realize the proper goal of the human form, and as a result it is unlikely that they will ever become truly happy.

It's all in the proper use of our bodies and minds—that's what makes us human. And, as humans, only by acting in our natural capacity can we become truly happy. As Krishna says in the Gita (2.62–63):

> While contemplating the objects of the senses, a person develops attachment for them, and from such attachment lust develops, and from lust anger arises. From anger, delusion arises, and from delusion bewilderment of memory. When memory is bewildered, intelligence is lost, and when intelligence is lost, one tends to plummet into the material whirlpool.

But why should we care? What's wrong with immersing ourselves in a materialistic kind of life? This is, after all, the way most people seem to spend their time. That being said, Krishna continues His thought in a most illuminating way: "One who is not in transcendental consciousness can have neither a controlled mind nor steady intelligence, without which there is no possibility of peace. And how can there be any happiness without peace?" (2.66)

In this verse, Krishna uses the Sanskrit words *bhavana* and *buddhi*, which can be translated as "mind" and "intelligence," respectively. These are words that are intimately related to *manushya*, mentioned earlier. The idea is simple: Man is meant to be thoughtful, as already stated. We are truly human only when we use our body and mind to pursue the spiritual element, to see in a deeper way. This, again, is what distinguishes humankind from the animals.

Now, there is a spiritual process whose terminology is also etymologically linked to the *manushya* concept. I'm talking about mantras. The word *mantra* actually means "mind-release." And so it all ties together. I guess I could summarize what I've been saying in the following way: We are human (part of humankind) if we use our minds (*mana*) to pursue the spirit. And the best way to do that is with mantras (mind-release).

Mantras, or sacred sounds, are used to pierce through sensual, mental, and intellectual levels of existence—all lower strata of consciousness—for the purpose of purification and spiritual enlightenment. The sounds of different letters, particularly Sanskrit letters, have been shown to affect the mind, intellect, and auditory nerves of those who chant and hear them. The seven energy centers (*chakras*) of the spinal column, as well as the *ida, pingala,* and *sushumna nadis,* or the three pranic channels of the subtle body, all respond to mantras, bringing practitioners to elevated levels of awareness.

In another category altogether is the Hare Krishna Maha-mantra, or "the great chant for deliverance." This is considered by scripture to be the most powerful of mantras, for it includes the potency of all others and does much more than any other sound vibration. It puts one into direct contact with God, for Krishna and His name are nondifferent.

The mantra runs as follows: Hare Krishna, Hare Krishna, Krishna Krishna, Hare Hare/Hare Rama, Hare Rama, Rama Rama, Hare Hare, and the Vedic literature particularly recommends it for the current age. Statements to this effect can be found in many Vedic and post-Vedic texts. It basically means, "O Lord, O divine energy of the Lord! Please engage me in Your service." Such selfless prayers make humans truly happy. This is the overall teaching of the Gita.

There are numerous subteachings, of course, and the Gita goes into elaborate explanations of why we are here, in the material world; what the best course of action is while we're here; and the various kinds of liberation available to us. In other words, it explains how to put an end to material suffering. The Gita thus includes elaborate analyses about the human condition, but, on an esoteric level, its ultimate conclusion involves the yoga of chanting, *kirtan*, and the glorification of God, for this is the recommended process of God-realization in the current epoch of world history.

Here's how it plays out: The Gita's final teaching is that surrendering to God is the essence of spiritual knowledge (18.66) and that nonsectarian, universal spirituality is a path that is open to all. The great masters of this yogic science tell us that this surrendering process is largely affected by chanting in a prayerful state of mind. Krishna Himself specifically says that the great souls are always chanting His glories with great devotion (9.14). In this way, chanting God's names, with a heart steeped in devotion (*bhakti*), is where Lord Krishna ultimately takes Arjuna, and, in that sense, it's also where the Gita leads its readers.

— 2 —

Who Are You?

The Gita assumes a certain metaphysical understanding of reality. Arjuna is quickly made privy to a conception of the self that transcends bodily identification. In addition, he is told that the living entity transmigrates from one body to another in a seemingly endless series of incarnations—endless, that is, until one awakens to one's original, spiritual nature and thus returns to the spiritual world, completing the cycle once and for all. In India, even today, this transcendental worldview is not uncommon.

In the West, things are a little different. Most people identify with their gross and subtle bodies, that is, the physical form and the mind/intellect that accompanies it. When asked who they are, they respond with a name, a profession, and a description of their religion (i.e., their acquired faith), or their political affiliations. Sometimes they identify with familial connections, their heritage, or their "roots." Others have a more psychological perspective: "I am sensitive; I would never hurt anyone; I am rational and honest, and I have close ties with others who have similar qualities."

Most readers would be able to identify with the personality traits suggested above or their endless variations. And at first it seems appropriate to define oneself using such words and concepts, at least in a practical, everyday sense. But do we cease to exist if we change our names? Or if we lose our jobs? Or if we convert to another religion? Or if our sense of morals or ethics become compromised? In fact, if all the above traits disappear, do we transform into a nonentity? The question remains: Who are we beyond these changeable, material designations?

Plato described existence in this world as *metasy*, "an in-between state." Living beings, to him, were a combination of matter and spirit, a spark of the eternal caught in a web of temporality, a quantum of knowledge drowning in an ocean of ignorance, a blissful entity captured in a world of pain and madness. Most forms of Eastern thought agree with this view.

According to ancient India's Vedic literature, living beings are essentially spiritual; creatures that take birth in the world of matter due to a series of complex
yet subtle desires. Such embodied souls are called in Sanskrit *tatashtha-shakti*.
The root *tata* signifies the hypothetical line that divides land from sea. Sometimes
water covers the land, and at other times it recedes. Living beings in this world are
sometimes covered by forgetfulness of their true nature, and sometimes uncovered.

Can anyone prove that we are essentially spiritual, or that we are eternal souls
temporarily living in material bodies? Some people feel that the answer may lie
in science. By examining other subatomic particles, scientists have learned much
about the unseen world all around us—perhaps they can find the soul through
similar methods. Subatomic particles are accepted as real because of the effects
they produce around them, even though the particles themselves remain unseen.
There is certainly virtue to this argument. But if souls are truly spiritual, they might
ultimately elude the scientific approach.

Consequently, direct perception will likely prove faulty when observing subtle
phenomena. One would do well to supplement this with a more intuitive approach.
J. Paul Williams of Mount Holyoke College, in his unpublished essay *Belief in a
Future Life,* ponders this truth:

> The fact that we have no direct experience of souls which do not exist apart from the
> bodies . . . need not force us to the conclusion that [the soul] does not exist. The ty-
> pical reaction of the materialists to this kind of reasoning is an appeal to stick to
> the known facts. But the materialistic scientist certainly does not limit himself to
> immediately experienced data. The limits of our experience are so narrow that if we
> did not permit our thinking to go beyond them, human thought would be puny
> indeed. Whoever experienced an atom or an electron? The whole conception of
> the atomic structure is an inference; it is believed because it is consistent with the
> way in which elements combine, because it explains why under certain conditions
> peculiar markings appear on photographic plates. Yet we do not accuse the physicist
> of irrationality when he says that solid matter, such as rock, is really composed of tiny
> solar systems in which electrons revolve at incredible speeds around protons. Let no
> one think he has reached perfection in his habits of thought if he accepts inferential
> logic in physics but rejects it in theology.[1]

Inferred evidence, then, is not exclusive to theological science; it is a basic tool
of the hard sciences and a part of our own daily lives. We have never seen the
hearts of our loved ones but we do not doubt that they exist. We have never seen
our ancestors, but our existence is proof enough that they, too, once walked the
earth. Perhaps it is the momentous significance of an unseen soul animating our
own body that makes its existence so much harder to accept than that of a proton.
What could be more shocking than realizing that we are not our bodies?

And yet this is the fundamental premise upon which the Gita rests. Its entire
second chapter argues for the existence of the soul in no uncertain terms. As soon
as Arjuna articulates his confusion and agrees to be instructed by Krishna, the
Lord asserts their eternality (2.12). He compares earthly existence to a change of

dress—people change bodies in the same way that they don new clothes from day to day (2.13). Thus, Krishna clearly establishes the existence of an entity in the body that is everlasting (the soul), as well as the concomitant truth of reincarnation.

In terms of modern science, one might say that a quantum of energy pervades the body, and that this energy, like all energy, cannot be created or destroyed. This is called the First Law of Thermodynamics. Since the energy that animates the body continues to exist after death, where does it go? One might argue that it somehow merges into the totality of existence. But Krishna says, "No." He argues that the quantum of energy simply inhabits another body, which it inadvertently chooses based on previous actions (*karma*) and desires (*kama*).

Karma is another fundamental law enunciated in the Bhagavad Gita. What exactly *is* karma? When looked at in modern terms, it can be seen as a sort of metaphysical extension of Newton's Third Law of Motion—for every action, there is an equal and corresponding reaction. This is a law, according to the Gita, which survives death. Thus, if in this life one's actions are not fully realized, that is, if they have not garnered a commensurate reaction, then a subsequent life is created to reap all that was previously sown (8.3).

Ultimately, whatever our beliefs, *something* separates living beings from inorganic matter. Something is present in life that is absent in death. The physical, chemical components of the body remain in place at death: heart, brain, skeletal structure, and every chemical present in the body during life; but something else, something nonphysical has been lost. Whatever one chooses to call it, this nonphysical life force distinguishes a living body from an inert chemical shell.

What do we know about this unique element that pervades the body? We know that classical science rejected it along with religious dogma—at least when referred to as "the soul"—and we know it has been accepted by religionists throughout history, with few exceptions. In the interest of finding terms acceptable to both classical science and religion, we will speak of "consciousness," for science studies consciousness as at least a potential nonmaterial force within the body, and religionists often accept consciousness as synonymous with or at least symptomatic of the soul.

THE SYMPTOM OF THE SOUL

Consciousness is the most fundamental part of human experience; nothing is more intimate or more immediate. Every sensorial impression—such as seeing the words on this page—has meaning because we are conscious. Unlike living beings, a chair, for example, registers no sensory impression; it is not conscious; it has no soul. But I do; I am; I have a soul. Or do I? Am I the possessor of the soul? Or am I rather a soul who possesses a body? In other words, do I have a soul or do I have a body?

Ancient scriptural texts, especially those from India, simplify fundamental ontological questions such as these. For example, in certain classical schools dating back to the Vedantic tradition, there is an elementary exercise that runs something like this: Can I be conscious of my body? Can I be conscious of my hand? My legs? My face? My heart? My mind? Yes, I can be conscious of any part of my body, its pleasures, and its pains.

Now, can the body be conscious of itself? The immediate answer is no. My body cannot be conscious of itself. Rather, *I* am conscious of *my* body. This simple reflection on the nature of consciousness makes it clear that there is a separation between the body and the self, the living being within who is conscious of the body.

To extend this idea, let us admit that we do not really know if the body is conscious of itself. *We do not know because we are not the body*. I cannot really tell if my finger, chest, or brain, for example, are conscious of themselves. Nor can they tell me anything about their (would-be) perceptions because none of them is a self, a personality. They are, at least empirically, unconscious. Therefore, Vedantic texts conclude, consciousness is personality and personality is consciousness.

The Vedic seers draw out various implications from these conclusions, and these, in turn, lead to other simple exercises in understanding: My finger is not a person. Nor is my leg, my nose, my ear, my brain, nor my entire body. These accoutrements of the self cannot tell me who I am or who they are, either individually or collectively, because none of them is a self, a personality. None of them possess self-experience. It is I who experiences through them and in them. It is concluded, therefore, that they are different than the person in the body who experiences—for that is me, the possessor of consciousness. Modern teachers of Vedanta often point out that the distinction between body and self is even reflected in our language, for the possessive pronoun suggests that *I* am different than *my* body.

This difference between the body and the self is perceived in everyday experience. Here is an example: If something were to touch my hand, it would not be empirically correct to say that my hand is conscious of that particular stimulation. If I think about it, I will admit that it is I, through my hand and in my hand, by a process of identification, who am conscious of the touch. The ultimate "self," if you will, uses the brain to pick up signals throughout the nervous system and is thus aware of the workings of the body.

It is also through this process of bodily identification that a person is able to say he or she is hungry, for instance, when, as a matter of fact, it is the stomach, not the person, which is demanding food. The concept of being hungry indicates that "I," the self, am conscious of the contractions of my stomach. If, however, my stomach is locally anesthetized, then the process of self-identification with the stomach is temporarily broken, and I cease to be conscious of its contractions. In other words, "I" would no longer feel hungry, although the body, of course, would still require food. The "self" here is actually the brain and its conditional responses to the world around it; the higher "self" is quite aloof from such perceptions and is not ultimately affected by them.

In this way, direct experience, inference, logic, religious faith, and empiric observation all concur: some sort of conscious energy exists within the body and experiences this world through the body. This conscious energy is the thinker of thoughts and feeler of feelings.

The body is an instrument; the conscious energy is the player of that instrument. I am no more my brain or nervous system than a guitarist is the guitar he plays. As a musician produces music with a musical instrument, so I—the thinker—produce thoughts with a thinking instrument: the brain.

Moreover, consider this: If an instrument is destroyed, is the musician necessarily destroyed as well? Analogically, if my body is destroyed, I am not necessarily destroyed along with it. If my guitar is destroyed, I would have to get another one to make music—or I would have to stop playing the guitar altogether. But I exist apart from the guitar, and my longevity is not dependent upon the longevity of my instrument. Guitars may come and go, but expert players live on. This conception is consistent with the First Law of Thermodynamics, or the Law of Conservation of Energy, as mentioned above. In other words, if the soul exists at all, then it must subsist in sustained existence. As the Gita tells us: "For the existent there is no cessation, and for the non-existent—like a dream or an illusion—there is no endurance" (2.16).

Where does the energy within the body go at the time of death? As stated earlier, the Gita tells us that the soul reincarnates. And nature supplies numerous hints suggesting that this is a sensible answer. Consider, for example, the changes our bodies undergo in this one life, from childhood, to youth, to old age—changes that occur while we remain in the same body. Physiologically, the cells of our bodies perpetually deteriorate and die so that after approximately seven years our cellular structure is completely new.

In a seventy-year lifetime, a person physiologically "dies" and is "reborn" ten times; and while these intermediate "deaths" do not involve reincarnation as such, they allow us the remarkable experience of looking back, in this lifetime, to previous lives: as infants, children, youths, and grownups. These past images are, in a sense, past physical selves that no longer exist. Different bodies, same person—a simple exercise in seeing the difference between the physical and spiritual self, in seeing who we appear to be and who we really are. This is the first major teaching of the Bhagavad Gita.

NOTES

1. Paul Williams, *Belief in a Future Life*, unpublished manuscript, n.d.

—3—

An Overview

The Gita begins about one-third into the larger epic, the *Mahabharata*. It opens with King Dhritarashtra, blind from birth, asking his secretary, Sanjaya, about the devastating battle that has just taken place. The king's hundred sons, known collectively as the Kauravas, had entered into mortal combat with their cousins, the Pandavas, who are the heroes of the epic. This was a family feud that had been escalating for generations, and it had now become a full-scale civil war.

Prior chapters of the *Mahabharata* inform readers that Lord Krishna, the Personality of Godhead, had become Prince Arjuna's charioteer—He rides on the side of the Pandavas, even if He had vowed not to actually take part in the fighting. In fact, He only drives the chariot because He so loves His devotee, Arjuna.

Taking up his bow, ready to fight, Arjuna sees the sons of Dhritarashtra and their seemingly countless soldiers in military array. Thinking deeply about the task before him, he asks Krishna to draw his chariot between the two considerable armies. Looking around him at people he has known for his entire life, Arjuna's mind becomes disturbed, perhaps for the first time ever, as he ponders the imminent death of his teachers, relatives, and friends, many of whom are on the opposing side. "What good is all this?" he wonders, throwing down his bow and deciding not to fight.

Chapter One makes clear his horror as he considers the oncoming confrontation. He sees only evil in the bloodshed that will inevitably follow, and it makes him feel unworthy in numerous ways. After all, he is a well-trained soldier, and he should do his duty. Still, even before the text moves into Chapter Two, Arjuna offers Krishna several arguments for refusing to fight.

Though his reservations stem from various sources, he particularly mentions the sinful reactions involved in killing. He expresses his concern for his close associates who will die on the battlefield. And he muses about the inevitable results of war, such as the ruination of dynasties, which leads to irreligion.

Feeling compassion for His well-meaning if confused devotee, Krishna begins to address Arjuna's concerns in Chapter Two. First, he expresses surprise that Arjuna would ask such questions—he is a highly qualified warrior and he should know better. Krishna explains that Arjuna's hesitation is merely a temporary weakness of heart, and that he should rise beyond it.

But Arjuna insists that there are great, virtuous men on the opposing side, and that he would be remiss if he were to enter into battle with them.

In response, Krishna smiles, explaining to Arjuna that his misgivings are ill conceived. With this, the Lord effectively begins His teaching. He starts with the actual nature of the self, saying that both He and Arjuna are eternal beings. And He explains this in various ways, using both logic and analogy. He further explains reincarnation and relativity, as well as the long march of the soul from illusion to enlightenment.

Additionally, Krishna reminds Arjuna of his duty as a Kshatriya, or an administrative officer. Legions of innocent people are depending on him, and his enemy—who was given ample opportunity to reconsider the war—must now be vanquished. Moreover, Krishna makes clear that this particular battle is consonant with His desire, thus making it a religious war in the most legitimate sense of the term.

Krishna tells him to avoid infamy by doing his duty, and to know that he is acting on God's behalf.

The Lord then elaborates on "the art of work" (Karma Yoga), saying that fighting in a mood of divine service is transcendental and will bring no sinful reaction. He tells Arjuna to learn to control his senses, which will then, in turn, allow him to do devotional work.

At this point, Arjuna's heart seems somewhat lighter, and he begins to ask pertinent questions. For example, what sort of characteristics, he wonders aloud, might one find in a self-realized soul—how does one recognize a saintly person? How do they walk, talk, think, and act? And so, for the remainder of Chapter Two, Krishna elaborates on the nature of one who is focused on the Supreme. He explains how they are in control of their senses, that they fully realize the distinction between self and body, and that their intelligence is fixed on God.

As Chapter Three opens, Arjuna is a bit bewildered by most of what he has heard thus far. Krishna's explanation of sense control seems incompatible with Karma Yoga. How can one engage in deep meditation and withdrawal of the senses and still function in the world, even as the Lord's instrument?

In answer to this question, Krishna goes into further detail about Karma Yoga, or reaction-free devotional work, and thus corrects Arjuna's mistaken idea that all work is self-centered or fruitive, leading to bondage. Krishna relates this idea to Arjuna's immediate dilemma of not wanting to fight. He tells him that avoiding sinful reactions through devotional work—in this case, fighting a war—is better than trying to escape reactions through renouncing work altogether. Krishna also argues that Arjuna should fight to set the proper example of doing one's duty. The conclusion, in any case, is that Arjuna should engage in warfare, but as a religious sacrifice, with knowledge and detachment.

After this, Arjuna wonders why the soul seems naturally drawn to improper action, almost as if by force. Krishna identifies the underlying reason as lust—selfish desire—saying that it comes in both gross and subtle forms and that it actually compels people to act improperly. He then again recommends that Arjuna regulate his senses, becoming fixed in his pure identity as a servant of the Divine. It is by this method, He says, that one can overcome the all-pervasive enemy known as lust.

Since Chapter Three had emphasized the importance of working for God with knowledge and detachment, the next chapter picks up on this theme, emphasizing "transcendental knowledge" as essential in spiritual life. Krishna opens with a pivotal point in the Gita's storehouse of spiritual teachings, and one that is often overlooked: that of learning the text's truths through the agency of authorized lineages (*parampara*). After this, He briefly mentions the mystery of His own appearance and mission, and He describes "devotional service" (*bhakti*) as the means of perfection and the goal of life. This chapter ends with Krishna glorifying transcendental knowledge and requesting Arjuna to arm himself with such knowledge—for it "burns all sinful reactions to ashes" and thus allows one to gradually approach the supreme destination.

As Chapter Five opens, Arjuna again asks for clarity. He still sees contradiction in Krishna asking for both renunciation and work in devotion—he wants to know, once and for all, which of the two is superior. Krishna responds by articulating a central teaching of the Gita: that real renunciation means detachment from the results or fruits of one's work. Avoiding work altogether is not the highest, He says. Rather, working for Him, in a spirit of love and devotion, is at the heart of true renunciation.

In the first five chapters, Krishna has explained what might be termed "Buddhi Yoga," or working with consciousness focused on Krishna and without fruitive desires. The various terms used to describe this process, from Karma Yoga to Buddhi Yoga, vary only in terms of emphases. Ultimately, they refer to different sides of the same coin—working for Krishna, or using body and mind in His service. Now, at the end of the fifth chapter and continuing on to the Sixth, Krishna explains Dhyana Yoga, or Ashtanga Yoga (also called Raja Yoga). An abbreviated version of this teaching has become popular in the modern world as Hatha Yoga

This is a difficult and somewhat mechanical technique meant to help practitioners gain control of their body and mind, thus allowing them, ultimately, to focus on God. Arjuna finds the entire procedure cumbersome and extremely difficult, at which point Krishna assures him that real meditation means focusing the mind on Him directly, and that the best yogis are simply His devotees. In fact, says Krishna, engaging in His devotional service is the perfection of yoga.

Since the ideal form of yoga centers on Krishna, Chapter Seven describes knowledge of Krishna, the process of obtaining that knowledge, and what one might expect when such knowledge is indeed accessed. After all, how can one meditate on Krishna if one doesn't know Him? How can one serve Him without knowledge of who He is and what He wants? Thus, Krishna begins to give Arjuna esoteric understanding of all such details, so that he might properly engage in the yoga process of "linking with God" (which is what the word "yoga" literally means).

The Lord identifies Himself as the Supreme Absolute Truth, and tells Arjuna that everything in existence is a combination of His material and spiritual energies. He is all-pervasive through these energies, and yet He remains distinct, as the Personality of Godhead. Because the material world's activities are governed by the three modes of nature—goodness, passion, and ignorance—of which He is the source, only those who surrender unto Him can rise beyond them. Four kinds of impious souls, Krishna says, will never surrender, while four kinds of pious ones, do. He gives indications by which one might identify these eight kinds of people, and He urges Arjuna to be among the pious four, in His service. By such proper action, Krishna asserts, one can focus on Him at the time of death and thus attain the spiritual realm.

Thus, Chapter Eight is almost exclusively devoted to the moment of death, an important juncture in man's sojourn in the material world. As the chapter opens, Arjuna asks Krishna seven questions: He wants to know (1) the nature of Brahman (the impersonal Absolute); (2) karma (causation); (3) the demigods; and (4) the material world; he also wants to know (5) how God resides in the body of every living entity, and (6) exactly where He is located in the body. Finally, he inquires as to (7) how one might be conscious of God at the time of death.

Krishna addresses most of these questions briefly, since He has already answered them in earlier portions of the Gita. The last question, however, is dealt with at length.

Whatever one focuses upon at the time of death, He tells Arjuna, becomes one's next destination. Thus, if one remembers Krishna, one goes to Him. To accomplish this end, the Lord should be meditated upon as the ultimate transcendental person who knows everything, who is the original controller, the smallest of the small, and the maintainer of everyone and everything. By such meditation, Krishna explains, one will go to the eternal spiritual world, never to return to matter again.

Then, after describing the various yogic methods for leaving this world, He advises Arjuna to be unconcerned with all such paths—whether Vedic study, conventional yoga, austere sacrifices, charity, the cultivation of knowledge, or karma—for their many fruits are all obtained through the performance of devotional service. Moreover, such practitioners of devotion will naturally reach the supreme abode, while others may get distracted and miss the essence.

In Chapter Nine, Krishna nurtures the plant He had begun to sow in Chapter Seven, that is, explaining details about Himself. He prefaces this information by revealing that it is "the most confidential knowledge" and the "king of education." Naturally, then, the chapter focuses on the Lord's actual transcendental nature, which "foolish people," He says, can never understand. He tells us that such *mudhas* (literally, "asses") deride Him when He descends in His humanlike form, and He contrasts them with *mahatmas* ("great souls"), who are always chanting His glories.

Krishna continues His sermon by enumerating various kinds of worshipers—those who prefer the impersonal Absolute, the demigods (highly empowered beings from upper planetary systems), pantheists, and so on—explaining that, ultimately, they worship only Him. It is He who is the true recipient of all religious veneration, however disguised He might at times be. His real identity remains secret to all but the most realized souls.

Those who worship Him directly, therefore, are in a better position to know His overall transcendental nature. Here, the Gita offers a strong monotheistic message. Krishna acknowledges that, for various reasons, people worship lesser manifestations of the Supreme. But He says that those who have actual knowledge worship Him alone, for He is the Supreme Personality of Godhead. In His own words:

> But it is I who am the ritual, I the sacrifice, the offering to the ancestors, the healing herb, the spiritual chant. I am both the butter and the fire of the offering. I am the father of the universe, the mother, the support, and the grandsire. I am the object of knowledge, the purifier of everything, and the mystical syllable Om. I am also the embodiment of the Vedas. I am the goal, the sustainer, the master, the witness, the abode, the refuge and the most dear friend. I am the creation and the annihilation, the basis of everything, the resting place and the eternal seed (9.16–18).

Thus, His devotees, by making Him, in His original spiritual form, the object of all their veneration, offerings, and austerities, free themselves from the bondage of karma and, ultimately, develop love for Him. He concludes the chapter by saying that those who focus on Him, with complete absorption, will achieve ultimate perfection in spiritual life and come to Him in the end.

In Chapter Ten, Krishna continues to describe His limitless opulences, as well as the uniqueness and sanctity of those who recognize these opulences. And then He recites what have come to be known as the four nutshell verses, wherein He summarizes the Gita's teachings in seven broad strokes: (1) Krishna is the origin of everything; (2) those who are wise thus engage in His loving service; (3) they always think of Him and (4) discuss His attributes; and this (5) brings them great pleasure. To such pure devotees (6) Krishna gives full enlightenment, and concomitantly (7) destroys their ignorance. (The verses themselves are fully translated elsewhere in this book.)

After hearing this summation of Gita theology, Arjuna takes a necessary if easily understandable leap of faith, affirming his acceptance of Krishna as the Supreme Lord. He now accepts all that Krishna has told him, he says, and wants to know more. Krishna's ensuing description is profound and thought-provoking: He identifies Himself as the light of the sun and the moon, the ocean, and the Himalayas. In fact, He is synonymous with all that is great, with anything that embodies primacy, in any major category. However, He concludes by saying that these wondrous phenomena merely suggest His limitless opulence. As He points out, "With but a single fragment of My divine being, I pervade and support the entire universe."

Arjuna feels that he is now free from illusion, seeing Krishna as He is, *and for what He is*. But he begins to consider others who might not be as fortunate. He wonders how they might be convinced of Krishna's supremacy. Thus, in Chapter Eleven, he requests Krishna to show His form as God—as the entire universe—so that there could be no question about His divinity.

Krishna then reveals to Arjuna His wondrous, effulgent, all expansive Universal Form, which includes everything in existence, including time. It defies all human and spatial categories. Unlimited universes appear in one place, and all beings, as effulgent as the sun, assume their true forms. Arjuna even sees the soldiers on both sides of the imminent battle, dying one by one, though this has not yet taken place. As Krishna's otherworldly, inconceivable spectacle unfolds before the great archer, He explains His form as time, the destroyer of all worlds, and requests that Arjuna, now made aware of the inevitable fate of all the warriors, become His instrument.

Arjuna, overwhelmed by seeing everything at once, glorifies Krishna as the original master, the Lord, and the cause of all causes. He begs Krishna to forgive any familiarity with which he may have treated Him in the past, as if He were an ordinary person.

For Arjuna, the Universal Form is unbearable, and he begs Krishna to return to the simple, familiar two-armed form, for which he now has new appreciation.

In response to Arjuna's fearful pleading, Krishna first shows His four-armed form as Vishnu, God of gods, before again returning to His original two-armed form. He then states that His two-armed form is special and can only be seen by pure devotees.

In Chapter Twelve, Arjuna, after witnessing Krishna's awe-inspiring Universal Form, wants to clarify his own position as a devotee, as being among the most intimate worshipers of the Supreme. He thus asks about a certain qualitative distinction on the spiritual path: Which is better, he asks Krishna, worshiping Him, the Supreme Lord, as a person, or worshiping the impersonal Brahman— God as an amorphous void or a nondescript light, as some indeed do? Krishna immediately responds that one engaged in His personal service is the topmost. For a person to relate to something impersonal, He says, is naturally quite difficult. And He does not recommend it.

Krishna then offers Arjuna a hierarchical list of possibilities for engaging in His service. That is to say, ideally, one should take up Krishna's loving service with mind fixed solely upon Him. The Lord recognizes, however, that most people are not sufficiently spiritually evolved for such unmotivated and uninterrupted service. And so, if this cannot be done, one should follow the rules and regulations of Bhakti Yoga, as enunciated in the scriptures, for this will purify a person so that he or she will soon be able to do so. Additionally, Krishna describes other processes that gradually lead to His pure devotional service.

Ultimately, this hierarchical list leads to a description of Krishna's pure devotees, and Krishna repeats at the end of each description that such a devotee "is very dear to Me." These devotees are free from material desires, material dualities, and false ego. Clearly, Krishna wants all beings to achieve this level of existence, even if it will, for some, take many lifetimes to get there.

Arjuna opens Chapter Thirteen by inquiring about "the field of activities" and "the knower of that field." This refers to the body and the soul within the body, respectively. There is a third factor here as well—the Master of the field. This is Paramatma, or Supersoul, an expansion of the Supreme Lord who accompanies the conditioned soul in his or her sojourn in the material world. Krishna explains all three with scientific precision.

To help Arjuna understand these three, Krishna also explains material nature, true knowledge, the real enjoyer of all activity (God), and the ultimate conclusion of knowledge, too. The understanding of material nature conveyed in this section is important, because by understanding nature's three modes, goodness, passion, and ignorance, one can understand the inner workings of the created world, along with the living entities and their conditioned responses. Ultimately, the chapter clarifies the interrelationship between matter, the soul, and God.

Chapter Fourteen is central to the philosophy of the Bhagavad Gita. Lord Krishna elaborates on the three modes—goodness, passion, and ignorance—discussed only briefly in previous chapters. He now shows how they are in fact forces that bind and control all conditioned souls within the material world. He points out that He Himself is beyond the modes (as their creator) and that an ordinary soul, too, can transcend them through devotional service.

Such transcendence is tantamount to liberation. Krishna says that when one rises beyond the modes, one concomitantly rises beyond birth, death, old age, and disease, and "can enjoy nectar even in this life."

Chapter Fifteen finds Lord Krishna expounding on the need to free oneself from matter's grip. He begins by comparing the material world to a gigantic, upside-down banyan tree, with roots shooting upward while its branches are facing down—the opposite of a normal tree. This Zen-like image is meant to provoke thought about the inverted nature of material existence, and how it is merely a perverted reflection of the spiritual world. Thus, by encouraging Arjuna (and future readers of the Gita) to contemplate earthly existence in a deeper way, seeing it as but a partial, shadowlike representation of ultimate truth, Krishna enables His devotees to see a higher reality.

But then He says something especially engaging: He declares that, "One who knows this banyan tree is the knower of the Vedas" (15.1). Why should one who knows the material world—an inverted reflection of all that is real—be seen as "the knower of the Vedas"? What Krishna means is this: the ultimate purpose of Vedic knowledge is to understand this entangling "tree" of the material world and, by such knowledge, extricate oneself from it. In effect, understanding the complexities of this banyan tree and how it relates to the soul and God have been the main subject of the Gita thus far, since Krishna has explained it in several ways using diverse terminology.

Next, Krishna extends the metaphor by elaborating on the means by which one might extricate oneself from the material world: "Using the powerful axe of non-attachment," He says, "one must cut down this banyan tree with determination. Thereafter one must seek a truly spiritual situation, from which one never comes back." He then describes the surrendering process and gives a brief description of His own kingdom. He mentions that His realm is self-illuminating and that one who goes there never returns—for such a person, the inverted banyan tree assumes it original form. Thus, instead of just pointing out the dark roots of material complexity, Krishna gives a taste of the sunny destination awaiting the aspiring spiritualist.

In this chapter, too, Krishna describes the various kinds of people in the material world, and He analyzes why they do the things they do. He shows us how all activity relates to the modes of nature, and how people can be understood by the types of austerities they perform, the types of food they eat, and so on.

This might be seen as Krishna's psychological study of man in the material world, which He began in the prior chapter. After looking at the banyan tree analogy and its implications in some depth, He concludes His teaching by stressing the importance of renunciation and devotion to God.

Since Krishna has already analyzed the various kinds of people in the world, as well as numerous processes of God-realization, here, in Chapter Sixteen, He narrows down personality types into two: divine and demoniac natures. The "divine people," as He calls them, are primarily in the mode of goodness, with qualities that are conducive for self-realization. The "demoniac" are weighed down by passion and ignorance, embodying qualities that are detrimental to spiritual progress. The divine persons generally live regulated lives, abiding by the authority of scripture. Gradually, they develop an innate desire to serve the Supreme and experience unending happiness. They invariably attain perfection. The demoniac tend to act whimsically and fall deeper and deeper into conditioned life, trapped by their own habitual responses to material nature and their burning desires. While they experience minimal pleasure as they start out in life, they become progressively more miserable as their years wear on.

After mentioning twenty-three godly qualities, Krishna explains the demoniac, which, He says, degrades the soul through arrogant, ignorant, and conceited pursuits of sense gratification and power.

He graphically describes the demonic mentality as follows: They see the world as ultimately unreal, without any spiritual dimension and produced only of sex desire. Taking shelter of lust, they think that to gratify their senses is the only real goal of life; to increase their wealth, they will not hesitate to engage in illegal activity. They often plot to do away with their "enemies" (competitors), thinking themselves the center of existence. Perplexed by illusory anxieties, bewildered by self-complacency, impudence, and sexual fantasy, they envy or denounce all that is good and true, often blaspheming real religion. These mischievous, sad-hearted living entities are repeatedly cast by Krishna into lower species and gradually sink to the most abominable forms of existence.

Their only chance is to change their ways over many births, or to receive the grace of a pure devotee.

Krishna ends the chapter by explaining that because lust, anger, and greed are often found at the outset of demonic life, all well-meaning, thoughtful people should give them up and understand their duty through faithfully following the scriptures.

Chapter Sixteen thus concludes with Krishna declaring that righteous people follow the scriptures while the demoniac do not. In the beginning of Chapter Seventeen, therefore, Arjuna asks for details about those who don't follow sacred texts, but who instead devise means of worship according to their own concocted ideas of transcendence. Krishna responds by saying that it all depends on how the modes combine in any given individual's life. According to each particular combination of the modes, a person will be inclined to a certain kind of faith, worship, eating, sacrifices, charity, austerity, and so forth. The chapter ends with Krishna affirming that real religion means serving Him, with love and devotion. Religion is meant for His satisfaction, He tells Arjuna, and all other forms simply miss the point. They may afford roundabout, indirect means of worshiping Him, and practitioners can certainly reach the goal in due course. But the direct process is always better.

The entire Bhagavad Gita is thus concluded in seventeen chapters, and so, in Chapter Eighteen, Krishna reviews the knowledge and procedures already presented earlier on.

Since Arjuna's basic desire to renounce his duty as a warrior was prompted by fear of sinful reaction, Krishna explains what renunciation really means, and how to transcend sinful reactions through (1) becoming renounced from the fruits of activities;(2) abiding by the order of the Supersoul; and (3) worshiping the Lord through the fruits of one's work—and one's proper work is determined by the modes and one's status in society. Krishna explains all of this as a complex science, both here, in His summing up, and throughout the earlier chapters of the Gita.

The chapter concludes by telling us that Krishna can only be known through surrender, by purely engaging in His devotional service. And only in this way—free from any other conception of religiosity or self-motivated desire—can one know true happiness and reach the perfection of yoga, or linking with God. He further tells Arjuna that, knowing this, he should not hesitate to do his duty, for it is consistent with His desire and the right thing to do.

The Lord then reiterates the most confidential knowledge: "Become My devotee, always think of Me, act for Me, worship Me, and offer all homage unto Me. Surrender unto Me alone. Do not fear sinful reactions."

After hearing the instructions of Lord Krishna, Arjuna is determined and ready to fight. His illusion now gone, he surrenders to the wondrous two-armed form of Krishna and moves forward to win the war.

— 4 —

Fight or Flight:
Violence in the Saga
of the Pandavas

"To win without fighting is best—though not always possible."
—Sun Tzu (*The Art of War*)

INTRODUCTION

The Bhagavad Gita opens on a battlefield at the onset of a major civil war. What exactly precipitated Arjuna's presence on the battlefield? Is the fight before him legitimate? Was he the right person to fight it? These are some of the questions addressed in this chapter.

To begin, let it be said that many of the Gita's readers, when first introduced to the text, find it disconcerting that it teaches *ahimsa* ("harmlessness" or "nonaggression") in the midst of imminent bloodshed, and that it talks of God while supporting the killing of His creatures.

Some have thus attempted to explain the Gita's violence as allegorical. Gandhi theorized that the text was not about historical war but rather about the battle that goes on in each individual heart. His interpretation was derived from the Theosophical Society, notably, the works of Subba Row, William Q. Judge, and Annie Besant, who were among that Society's earliest members. They conveyed to him their metaphorical approach to the Gita, which spoke to his purposes directly. Here was a way to accept the scripture of his motherland and to use it to support his doctrine of nonviolence. Others have also viewed the Gita as a metaphor, either comparing Arjuna to Everyman, or saying that the five Pandavas—the heroes of the Gita—represent the five senses, and so on.[1]

Stephen Mitchell, translator of a recent edition of the Gita,[2] has attempted to refute allegorical readings. He writes, "If Arjuna is the mind or ego in every person, what can it possibly mean, for example, to say that he is 'born with divine traits' (16.3), whereas other people have 'demonic traits'? Who can these others be if Arjuna stands for us all?"[3] While this logic is appropriate for the allegorical readings of Arjuna as Everyman, it falls flat when applied to other allegorical interpretations, as when, for instance, Arjuna represents only our higher nature, or one of the five senses.

Frankly, there is a reason why people adopt the metaphorical approach: In the first verse of the Gita, Kurukshetra (the battlefield on which the Gita is originally spoken) is referred to as "Dharmakshetra," the field of *dharma*, of duty and righteousness. The implication is that the Gita's teaching transcends its battlefield surroundings. The conflict portrayed in the text involves eternal rivals: justice and injustice, good and evil, reality and illusion, and matter and spirit. And this is all true enough. But it is likely that the allegory stops there. Though there are traditional commentaries giving credence to allegorical interpretations,[4] it is clear that these readings of the text are always considered subservient to a literal understanding—an additional perspective that can illuminate inner teachings. But the allegorical version never stands on its own. Even if the Gita *is* taken as an allegory, the militaristic imagery can still lead to violence, and a war of astounding proportions still ensues in the *Mahabharata*.

This chapter will argue that even if one interprets the Bhagavad Gita literally, there is still rhyme and reason to the war alluded to in its pages, and, more, it is still justifiable in terms of *ahimsa*, or nonviolence. This is so because the hero of the Gita preferred a peaceful solution, and because the teachings of the Gita in no way encourage killing, except in this very specific situation. Only as a last resort did Krishna direct Arjuna to fight. Gita scholar Mahesh Kumar Sharan has rightly pointed out that, "because people do not realize the circumstances under which the Gita was spoken, and take it as a book of isolated teachings . . . they commit the grievous mistake of saying that it inculcates manslaughter."[5] Sharan goes on to suggest that one must understand the Gita by understanding its context. That is precisely what we attempt to do here.

Thus, the subject of violence in the Bhagavad Gita is complex. This being so, I will begin with a brief overview of the story of the *Mahabharata*, a story that is itself multifaceted and difficult to understand. After this, I look at who Arjuna actually was, and whether it was legitimate for him to engage in warfare. This includes an analysis of Kshatriya-*dharma*, or the duty of the warrior class in ancient India, and an exploration of the "just war" concept in the world's major religious traditions. I conclude by summarizing the Gita's essential teachings and by reassessing the subject of violence in the Bhagavad Gita in light of all that has been discussed up to that point. By the end of this chapter, it is hoped, the reader will have sufficient background to appreciate the complexity and overall meaning of violence in this most sacred of texts.

THE WAR TO END ALL WARS

The Bhagavad Gita is a text with a definite context. And this context can be found in the labyrinthine tome known as *Mahabharata*, one of India's greatest epics. In a sense, looking at Bhagavad Gita without reference to the larger epic is like walking into a room in the middle of a conversation, when someone is halfway through telling a story. In fact, this is precisely what it is—the Gita appears in the middle of the larger work. It can be found in the *Mahabharata, Bhishma-parvan,* Chapters Twenty-Three to Forty, to be exact. Thus, as indicated above, any attempt to unravel the truth behind the Gita's "violence" will fall short without recourse to the larger epic.

The *Mahabharata* begins with a detailed genealogy that helps answer the question of why the war took place: While reading the intricate "who's who," we learn that demons incarnated to take over the world and *devas* (demigods) took birth to stop them. Clearly, to understand the underpinnings of the war, we must delve into the theological background of the larger story. According to the epic itself, the war is part of God's *lila,* or "spiritual pastime." If we study the book with this in mind, the story's otherworldly dimensions will make sense and the *Mahabharata*'s internal perspective on war will come through.

Indian sages have carefully preserved the details of the civil war that took place at Kurukshetra (a vast land area that still exists today, about eighty-five miles north of modern Delhi), and have made it the centerpiece of the *Mahabharata.* Guinness calls this epic "the longest poem ever written." It is seven times the length of the Iliad and the Odyssey combined or nearly three times the size of the Judaeo-Christian Bible.

While the date of the *Mahabharata* war is debated among Western scholars, tradition says that it occurred 5,000 years ago, and that the great sage Vyasadeva put the Gita and the rest of the *Mahabharata* into written form at that time.

The focus of the story is courtly intrigue, a deep-rooted conflict involving an important political family of the period. This family consisted of the Kauravas and the Pandavas, two groups of feuding cousins. King Dhritarashtra, the father of the Kauravas, was congenitally blind. Thus, the throne that would have been his, was instead given to his younger brother Pandu, father of the Pandavas. Dhritarashtra resented Pandu for securing the throne and never forgave him.

After Pandu's early death, Dhritarashtra received at his court Pandu's five sons, the Pandavas: Yudhishthira, Arjuna, Bhima, Nakula, and Sahadeva. Though the foreign names might be daunting to the average Western reader, these five, at least, should be remembered—they are the heroes of the *Mahabaharata.*

Pandu's eldest son, Yudhishthira was the rightful heir to the throne. But Dhritarashtra didn't want to hear this. He wanted his own boys, the Kauravas, to rule. Still, out of duty, he raised the Pandavas with his own children. All the boys were trained as warriors (*kshatriya*) according to ancient standards of military excellence and chivalry that are today all but lost.

Even when the Kauravas and the Pandavas were young boys, rivalry developed between them. The Kauravas became devious; the Pandavas, virtuous. As they grew older, the Kauravas used their military might for selfish reasons, while the Pandavas were greatly loved and spiritual minded political leaders. Dhritarashtra, as blind spiritually as he was materially, naturally favored his own boys, even though it was clear that the Pandavas were better suited to rule the kingdom.

The sons of Pandu were eventually given territory of their own, where they erected a great city. However, Duryodhana, the eldest son of Dhritarashtra and leader of the Kauravas, was jealous and plotted to take the territory of the Pandavas by dubious means. To this end, he arranged a game of dice in which the eldest son of Pandu, Yudhishthira, was sure to lose. The plot succeeded, Yudhishthira lost his kingdom, and the Pandavas were sent into exile for thirteen years.

As true Kshatriyas of their day, the Pandavas honored their (albeit rigged) defeat and entered the forest, believing they would regain their kingdom upon their return. But after the thirteen years, Duryodhana denied them the kingdom that was rightfully theirs. They then asked for five small villages, because, as Kshatriyas, life lacked meaning without kingdoms over which to rule.

Duryodhana, however, was cruel. "If they want as much land as fits under a pin," he sneered, "they will have to fight for it." Thus, by his humiliating response and his refusal to grant them even small villages to rule, he instigated what was to become a devastating battle.

By this time, the Kauravas had become infamous as exploitative kings. In contrast to the five sons of Pandu, whom the *Mahabharata* describes as incarnations of godly personalities (Adi-parvan 109.3), Duryodhana is seen as the Kali Purusha—the demon Kali in human form (Adi 61.80). In other words, he could be seen as the Hitler of his day. As a group, Duryodhana and his brothers embodied "the brood of ego-centric desires and passions like lust, greed, hatred, anger, envy, pride, vanity, and so on, to which the empirical ego is firmly attached and to which it clings desperately."[6] Their rampant mistreatment of the Pandavas—and of innocent citizens—multiplied with their years.

The Kauravas were "evil-doers" by any standard. From the Vedic point of view, they were guilty of six acts for which lethal retaliation is justified: (1) administering poison; (2) setting fire to another's home; (3) stealing; (4) occupying another's land; (5) kidnapping another's wife; and (6) attacking with a deadly weapon. Numerous chapters of the *Mahabharata* detail how Duryodhana and his men were guilty of these crimes.

Duryodhana, for his part, had fed Bhima a poisoned cake in one of several attempts to kill him; he had arranged for a house made of lacquer to be built for the Pandavas and then had it set ablaze while they and their mother were still inside; the Kauravas stole the Pandavas' land on several occasions; they kidnapped the Pandava wife Draupadi; and now, with war pending, they were about to attack them with the most lethal of weapons. Such aggressors, or criminals (*atatayi*), say India's sacred texts, should be killed by protectors of the righteous. *Manu-samhita* 8.350–51 says: "Whether he be a teacher ... an old man, or a much learned Brahmin, if he comes as a criminal (*atatayi*) in any of the above six ways, a Kshatriya should kill him.... There is no sin in killing one so heartless." In fact, tradition teaches that, "such a criminal is in reality killing himself by his own outrageous behavior."

Again, the Pandavas were not the exclusive focus of the Kauravas' hatred. As the latter's unjust reign grew, they wreaked havoc throughout the country, causing hardship for all their subjects. So the Pandavas' retaliation was not a vendetta but an attempt to save their fellow men. Professor Pandit Rajmani Tigunait paraphrases the *Mahabharata* when he summarizes the reign of the Kauravas during the Pandava exile:

> During this period of exile, the false king and his sons gathered an enormous military force, stockpiled weapons, and formed alliances with neighboring countries. Their subjects were miserable—taxes were heavy, with every penny used to increase the strength of the army; corruption was rampant, and women and children were not protected. People were praying for the rightful king and his four brothers to return from exile. When they did, the rightful king sent an emissary to the court with a proposal for getting his kingdom back. The emissary was mistreated and the proposal spurned.[7]

It should be underlined that the Pandavas preferred peace—and the *Mahabharata* carefully records this important fact. Indeed, the *Udyoga-parvan*—interestingly, "the Book of Effort," highlighting the intense endeavor made by the Pandavas to avoid the war—cites several instances in which both Krishna and the Pandavas pleaded for an end to the senselessness that lay before them. But all such requests, heartfelt though they were, fell on deaf ears.

Queen Draupadi insisted on war—she sought revenge for the injustices brought upon her husband, Yudhishthira. Others chimed in, too, saying that the disrobing of Draupadi should not go unpunished. The consensus was that the Kauravas should not be allowed to continue. Krishna, however, would not easily acquiesce to war, saying that serious conflict should be avoided if at all possible. War, He said, should never be waged for revenge, personal insults, or venting anger. At this point, it becomes evident that far from endorsing war, the heroes of the *Mahabharata* go to great pains to see that it never happens. But the die was cast—the battle became inevitable.

That the Pandavas clearly preferred a nonviolent alternative is eloquently expressed by Arjuna's eldest brother, Yudhishthira (*Udyoga-parvan* 70.55–58):

> War is evil in any guise. What killer is not slain in return? To those who die on the battlefield, victory and defeat are equal. . . . He who survives is also a loser: As time goes on, someone will perhaps kill one of his loved ones, as *karma* decrees, or he will otherwise regret his violent acts. . . . It is the righteous warriors, truly noble and with a mood of compassion, who are generally killed in war. And the lesser men escape. There is naturally remorse after the killing of others, especially in the hearts of warriors who know the value of life. Only pain can come from battle.

Yudhishthira, more than any other character in the *Mahabharata*, questions the whole premise of Kshatriya-*dharma*, saying that it inevitably leads to pain and regret. Nonetheless, without any other recourse, a major war soon came to be.

Lord Krishna, known by the cousins as God incarnate, was acting as the leader of the Yadavas from Dwaraka, a magnificent city on India's western coast. He offered Himself and His entire army to the cause of the upcoming battle. But both parties would have to choose one or the other. Krishna stipulated that He would do no battle—the side that chose Him would have to be content with His moral support. He would also act as a charioteer. The opposing side would have His nearly endless group of warriors, all highly trained.

Materialistic Duryodhana quickly chose the armed battalions. The righteous Pandavas, on the other hand, asked for Krishna alone, confident that God's grace offers more than any material facility. Krishna, the *Mahabharata* tells us, in letting the two sides choose Him or His army, shows that God is unbiased—if one turns to Him, to whatever degree, He reciprocates accordingly.

Thus, with Krishna as Arjuna's charioteer, the Bhagavad Gita begins. Both armies are arrayed and ready for combat. But before the war actually begins, Krishna pulls Arjuna's chariot into the middle of the battlefield, where the fabled bowman can see that on both sides there are friends, relatives, and countrymen. Arjuna becomes paralyzed with fear, with second thoughts about committing to the massive war that lay ahead, in which no one can really win. And Krishna begins to speak, or, rather, to sing.

Hinduism scholar Barbara Powell, author of *Windows into the Infinite: A Guide to the Hindu Scriptures*, nicely summarizes Krishna's song, the Bhagavad Gita, with special attention to the subject of violence:

> Initially one might expect Krsna to applaud Arjuna's decision [not to fight]. After all, by embracing nonviolence he appears to have assumed a morally superior stance. But Krsna shows a deeper truth. He will surprise us.
>
> "Coward!" He reprimands. "Such behavior is unfitting to a man of your station. Get out there and fight!"
>
> Is the Gita advocating violence? Of course not. In many other places in the text, Krsna will extol gentleness and nonviolence, even passivity. If there's one generalization we can make about the Gita, it's that it embraces diversity. No one occupation, standard of conduct or spiritual path is appropriate for everyone. Different people require different paths. Arjuna is a *kshatriya*, a soldier by profession, and it is his moral and spiritual imperative to attend to the duties, the *dharma*, of that profession. Were Arjuna a priest, a spice merchant, or a housewife, Krsna would have given him very different advice, for violence is never acceptable for these people. But the question of war and peace is not the issue here at all. The issue is action and inaction. If Krsna were talking to an exhausted mother with five screaming children all needing her attention at once, she might tell Him, "Krsna, I can't face it. There's no way I can be a mom today." His reply would be, "Yes you can. In fact, you must. It's your duty. Get in there and fight!" The war of Kurukshetra merely provides a context in which to examine the subtler truths of life and death, liberation and bondage. The battlefield represents life in the world, with all its perils, temptations, and vicissitudes. Each day we have new battles to fight, the greatest of all being the battle against our own lower natures, the struggle for spiritual emancipation.[8]

Powell makes several important points here, though to say that the Gita "in no way" advocates violence might be a bit extreme. In this particular case, to this particular person (Arjuna), the Gita is in fact advocating violence. Of course, in a larger sense, Krishna is addressing the more general question of "doing one's duty," or of "action versus inaction." But this doesn't change the fact that here, for Arjuna, violence is the path to righteousness. So, for Powell's analysis to be more accurate, she should have perhaps asked, "Is the Gita advocating violence for all people in all circumstances?" Then, her answer, "Of course not," would be appropriate.

"Does the Gita advocate violence?" The most honest answer would be, "In some circumstances, yes."

Powell goes on to say that "the war of Kurukshetra merely provides a context in which to examine the subtler truths of life . . . The battlefield represents life in the world. . . . " This again takes the metaphorical approach too far. While the battlefield context teaches us much about life and engaging in duty despite the most extreme of situations, it is simply a fact that some people do find themselves in this situation, as Arjuna did, and the Gita explains how to best react when confronted with such real life hardships.

WHO IS ARJUNA?

One step toward understanding violence in the Gita is to understand its main protagonist, Arjuna, who was quite literally a soldier. He was part of the ancient *varna* society, which is mentioned in the Gita (4.13) as a natural social system emphasizing quality (*guna*) and work (*karma*). The Gita explains that this system takes into account each person's individual nature, not merely birth status.

Basically, the *varna* system is comprised of four groups (1) priests and intellectuals; (2) political and military leaders; (3) farmers and merchants; and (4) the proletariat, including artisans—four natural social divisions found in one form or another in any given society. In India, these four are known as Brahmins, Kshatriyas, Vaishyas, and Shudras, respectively. A similar social structure is mentioned by Plato in *The Republic*, though slaves, in his system, take the place of Shudras. Many scholars say that the similarity is too great to be accidental—the connection, it is often thought, must have come through the Pythagoreans, whose teachings have much in common with those of ancient India. More on this social system and its connection with Plato will appear in an upcoming chapter.

The "quality and work" components sharply distinguish *varna* from the much later caste system, which divides society according to birth. Basing one's class solely on family considerations can cause problems. The son of a priest or an intellectual, for example, is not necessarily inclined to the same kind of work as his father. Or, to give another example, imagine a talented artist trying to convince his or her daughter that the little girl was born to paint, even though, despite all endeavor, she is unable to draw a straight line. The point is straightforward: Simply because one is born in a particular family does not mean that one will adopt the qualitative traits of his or her parents. However, everyone does have some natural inclination (either from birth or later acquired) and should therefore be engaged in their respective field. This is the *varna* system.

It should also be pointed out that *varna* was meant to be a form of yoga, or a way of uniting with God, and the saintly kings of Arjuna's time approached it in that way. They saw it as a type of *yajna*, or sacrifice, which was specific to one's psychophysical makeup—an opportunity to serve God in a way that is appropriate for the individual. For a Kshatriya, like Arjuna, this system teaches that death in battle is the highest duty, a religious sacrifice, and a sacred rite. The *Mahabharata* describes the Kshatriya arena of worship: His bow is his sacrificial stake, his bowstring the cord for tying the victims, his shafts are the small ladle, and his sword the large one. His chariot is the altar and the blood he pours on the battlefield is the clarified butter. His wrath is the fire of the sacrifice and the four steeds yoked to his vehicle are the four sacrificial priests (*hotri*). After spilling his own life-breath (*prana*) and that of his foes as libations upon the sacrificial fire of the battlefield, he becomes freed from sin and secures a place for himself in heaven (*svargaloka*).[9]

For the ideal Kshatriya, the sacrifice of battle becomes a form of total renunciation (*tyaga; sannyasa*) in which one puts one's own life on the line (*atmayajna*). Arjuna, says the Gita, knowing this full well, should not abandon his responsibilities nor pursue his own narrow interest, however noble or pacifistic it might seem at the moment. Instead, he must dedicate his life to the larger concern of human protection (*lokasamgraha*), undistracted by family ties and without attachment to the results of his actions. The sacrifice he performs then becomes an act of yoga due to its one-pointed focus on the task before him, in service to God.

Consequently, in Arjuna's world, war was seen as the proper sacrifice for the warrior (*kshatriya*), a sacrifice that potentially included the loss of one's life on the battlefield. It is this notion of unattached action (in contrast to the Vedantic renunciation of action itself) that distinguishes the teaching of the Gita. From here it becomes clear how all people can sacrifice their work to God, as opposed to sacrificing work altogether. Ultimately, all human activities—in any of the four *varnas*—could become a type of yoga, or sacrifice, provided that the fruits are dedicated to the pursuit of the spirit. This, of course, begins as Karma Yoga, or action on God's behalf, and, when imbued with devotion, becomes Bhakti Yoga.[10]

With this much background on Kshatriya-*dharma*, let us again look at Arjuna's particular predicament. Although a highly trained soldier, Arjuna does not want to fight. He shrinks from the act of killing. Given what we have just learned about *varna*—that it is judged according to quality and work—a legitimate question arises: Is Arjuna a genuine Kshatriya? After all, he argues in the Gita against fighting, and a true Kshatriya virtually lives for battle. So, although he may have been reared as a Kshatriya, cultivating the qualities of a warrior from childhood, does he actually have what it takes? Is it in his skin? In his blood?

Although in this case Arjuna has an aversion to war, he is nonetheless a genuine Kshatriya. How so? If his repugnance to the battle is merely a moment of weakness, a second thought, a solitary feeling of "Am I doing the right thing?" then Arjuna's status as a Kshatriya cannot be taken away from him. Despite one's natural inclination to a particular form of work, it is just as natural to periodically reconsider one's course of action, to ponder other possibilities, especially in extreme situations. Was this the case for Arjuna, or was he really something other than a Kshatriya?

To answer this with some certainty, we must, again, go back to the *Mahabharata*. There, we learn that Arjuna is actually the son of Indra, the warrior god of the Vedas (*Adi-parvan* 114.21). Implicitly, he was born for combat. But, as we have learned, birth is not enough. So, the *Mahabharata* goes further, stating that Arjuna not only studied under Dronacharya, arguably the greatest warrior-Brahmin of his time, but he is described as Drona's greatest student as well, his protégé (*Adi-parvan* 121). Arjuna stands out among all his brothers as the most skillful of Kshatriyas—he enjoys the hunt, wins awards, and takes to military life as a bee takes to honey (*Adi-parvan* 119). Arjuna feels that no other activity is as natural for him, and, prior to the event at hand, he lives the Kshatriya's life with great determination and pride. Indra himself tells Arjuna: "No one in existence, even on higher planets, can vanquish you. Your talents are beyond measure—you are unbeatable, matchless in the game of war (*Aranyaka-parvan* 165.2). And further, "No one living can compete with you as a soldier. Truly, the Kshatriya tendency is in your blood" (*Aranyaka-parvan* 171.2–3).

Acting within the *varna* system, then, Arjuna was clearly a Kshatriya, and to execute this properly was his *dharma*, his service to man and God. As a sensitive human being, he naturally questioned the propriety of such an all-encompassing war. But he was definitely a fighter, a soldier, and wanted nothing else out of life. With this now established, we can understand his plight by looking closely at the Kshatriyas' duty and the codes by which they lived. The etymology of the word is itself revealing: *kshat* means "hurt." And *trayate* means "to give protection." By this definition, one who protects from harm or violence is called a Kshatriya.

Kshatriyas like Arjuna were compared to gardeners. It was understood that they were to take care of "the field" in ways that the common man could not, keeping the garden healthy by plucking out weeds and other plants that were detrimental to the overall health of the garden. As Srila A. C. Bhaktivedanta Swami Prabhupada, Gita commentator and leading Vaishnava, writes:

> As in the paddy field the unnecessary plants are taken out, so it is expected from the very beginning of these topics [Bhagavad Gita] that in the religious field of Kurukshetra, where the father of religion, Sri Krishna, was present, the unwanted plants like Dhritarashtra's son Duryodhana and the other Kurus would be wiped out and the thoroughly religious persons, headed by Yudhishthira, would be established by the Lord.[11]

The gardener analogy is not meant to make light of Kshatriya violence. In fact, it was conceived in a Brahminical setting to acknowledge that Kshatriyas must sometimes do harm. A Kshatriya is a defender, a protector—a person who will resort to physical means to cultivate the field of life. He is not violent, but, rather, as stated, he protects others from violence. This is a necessary evil, since adverse conditions are an inescapable part of this world. These conditions, and the people at their root, are like weeds that, left unattended, destroy humankind's peaceful garden. Apropos of this, there must always be protectors of the innocent. To this end, a Kshatriya is trained in the military arts. He is noble and chivalrous. And, if necessary, he will employ combative tactics. Because there are people who perform evil deeds, Kshatriyas such as Arjuna are needed. And when Kshatriyas fight according to fair standards of warfare, only to protect and never as an aggressor, they serve an important function in society.

THE SPIRITUAL WARRIOR

Fair principles of war are similar in every civilized nation, even if said principles tend to be exploited by religious fanatics. From the Islamic jihad to the Crusades, men have fought each other in the name of religion—if not always in religious spirit. Historically, most "holy wars" are waged by political leaders who are generally unconcerned with true religious principles, even if they give lip service to sectarian affiliation. As Professor Stephen L. Carter writes in *God's Name in Vain: The Wrongs and Rights of Religion in Politics*:

> Wars are fought by countries, for causes in which the leaders believe. Critics of religious participation in politics are fond of arguing that religion has been the cause of many wars in the past. Partly true—but only partly. The religious wars, almost always, were fought by princes and their armies for some tangible benefit, such as territory or trade routes. Religion was often a convenient excuse, but it was rarely the underlying purpose.[12]

Lest one applies this idea to the *Mahabharata* war, a few additional points should be emphasized at this time: While the battle of Kurukshetra was ostensibly based on family squabbles and issues of land ownership, there were much deeper concerns at stake as well, such as saving the world from tyrannical rule and the devastation caused by powers of evil. On a deeper level still, Krishna Himself ultimately sanctioned the war, not some political-cum-religious representative with ulterior motives.

Another point: Although the Gita says that Krishna's philosophical arguments are universally applicable, His direction to kill is specifically meant for Arjuna. One should not thus use Krishna's words as a justification for violence. And the Vaishnava tradition—or the religious tradition based on the Gita's teachings—is clear on this: Only if God is personally in front of you, telling you to fight, should you engage in warfare.

In this rare situation, one becomes an instrument for the Supreme. Along these lines, it is interesting that Arjuna does not want to fight on his own behalf. Although the Kauravas have treated him and his brothers unfairly, to say the least—and caused havoc throughout the kingdom—he still remains softhearted and wishes to forgive them. This is a devotee's natural demeanor, and Arjuna is thus seen as Krishna's perfect devotee, the ultimate Vaishnava. Further, despite his own wish to set personal injustices aside, he has the larger vision of protecting the people who are depending on him, and, larger still, the understanding that Krishna, God, is personally telling him to fight. Thus, it is not on his own behalf that he engages in war, but on God's behalf. This is called the service of "agency." In the words of S.S. Rama Rao Pappu, scholar of Hindu Studies:

> Krsna urges Arjuna to act as His agent. In other words, though the material accountability for discharging the responsibilities of his role as a warrior fell on Arjuna, the formal, and the ultimate, responsibility of Arjuna's actions belong[s] to Lord Krsna.... [T]he [divinely] detached individual . . . is not responsible for the consequences of his actions in two senses: (a) His responsibilities, if any, are not "actor-responsibilities" but "agent-responsibilities;" (b) He is not an "actor," too, since his Self is not invoked in the production of (desirable) consequences.[13]

To make this clear by using an analogy: If a man kills for his own purposes, as an independent agent, he is considered responsible for his actions and must himself suffer the consequences. But if he kills as a representative of the armed forces, his government claims responsibility for his actions. In other words, if one acts independently, one sows what one reaps. But if one acts as another's agent, the reaping is properly done by he or she who sponsors the act.

This, again, is not meant to encourage irresponsible violence "on God's behalf," nor should such violence be engaged in frivolously. Rather, *Mahabharata* culture had strict standards for discerning whether or not one was truly acting for God. And in a situation where something as extreme as war was called for, the standards were higher still. Warriors in Arjuna's time never engaged in battle because a human being claiming to know God's will told them to. In fact, nothing short of God's presence and His direct affirmation of the war were acceptable. Needless to say, such occurrences in history are few and far between.

That Lord Krishna, the Personality of Godhead, was present during Arjuna's specific battle sharply distinguished the war of Kurukshetra from war in general, even those supposedly fought for religious purposes. Unlike modern combatants, the five Pandavas were neither pietistic generals, nor religious fanatics, nor misguided victims. They were pure servants of God, carrying out His divine plan. This, I know, begins to sound uncomfortably familiar. Warring nations often claim divine sanction. "Praise the Lord and pass the Ammunition" was a hit song in America during the Second World War. At the same time, Nazi storm troopers chanted "Gott mit uns," or "God is with us." In the more recent war between Iran and Iraq, soldiers on both sides shouted "Allah-U-Akbar!" ("God is Great!") But claiming divine sanction and actually having it are two different things. One may well ask, "Does God ever approve of war?"

Satsvarupa Dasa Gosvami, a contemporary devotee of Krishna and author of over a hundred books on Vaishnava traditions, writes:

> Those who fight for selfish and nationalistic interests forfeit any claim to God's sanction, despite their sanctimonious rhetoric. Such sectarian parties may claim God's sanction, but their claim is as meaningless as the goals for which they fight. God, the father of everyone, is equal to all; He doesn't favor a certain nation, group, or person. But to accomplish His mission of establishing the principles of God consciousness, protecting His devotees, and punishing the sinful . . . He may have His surrendered devotees fight on His behalf.

> Devotees of God are by nature nonviolent in the deepest sense: in the normal course of events they refrain from hurting any other living entity, and they strive to propagate the knowledge that can release one from the painful cycle of birth and death. Yet devotees also understand that war, when fought for the right cause—the cause of God—has its place in the world. The War of Kurukshetra was one among . . . such instances related in the Vedic literature.[14]

The war of Kurukshetra, especially, was fought according to sophisticated religious principles of fairness: "In the course of the battle, if one fights with speech, he should be opposed by speech only. One who, for any reason, leaves the midst of the battle should not be killed. A warrior on a chariot may only be fought by a warrior who is also on a chariot. One must fight opponents in fair ways, and no one who does not wish to fight is to be so engaged" (*Bhishma-parvan* 1.28–32). The rules of the *Mahabharata* battle are summarized by Gita expert Winthrop Sargeant:

> The great battle was supposed to be fought according to certain rules of knightly etiquette, which were, in fact, adhered to in the very beginning. Fighting was to take place only in daylight. After sunset, everybody mixed in friendship. Single combats were supposed to be only among equals. Anyone leaving the field or sitting in Yoga posture was supposed to be immune from attack. Anyone who surrendered was to be spared. Anyone momentarily disengaged was prohibited from attacking one already engaged. . . . Animals were not to be killed unnecessarily or deliberately.[15]

The Roman Catholic doctrine of just and unjust wars, too, evolved along similar lines. The original idea can be traced to St. Augustine, who said that a war is "only just when it is engaged in as a last resort; when it is declared by a legitimate religious authority; and when it is morally justifiable."[16] Once these criteria are discerned, the religionists who would go to war must consider the strategy by which the war will be fought. This consists of a rule of proportionality and a rule of discrimination.[17] Proportionality requires the use of only the minimal force necessary to emerge victorious; discrimination refers to just who is involved in the war: if someone is a civilian, an innocent bystander, or a noncombatant, they should not be harmed. These principles are similar to those employed by the Pandavas.

Interestingly, the Gita itself is nearly devoid of violence (barring the actual battle, which occurs after the Gita's final verses). To be accurate, in the Gita's Eleventh Chapter, Arjuna is given a mystical vision of the war that is yet to come: "All the sons of Dhritarashtra along with their allied kings and Bhishma, Drona, Karna—and our chief soldiers also—are rushing into Your fearful mouths. And some I see trapped with heads between Your teeth" (11.26–27). Here, the context of the Gita seems clearly martial, and Arjuna is being urged to fight an actual war. As Krishna says (11.34) "Drona, Bhishma, Jayadratha, Karna and the other great warriors have already been destroyed by Me. Therefore, kill them and do not be disturbed. Simply fight, and you will vanquish your enemies in battle."

That being said, the "violence" of the Gita centers on conquering our own lower self. We must defeat this opponent, the Gita tells us, with all the attributes afforded us by our higher nature. In other words, we must overcome our conditioning by gaining mastery over our mind and senses. Only then will we be able to see beyond the illusions of material existence and penetrate the higher reality of *bhakti*, or devotion for God. As the Gita says, "One must liberate himself with the help of his mind—not degrade himself. The mind is the friend of the conditioned soul, but it can be his enemy as well. For the person who has conquered the mind, it is the best of friends. But for one who has failed to do so, it will remain the greatest enemy" (6.5–6).

As alluded to in the beginning of this article, the Gita itself praises harmlessness (*ahimsa*) throughout its pages. In 10.4–5, *ahimsa* is glorified as a quality created directly by Krishna; in 13.8–12, it is described as knowledge as opposed to ignorance; in 16.2–3 it is a characteristic of divine nature, as opposed to the demoniac; and in 17.14 it is lauded as a desirable austerity of the body. Therefore, to reject the Bhagavad Gita because it superficially seems to support violence is missing the point of the text; the Gita itself rejects violence, and the *Mahabharata* (*Anushashana-parvan* 116.41) even praises *ahimsa* as the greatest of duties (*ahimsa paro dharmo*). Most followers of the Gita, in fact, have taken *ahimsa* to the point of vegetarianism—such persons would not even kill animals, much less humans.

The extreme nonviolence of those who embrace the Gita is confounding to those who think the text endorses war. And it is not only *ahimsa* that is taught in the pages of the Gita—it promotes many other qualities uncommon in martial texts. For example, Krishna explains that the truly enlightened person is *pandita sama-darshi*, or "a wise person who sees everyone equally"(5.18). If someone sees all beings as equal, how does he or she see them as enemies, or as representing an opposing army?

The ancient Indic culture in which the Pandavas reigned was a fair, even minded culture that, on the whole, preferred peaceful dealings. However, when evil appeared, in whatever form, the Kshatriya responded appropriately. In the Vedic literature, war against self-centered, destructive people, nonreligious forces, and untruth is praised as an act of purification (Rig Veda 8.104.1,7,12,13,19). While Vedic culture legitimates a rare form of violence based on religious principles, it sanctifies nonviolence as the best course of action. While it justifies war, it valorizes peace. The basic premise of Vedic culture teaches this: The ultimate solution to the mind-set that leans toward violence, conflict, and war, is, indeed, religion, or spirituality, which seeks to transform the consciousness. Only when every human is thus transformed by spiritual truth will violence appear foolish and aberrant, as it truly is. Until then, violence will necessarily, if unfortunately, play a part in life on earth.

It should again be underlined that not everyone is a Kshatriya, and Arjuna's dilemma is specific to his circumstance—not everyone in his position should fight. A Brahmin, for example, should not engage in warfare, nor would he generally find himself on a battlefield. Nor is he properly trained for engaging in battle. But a "born" warrior, like Arjuna, *must* fight. He would be acting inappropriately if he didn't fight, and this is Krishna's main point. The truth of this statement is so obvious that Gandhi, who otherwise endorsed nonviolence in all circumstances, wrote as follows:

> Let us suppose that Arjuna flees the battlefield. Though his enemies are wicked people, are sinners, they are his relations and he cannot bring himself to kill them. If he leaves the field, what would happen to those vast numbers on his side? If Arjuna went away, leaving them behind, would the Kauravas have mercy on them? No. If he left the battle, the Pandava army would be simply annihilated. What, then, would be the plight of their wives and children? . . . Arjuna, therefore, had no choice but to fight.[18]

That being said—and it was no easy thing for Gandhi to admit—it becomes obvious that sometimes fighting is necessary, as has been pointed out earlier. And this may be a good time to remember that, in a nonliteral sense, we are all Kshatriyas—we are spiritual warriors; and we all have no choice but to fight. There is a real life skirmish that must be fought and won. We must defeat our lower selves and emerge victorious. But we must fight on God's behalf. This is the essential message of the Bhagavad Gita. This is how the military symbolism applies to those of us who are not actual Kshatriyas. We must fight, as Arjuna fought, but our foes may be more abstract, more subtle, and, in this sense, more difficult to overcome.

The metaphor of spiritual seeker as warrior is a common one. Ancient Shaman-istic traditions speak of the truth seeker as "the true warrior." Taoism recognizes "warrior-monks," and so on. Such usage is pervasive for good reason. The spiritual pursuit is like a battle. Our material body, mind, and senses are immediate—they are in our face, as it were. The spiritual side of life needs to be nurtured, or uncov-ered. For most of us, it is far less immediate than our material circumstances, and so it becomes a struggle to make it a substantial part of our lives. Why should this be so? Is not spirituality our birthright, as Arjuna was born to be a Kshatriya? The Gita's answer is that we have lifetimes of conditioning to overcome, ages of deeply imbedded mental impressions that bind us to the bodily concept of life. Because of this conditioning, our natural spiritual nature remains covered; our material life enjoys prominence. To set aside the material in favor of the spiritual, then, is, in a sense, like swimming against the current. Along these lines, the Gita teaches that we have two choices: to float down the dry banks of material life, or to swim upstream to spiritual enlightenment.

CONCLUSION

Regarding the subject of violence in the Gita: It should be remembered that none of the soldiers—either among the Pandavas or the Kauravas—were draftees. All of them were voluntary, professional soldiers who wanted to be in the battle of Kurukshetra. Further, the Pandavas, for years, had begged the Kauravas not to fight, and had done everything in their power, including giving up their kingdom, to avoid the violence. But the Kauravas forced their hand.

Arjuna's plight might be better understood by imagining the following situation: What would you do if you woke up one morning and found that the U.S. government had been overthrown in a military coup and that the constitution was suspended? What if you then heard that half the military, loyal to the constitution and the rightful government, was fighting to reestablish law and order? Would you criticize the soldiers loyal to the constitution—who were defending your rights— for fighting to reestablish the real government? That's exactly what the Pandavas were doing.

Were they wrong in doing so? Would it be wrong to stop a Hitler, even if one had to use force? Let us assume for a minute that the reader is convinced that the Gita is justified in its use of war. What is it trying to show us? What is the larger picture, beyond the militaristic imagery? What is it that we are meant to learn from the Gita, at least in regard to violence? Asian Studies professor Chris Chapple leads us in the direction of an answer:

> In reading the Bhagavad Gita, which provides most people with their first introduc-
> tion to the *Mahabharata*, one could easily assume that the basic premise of Krishna's
> teaching glorifies war. Many a reader has winced when Krishna urges Arjuna to take
> up arms and Arjuna finally resolves to do so. A larger reading gives an utterly different
> picture: the war on Kuruksetra becomes a holocaust wherein the winners find no
> enjoyment in their spoils.... Furthermore, the gruesomely graphic detail of battle
> presented in the narrative has the impact not of an advertisement to join the armed
> forces, but rather of an anti-war film that exhausts, repels, and instructs its viewers
> regarding the horrors of war. One yearns for resolution to this seemingly endless
> conflict, hopes that this might be a war to end all wars, a hope that ultimately is
> not found in the realm of winners and losers but in the realm that transcends both
> winning and losing, the dissolution of the veil of otherness and alienation. This place
> beyond both, revealed in the final scene, is a realm of pacification ... where the blind
> see and all illusions are removed.[19]

This, in fact, is the real end to which the Gita hopes to bring its readers. It is not about violence or nonviolence but about transcending illusion and developing love for God. The battlefield scenario only serves to make this truth more poignant: If you had to sacrifice everything for God, would you be ready to do so? This same question is raised just as forcefully by Jesus, the Prince of Peace, in the Bible:

> Do not think that I have come to bring peace to the earth; I have not come to bring peace, but a sword. For I have come to set a man against his father, and a daughter against her mother, and a daughter-in-law against her mother-in-law; and one's foes will be members of one's own household. Whoever loves father or mother more than me is not worthy of me; and whoever loves son or daughter more than me is not worthy of me (Matthew 10:34–37).

These words could have easily been spoken by Krishna on the battlefield of Kurukshetra. Arjuna literally had to raise sword against family, because Krishna, God, asked him to. He had to show that he loved Krishna more than anything or anyone else. Jesus' statement as quoted by Matthew points to the same truth: One must love God before all others, even family. It is not that one shouldn't love family and friends, but that one's love of God should come first.

The ultimate test of one's love for the Divine would be if one were on a battlefield opposite all one's relatives (who were themselves opposed to the principles of religion). This was precisely Arjuna's plight, and this is why both the Gita and Jesus use militaristic imagery. It is meant to show us the ultimacy of a test that only the most devoted could ever pass.

These are subjects that are hard to deal with, and, when the words "violence" and "religion" are mentioned in the same sentence, it is natural to fear exploitation and abuse. Even if we are willing to admit that there may be some basis for righteous violence under the most extenuating circumstances, it is equally clear that unnecessary violence could be rationalized as religious duty. Such violence has already stained the pages of history. Innocent and sincere people have been exploited and victimized in the name of God since the beginning of recorded time; the concept of "holy wars" has been terribly abused through the centuries. This creates a natural fear and distrust of religious institutions, particularly when they use religion to justify unjust behavior to their fellow human beings. But does this mean that violence is never justified, or that violence is always violent?

Gandhi, to again quote this well-known supporter of the *ahimsa* ideal, writes that sometimes it is wise to see nonviolence in activities that may externally appear otherwise: "I have come to see that which I did not so clearly see before, that there is sometimes nonviolence in violence. . . . I had not fully realized the duty of restraining a drunkard from doing evil, or killing a dog in agony or one infected with rabies. In all such instances, violence is in fact nonviolence."[20]

Indian historian S. Dasgupta is quoted in *Mohandas Gandhi* as asking and answering the following question: If a dangerous beast enters a cattle shed, should one kill the beast or let it destroy the valuable cattle? Kill the beast, he concludes, for the principle objective is to maintain social order and the well-being of the people.[21] According to the Gita, this principle supercedes any abstraction, such as unqualified nonviolence (which is often an extremist position), which may result in more harm done than good. Dasgupta further asks us to consider if it is "violent" to engage in acts of self-defense. This was clearly the situation that Arjuna and his brothers were in.

The *Mahabharata* (*Shanti-parvan* 276.34, 110. 14, 15) asks us to consider other extreme cases where morals and ethics might be suspended for a higher good. For example, is it ever appropriate to tell a lie? The epic asks us to imagine a group of innocent people hiding in a forest. They are pursued by a heartless murderer who wants to kill them. The murderer approaches you and asks where they are. What do you do? Do you tell the truth, allowing the group of innocent people to be murdered? The *Mahabharata* advises: "In such a situation, do not speak unless you are asked. If possible, act like one who is dumb or ignorant. If you cannot escape without speaking, or if not speaking will arouse suspicion, in this context it is better to tell a lie than the truth." In other words, the epic encourages going to great lengths to avoid lying but recognizes that sometimes it is preferable to telling the truth. This same wisdom applies to the violence of the *Mahabharata* war.

Nonviolence, of course, is a quality cherished by many—and especially by those who follow the Bhagavad Gita—but it must be approached with practicality. Total nonviolence may be a diplomatic ideal, but it is never fully realized: Even when we breathe, we unintentionally kill tens of thousands of microorganisms. As long as breathing is a part of life, then, "violence" will be unavoidable.

And yet, the *Mahabharata* makes it abundantly clear that nonaggression or nonviolence (*ahimsa*) is the highest duty, as already stated. How is it, one might ask, that Arjuna achieved perfection while clearly abrogating the highest duty? How could he please God by acting contrary to the principle of reverence for life? This question leads to the Gita's esoteric teaching—the higher truth that the Gita seeks to give its readers. This truth is more profound than "reverence for life" or even meditation and yoga. This is the truth of love of God. Ultimately, the *Mahabharata*, taken as a whole, that is, including the Gita, goes beyond *ahimsa* as the greatest of all *dharmas*. It affirms that, in the normal course of events, nonviolence is the laudable path of all true spiritualists. But the Gita's final teaching is, "Abandon all *dharmas* and simply surrender unto God. He will protect you from sinful reactions. Do not fear, worry, or hesitate" (18.66). The ultimate or greatest duty is to surrender to Krishna, adhering to principles of nonviolence whenever possible. This secret is revealed in the *Bhagavata Purana* (1.2.6), too: "The highest *dharma* for all humanity is that by which one can attain to loving devotional service unto the transcendent Lord. Such devotional service must be unmotivated and uninterrupted to completely satisfy one's inner being." In other words, the Gita teaches that spiritual perfection lies beyond selfishness and violence—it lies in the realm of selflessness and love. This is the realm of pure devotion, where all dualities, such as violence and nonviolence, lose meaning, and become subsumed in Krishna's Divine service.

NOTES

1. For more on the origin of allegorical or metaphorical versions of the Gita, see the commentary of Abhinavagupta in Arvind Sharma, *Gitarthasangraha* (Leiden, Netherlands:

E.J. Brill, 1983). Robert Minor, a leading Gita authority, warns, "These allegorical inter-pretations are not in any way explicit in the Gita itself. The writer [of the Gita] does not seem to intend an allegory." See Minor, Robert, *Bhagavad Gita: An Exegetical Commentary* (Columbia, MO: South Asia Books, 1982), p. 2.

2. Stephen Mitchell, *Bhagavad Gita: A New Translation* (New York: Harmony Books, 2000).

3. Ibid., p. 206.

4. See V.S. Sukthankar, *On the Meaning of the Mahabharata* (Bombay, India: The Asiatic Society of Bombay, 1957), in which he explains that there are three levels of meaning to the text—the literal, ethical, and metaphorical levels. He bases this approach on the great teacher Madhvacharya, who, in his *Mahabharata-tatparya-nirnaya* (trans., B. G. Rao, Bangalore: 1941), mentions the three layers of meaning, one being allegorical.

5. Mahesh Kumar Sharan, *The Bhagavad Gita and Hindu Sociology* (Delhi, India: Bharat Bharati Bhandar, 1977), p. 10.

6. See Julian Woods, "Destiny and Human Initiative in the *Mahabharata*," unpublished Ph.D. Thesis, McGill University, 1993.

7. Pandit Rajmani Tigunait, *Yoga on War and Peace* (Honesdale, PA: The Himalayan International Institute, 1991), p. 77.

8. Barbara Powell, *Windows into the Infinite: A Guide to the Hindu Scriptures* (Fremont, CA: Asian Humanities Press, 1996), pp. 37–38.

9. Julian Woods, op. cit.

10. Ibid.

11. His Divine Grace A. C. Bhaktivedanta Swami Prabhupada, *Bhagavad Gita As It Is* (Los Angles, CA: Bhaktivedanta Book Trust, 1989, reprint), 1.1 purport, p. 37.

12. Stephen L. Carter, *God's Name in Vain: The Wrongs and Rights of Religion in Politics* (New York: Basic Books, 2000), pp. 125–136.

13. S.S. Rama Rao Pappu, "Detachment and Moral Agency in the Bhagavad Gita," in *Perspectives on Vedanta: Essays in Honour of Professor P.T. Raju* (Leiden, Netherlands: E.J. Brill, 1988), p. 156.

14. Satsvarupa Dasa Gosvami, "Can War Have God's Sanction?" in *Back to Godhead Magazine* 17:8, August 1982, p. 32.

15. Winthrop Sargeant, trans., *The Bhagavad Gita* (Albany, NY: State University of New York Press, 1984), p. 27.

16. Carter, op. cit.

17. Ibid.

18. *The Bhagavad Gita According to Gandhi*, ed., John Strohmeier (Berkeley, CA: Berke-ley Hills Books, 2000), p. 34.

19. Christopher Key Chapple, *Nonviolence to Animals, Earth, and Self in Asian Traditions* (Albany, NY: State University of New York Press, 1993), pp. 78–79.

20. Quoted in Mark Trivedi, *Mohandas Gandhi: The Man and His Vision* (Calcutta, India: Time Publications, 1968), p. 10.

21. Ibid., p. 15.

—5—

Krishna's Jewel Box

Throughout the centuries, numerous travelers have sought wealth in India. Colorful rubies and exotic gems of unimaginable value were brought back to Western shores as the sacred land of the Ganges was repeatedly pillaged for its considerable assets. This chapter will focus on an ancient text that also originated in India—the Bhagavad Gita—a metaphorical jewel box with secret treasures.

The first in the Gaudiya Vaishnava lineage to describe the Gita as a jewel box was the eighteenth-century philosopher and spiritual master, Vishvanath Chakravarti Thakur. In his commentary on the Bhagavad Gita, known as the *Sarartha Varshini Tika*, he divides the Gita's eighteen chapters into three sections: He writes that the first six are primarily concerned with *karma*, or the "actions" that bring one closer to God, and that the final six focus on *jnana*, which uses "knowledge" in pursuit of the Divine. The middle six chapters give us *bhakti*, or devotion—the Gita's essence and its highest prize. Vishvanath Chakravarti writes,

> The final six chapters of the scripture, Sri Gita, are jewels of spiritual education. They form part of a treasure chest containing the rarest secret of *bhakti*, or devotional service. The first six chapters dealing with *karma* form the golden, lower part of the chest, and the third six chapters dealing with *jnana* form its gem-studded cover. The *bhakti* found within is the most precious treasure in the three worlds. It has the power to bring Sri Krishna under one's control.

In commenting on the above, Vishvanath's disciple, Baladeva Vidyabhushana, takes the analogy further. According to Baladeva, the following verses are like a confidential inscription on the box, revealing its true meaning and value: "Because you are My very dear friend," Lord Krishna says to Arjuna, His exemplary devotee, "I am speaking to you the most confidential part of knowledge. Hear this from Me, for it is for your benefit. Always think of Me and become My devotee. Worship Me and offer your homage unto Me. Thus you will come to Me without fail. I promise you this because you are My very dear friend" (Bhagavad Gita 18.64–65).

Verse 18.65, in particular, is the only one in the entire Gita that Krishna repeats twice—He first utters this truth directly at the Gita's center (9.34), or in the heart of the *bhakti* section. In other words, this verse is so significant that He decides to repeat it, emphasizing this fact with the Sanskrit word *bhuyah* "again," in 18.64, where Krishna also underlines the fact that this teaching—always thinking of Him and becoming His devotee—is the most confidential knowledge and the most important part of the Gita.

THE THREE-FOLD DIVISION

The Gita's tripartite division, as expressed by Vishvanath Chakravarti, actually goes back to Yamunacharya, a tenth-century Vaishnava saint in the Sri lineage, who mentions it in his thirty-two-verse composition, the *Gitartha-samgraha*. Another great Vaishnava teacher, Ramanujacharya, who follows in Yamunacharya's line, develops the idea in his *Gita-bhasya*. Madhusudana Sarasvati, too, though ostensibly representing an alternate philosophical tradition, makes use of the same schema in his poetic work, the *Gudartha-dipika*. Finally, Vishvanath Chakravarti and Baladeva Vidyabhushana, as stated, give it new life in their respective commentaries on the Gita, adding Gaudiya Vaishnavism's signature "sweetness." Vishvanath, especially, uses diverse imagery to make his point: He writes that *bhakti* gives life to both *karma* and *jnana*, which are useless without it; that it nourishes *karma* and *jnana*, and so it is strategically placed in the text so that it touches both; as a lamp placed in a doorway sheds light on both sides of a door, so the middle section on *bhakti* illuminates *karma* and *jnana*, and so on. Thus, for Vaishnavas, the jewel box analogy is alluring, confirming that *bhakti* is the Gita's "special gem."

Following Baladeva, His Divine Grace A. C. Bhaktivedanta Swami Prabhupada uses this three-part division, too, and he is perhaps the first to do so in the English language. He sums up the idea as follows: "Chapters seven through twelve are the essence of the Bhagavad Gita. The first six and the last six chapters are like coverings for the middle six chapters, which are especially protected by the Lord."

While there is considerable overlap—that is, one can certainly locate elements of *jnana* in the middle section, *bhakti* in the last one, and so on—the great masters in disciplic succession did decide to describe the Gita in terms of these three sextuplets. In fact, if one looks at the text with an awareness of these dividers, one can make out just what the *acharyas* are talking about: chapters one to six establish the spiritual nature of the self and the importance of working (*karma*) for the Divine; its third chapter is even called "Karma Yoga," and the title of the fifth chapter reiterates this emphasis. Here we learn of the self, duty, yoga, and the culmination of yoga, which is to focus the mind and heart on Krishna, God; this is, of course, Bhakti Yoga, or devotional service. It is on this note that the first section ends, serving as an introduction, of sorts, to Chapter Seven, the beginning of the middle section.

The word "*bhakti*" proper does not arrive until the seventeenth verse of the seventh chapter, and it is not defined until the twenty-first verse. Chapters seven to twelve thus teach us about God, how to see Him in the world and beyond the world, and how to serve Him. Here we find the four "nutshell" verses through which the entire Gita is summarized. These verses are translated as follows:

> Krishna says: "I am the source of all material and spiritual spheres. All things emanate from Me. Those who know this perfectly are truly wide and therefore engage in My devotional service and worship Me with the entire being (10.8).
>
> "Those who are greatly devoted focus their thoughts on Me. Their lives are dedicated to Me. And they derive great pleasure, even bliss, by discussing My glories and enlightening one another about My transcendental activities (10.9).
>
> "I only reveal Myself to those who worship Me with such loving ecstasy. And I further give them the understanding and transcendental intelligence by which they can come to Me (10.10).
>
> "Because I have special compassion for them, I, who dwell in their hearts, destroy any shred of ignorance that may somehow remain—I accomplish this by using the lamp of true knowledge" (10.11).

This summarization focuses on service to Krishna (Bhakti Yoga). The last chapter of this section is even called "Bhakti Yoga," underlining the emphasis of the six preceding chapters.

Finally, in chapters thirteen to eighteen, we find an analytical study of material nature, with elaboration on consciousness and the way in which the world works. Arjuna opens the thirteenth chapter with a series of questions, showing his desire to understand all that Krishna has taught him. The Lord then expounds on the three modes of material nature—goodness, passion, and ignorance—and on how these modes impact everything that we see, hear, smell, taste, and touch. Overall, these chapters offer intellectual apparatus by which readers can learn to see and serve the Lord. In addition, this section examines the principle of renunciation, which is associated with true knowledge (*jnana*) and leads to surrender—the ultimate teaching of the Gita. The last chapter is essentially a summary of the text as a whole.

FIVE MAJOR TOPICS

The jewel box known as the Bhagavad Gita is home to many lustrous pearls that radiate pure knowledge and love of God. Traditionally, it is said that five such pearls, in particular, make up the Gita's special wealth: God (*ishvara*), the soul (*jiva*), material nature (*prakriti*), time (*kala*), and the intricacies of action and reaction (*karma*). Though these topics are also discussed in other sacred texts, the

Gita offers a most detailed analysis of them, as well as their implications in terms of the ultimate goal of life, devotional service to Lord Krishna.

Out of these five, the Lord, the living entities, material nature, and time are eternal. But karma is not—it comes and it goes. We receive the fruits of our actions, and then we move on, although the reactions may impact our lives in ongoing and countless ways. The manifestation of material nature, as we see it today, too, may be temporary, but it is not false, as some schools of philosophy claim it is. According to the philosophy of the Bhagavad Gita, the world is real but temporary. It is compared to a cloud that gradually moves across the sky, or the coming of the rainy season, which facilitates the growing of grains. As soon as the clouds are gone, or the rainy season is over, a farmer's crops will dry up. But next season the same process will repeat again, and after that, yet again. Similarly, this material manifestation takes place at certain intervals, stays for some time, and then disappears. Nonetheless, the cycle is going on eternally.

The Gita unpacks these terms more fully as the text moves from chapter to chapter. As one reads the Gita, one realizes that the term Ishvara ("Lord") implies monotheism—in its ultimate sense, it refers exclusively to one Supreme Godhead. Thus, the Gita informs readers of the distinction between *devas* (demigods, in the plural)—empowered beings from higher planets—and the Lord whom they serve. In fact, all other beings (*jivas*) are subservient to Ishvara, who is identified in the Gita as Krishna. Though *jivas* are eternal and fully spiritual, like Ishvara, they are small whereas He is great. The traditional example is that *jivas* are to Ishvara as drops of water are to an ocean—chemically analyzed, they are the same. But the ocean is great and the drop is tiny. Thus, the *jiva*—you and I—are not products of the material world (*prakriti*). Rather, we are of a higher, spiritual nature. Accordingly, we do not perish over the course of time (*kala*) but instead exist in a cycle of birth and death, reaping what we sow (*karma*) until we surrender to Krishna with love and devotion, at which point we stop reincarnating and join Him as loving devotees in the spiritual world. These points are important to understand if one is going to gain access to the Bhagavad Gita.

CONCLUSION

The Gita now enjoys immense popularity throughout the world and is traditionally considered one of the "Five Jewels" (*pancharatnani*) of the Mahabharata, along with other prominent episodes, such as "Thousand Names of Vishnu," and the "Teachings of Grandfather Bhishma." Perhaps it was this that inspired Vishvanath and Baladeva to restructure Yamunacharya's original jewel box analogy. Or they might have gotten their cue from the Gita itself: At the beginning of the Gita's most confidential middle section, in Chapter Seven, we read:

Krishna says: "O winner of wealth [Arjuna], there is no truth superior to Me. Everything rests upon Me, as *pearls are strung on a thread*" [italics added].

In this verse, Krishna refers to Arjuna as Dhananjaya, which means "winner of wealth." He also compares everything in existence to pearls, the valuable commodities one might find in a jewel box. Clearly, by the end of the Gita, the most precious wealth certainly belongs to Arjuna—he has submitted to Krishna and engages in His service, with love and devotion. In other words, the "jewel box" is his for the taking, and he indeed takes it like a man possessed, following Krishna's desire to the letter. This is the conclusion of the Bhagavad Gita.

The *Gita-mahatmya*, a series of verses glorifying the Gita and found in the ancient Padma Purana, gives us a hint of how valuable the Gita is:

> If one reads the Bhagavad Gita with great sincerity and determined seriousness, then by the grace of the Lord the reactions of his past misdeeds will not act upon him (*Gita-mahatmya* 2).

> Because the Bhagavad Gita is spoken by the Supreme Person Himself, one need not read any other Vedic literature. One need only attentively and regularly hear or read the Gita. In the present age, people are consistently absorbed in mundane activities and it is thus not possible for them to read the many existing Vedic texts. But such reading is not even necessary. This one book, the Bhagavad Gita, will suffice, because it is the essence of all Vedic literature and because it is spoken by the Supreme Personality of Godhead (*Gita-mahatmya* 4).

Thus, to achieve the Gita's jewels, as Arjuna did, is the greatest wealth in all of existence.

—6—

The Bhagavad Gita in Black
and White*

Thank you. I'm really happy to be here. It's been more than thirty years since I graduated from this school, and, as many of you may now know, I immediately joined the Hare Krishna movement after graduating, as did a good number of my friends from this school—maybe it's something you're serving in the cafeteria!

All kidding aside, though, the Krishna movement engaged my sense of art and color from the get-go. I was intrigued by the paintings, the incense, the temple worship, the singing and dancing—Krishna consciousness is an exotic world of colors, sounds, shapes, and fragrances. It engages the senses in so many ways. That's what I initially liked about it, coming from an art background.

I remember, in those days, in the early 1970s, I thought that spiritual life necessarily meant renunciation, giving up all pleasures in pursuit of God. I wasn't that far off. But it doesn't have to be dry renunciation, where the senses are starving for engagement. Just the opposite—I found out in Krishna consciousness that real renunciation means *using the senses* for higher spiritual ends, not starving them altogether. Why would God give us senses if we weren't intended to use them?

So, for those who think the Krishna movement is a place of dry asceticism—you can only call devotees "aesthetic ascetics," if ascetics at all. The philosophy is based on using this world in a God-conscious way, not renouncing the world in the usual sense of the word.

This is one of the main teachings of the Bhagavad Gita, the primary text of the Krishna movement. The Gita is one of the most famous philosophical poems of all time. It's part of the *Mahabharata*, one of the longest and most magnificent works of world literature. The Gita itself centers on a conversation between Krishna, God Incarnate, and His devotee, the warrior Arjuna. They are on a battlefield, just before the onset of a war of major proportions.

---

*A Lecture Delivered at the High School of Art and Design, New York City.

Now, Krishna and Arjuna exist in spiritual symbiosis, of sorts. Arjuna personifies the state of physical, mental, and spiritual suffering—he sees his relatives, friends, and teachers on the opposing side and begins to question the need for war at all. Arjuna represents a most difficult state of the human condition, like many of us today. Those family members and friends to whom he would rather feel loyalty have betrayed him—they have betrayed the world, too, wreaking havoc throughout the kingdom.

But, more personally, Duryodhana and his other cousins and half-brothers—who are on the opposing side—tried to kill him, to kill his brothers and his wife. These were bad seeds, known as the Kauravas, who, by the way, successfully banished the Pandavas, as Arjuna and his brothers were called, for thirteen years, and turned deaf ears to their pleas for peace and reconciliation. Even Krishna failed in His attempts to negotiate a settlement. As a result, Arjuna all but collapsed under the pressure. He says: "My limbs have become weak, my mouth dries up, my body trembles." In the first chapter he is depicted as a person riddled with sickness, doubt, illusion, and overall instability.

Krishna will have none of that. He presents to Arjuna the spiritual ideal, both in His own person and in His descriptions of what is to be done and what is not to be done. To make a long story short, Arjuna's encounter with Krishna gives him release from his hesitancy, from his doubt, and he enters the battle. By doing so, he not only does the righteous thing—for those on the opposing side were causing worldly torment and ruination—but he also attains spiritual enlightenment.

Part of this enlightenment is the awareness that man must call out to God in love and devotion. Krishna tells Arjuna that the great souls are always chanting His glories. They chant His glories to be in close touch with Him. And this is possible through chanting because God and His name are nondifferent, being composed of purely spiritual substance. Since God is absolute, His name, fame, form, and pastimes are the same. So, lovers of God keep closely connected to Him through chanting His name, and those of us who do not love God can attain that love by chanting, too. All religious traditions, in fact, mention chanting: Mohammed says, "Glorify the name of your Lord, the most high" (Koran 87.2). The biblical tradition teaches, "From the rising of the sun until its setting, the Lord's name is to be praised" (Psalms 115.3). These are just two examples of many.

The name "Krishna" is especially significant, though, because it refers to God on His own terms, in His own realm. What do I mean by that? Please consider this with an open mind: According to the ancient Vaishnava tradition embodied in the Krishna Consciousness movement, there are internal names of God and external names as well. The external names are those with which we in the Western world might be familiar—they refer to His nature only as He relates to us in the material world. You know, God as Creator, as Father, and so on. All religious traditions refer to such names in their respective languages.

But what about God in His own kingdom? What about His self-existent nature in heaven? What about His own internal life, in the realm of His pure devotees? These names are revealed in the Vaishnava tradition—they tell us of God as He interacts in an eternal world, with eternally liberated associates, in lush, beautiful landscapes of love. This is a land beyond time, where dedication and selflessness reign supreme. Such names, like Govinda, Nandanandana, and Gopala, will have little meaning to us—or merely seem "Indian"—if we are not studied in the ancient texts that reveal this transcendent world in full.

And of all such names and pastimes, Krishna reigns supreme, for here is the name and manifestation that suggests the greatest intimacy. It means, quite literally, the "All-Attractive one." And it refers to a hauntingly beautiful divinity who necessarily leaves management of the material world to His lesser manifestations. For His part, His sole activity revolves around pastimes of love; His only absorption is personal exchange and intimacy. Again, the aesthetic sense has opportunity to be fully engaged in the Krishna tradition, and if you see Krishna's form you'll know why.

But there's something more about the name "Krishna" that will appeal to the artist in each of you. Krishna also can mean "black." (Sanskrit is a complex language, and so the word "Krishna" can be understood in numerous ways.) And Arjuna means "white." As students of art, you'll immediately see implications here. In other words, God and the living being are never the same—they are as different as black and white. And I say this in spite of what many commentators have said. Those commentators who try to claim that Krishna and Arjuna are in some sense one—these are scholars and historians who obviously knew precious little about the actual Krishna tradition. All of the truly authorized commentators who are actually a part of the tradition are quite clear: God, Krishna, and Arjuna, His devotee, are never one. God is God, and the living being is the living being. And there's no getting around that, at least according to the Gita. I know that popular forms of Hinduism and numerous yogis from India claim that somehow man is God, and God is man. But no, not according to the Gita. Black and white. It's that simple.

Now, there *is* a sense in which God and the living being are one. Tradition asserts that we are one with God in quality, but definitely not in quantity. This means that just as God has various qualities, such as knowledge, wealth, strength, fame, and so on, we can possess these qualities as well—but God has them in unlimited proportions, whereas we have them in a limited sense. Sometimes in a very limited sense, no?

This notion of unity and diversity when it comes to God and the living entity is a school of thought called Achintya-bhedabheda Tattva, or the truth of our inconceivable oneness and difference from God. Most commentators, at least those with whom we are familiar in the West, tend to overstate the oneness with God. In actuality, the difference is far more significant, since the whole goal of a devotional text like the Gita is to remind us of our constitutional position as God's servants. If we're one with Him, there's no question of service. It's only by acknowledging our distinctness that serving Him has any meaning.

So let's look at this black and white component a little more closely. Those of you who have studied "Art theory" know that black is the absence of all color. It's unique in that sense. No other color is like that, just as no one is like God. He's in a category of his own. Conversely, white reflects all colors—it's a multiplicity, right? In that sense, white is like the living entities—we are part of a larger category. God is one, and we are many.

Let's see if I remember how it's taught: white light is said to be composed of all colors, and this is proven with a triangular prism, right? In nature, things appear white because they reflect all colors, whereas objects that seem to be of some other color absorb all colors except the color that they appear to be. For example, things that appear green absorb all colors of the spectrum except green, which they reflect, correct?

Superficially, this might appear to be saying that the ordinary living entity is greater than God, and that we absorb all colors but God is denied that particular asset. But think about what it's really saying: It's saying that the entire spectrum of colors has light in common, and that's all. Or, look at it this way, we could say that I reflect you and that you reflect me—we're both living entities, and so we reflect each other's qualities, in a sense. There is a sameness to us. That's all it's saying. God is in a different category altogether. Blackness reflects that unique position—it doesn't reflect all colors as white does, because it is totally Other. Like God.

Anyway, before we get too far adrift, let's remember that this is only an analogy—Krishna consciousness teaches that all living beings are like so many colors of the spectrum. And that God is one. There are so many analogies using color in the Krishna tradition, and in the Bhagavad Gita in particular. Take the three modes of nature, for example. This is a pivotal teaching in the Gita. There are three constituent qualities of material nature: goodness, passion, and ignorance. The entire world can be broken down into these qualities, and they affect us in numerous ways. Goodness is truth, righteousness, alertness, wisdom, joy, altruism, and so on. Passion is action, ambition, greed, frustration, and anger. Ignorance is characterized by idleness, sloth, and delusion. You can see how we're each affected by these modes.

They are compared to three primary colors: red, blue, and yellow. Now, as artists you know that we sometimes use these colors in their pure forms, but, more often than not, they're mixed in limitless ways. So, too, are the modes mixed in our lives, and thus few people represent pure goodness, pure passion, or pure ignorance. The Gita is a scientific approach to the modes, showing how to gradually evolve through goodness to pure goodness, and then to achieve perfect transcendence by learning how to serve God in a spirit of true devotion. While there is a lot more to the Gita and to Krishna consciousness in general, I think I'll leave you with that. This is, after all, the basic teaching of the text; it's what I've been working on for the many years since I graduated A & D. There are various nuances, but there you have it. This is the Bhagavad Gita in black and white.

— 7 —

Guru Tattva:
Transparent Medium
to the Divine

Implicit in the Bhagavad Gita is the need for a bona fide spiritual master, or guru. "Just try to learn the truth by approaching a spiritual master," Krishna says to Arjuna, "ask him relevant questions and render him some service. Such a qualified teacher can bestow his directly perceived knowledge on sincere disciples" (4.34). Earlier in the same chapter, Krishna makes it clear that authorized gurus come in traditional lineages. He further says that the Gita's considerable wealth is bequeathed to those who properly align themselves with such lineages (4.2). The reason this teaching is so important is that it is difficult to apprehend spiritual science without the benefit of an authentic preceptor. Thus, formal acceptance of a teacher is the first step in the pursuit of the Gita's teachings.

The value of a good teacher should be evident in all serious areas of endeavor, even if, for some, this is hard to admit. Nonetheless, if one is serious about learning a difficult subject, he or she would be wise to search out someone who is more experienced, at least for some initial guidance. This is all the more true when pursuing the Absolute Truth, which is complex and difficult to understand. Here's the problem: it requires humility and a sense of determination to admit that one needs a teacher. These are qualities that "level the praying field," to borrow Larry Dossey's catchy phrase. Few people have such qualities in any abundance. And yet it is precisely these qualities that allow one to appreciate the spiritual principle of Guru Tattva, or "Guru Reality," and all that it affords a sincere practitioner.

The term *guru* is itself interesting: It points to a metaphorical interplay between darkness and light, in which the guru is seen as the dispeller of all nescience. In some texts it is described that the Sanskrit syllables *gu* and *ru* stand for darkness and light, respectively:

The syllable *gu* means shadows,
The syllable *ru*, he who disperses them.

Because of the power to disperse darkness
the guru is thus named.
        —*Advayataraka Upanishad* (14.18.5)

Early Vedic texts teach us that the word is also an adjective meaning "heavy." It derives from a Sanskrit root whose cognates are the Greek *barus* and the Latin *gravis*—both also meaning heavy. Thus, the word *guru* is connected to "gravity" or "gravitas," indicating someone who is both "grave" and "heavy" with knowledge.

THE TRANSPARENCY FACTOR

A true guru is like a clear sheet, a transparent medium. Although the word "medium" might conjure up someone who speaks to spirits or communes with dead loved ones, that's not what I'm referring to here. The guru is a medium through whom one can actually see the Divine.

This transparent quality and the phenomenon of the guru as being heavy might be understood in relation to each other by way of a metaphor: Just as ice, water, and vapor, which are generally see-through, embody various degrees of heaviness, so does the Vedic literature describe three levels of perfect masters, one heavier than the other—though all are "see-through":

1. The Kanishta-adhikaris are those teachers in whose hearts a slight trace of material desire remains because of the influence of the mode of goodness (*sattva-guna*). In this type of perfected soul, desires, although present, remain dormant due to engagement in spiritual practice. Eventually, these desires are completely eradicated at their root (because of service to his or her own spiritual master). Such spiritual masters have two feet in the material world, but their eyes are fixed on the spiritual world.
2. The Madhyama-adhikaris, although residing in a material body, have no desire other than to serve the Lord. Such spiritual masters have one foot in the material world and have extended the other into the spiritual world of Krishna's eternal pastimes. There are other kinds of Madhyama-adhikaris, too, who have both feet in this world, but who distinguish themselves as preachers—by their intense desire to share knowledge of Krishna with others, they qualify themselves to be guru.
3. The Uttama-adhikaris are those who have attained their spiritual form in Krishna's eternal pastimes, whether or not they have given up their material body. Such gurus rarely appear in the material world. Their natural disposition is to see all living beings equally, but they bring themselves to the Madhyama level, whereby they are able to see distinctions between living beings and thus evaluate who they might help—in this way they function as spiritual masters. They have two feet in the spiritual world and extend their hearts to aspiring spiritualists out of compassion.

The third category of perfect souls listed above is ideal, and disciples can achieve the greatest benefit from submitting to such a spiritual master. Those in the first two categories of guru are servants of Uttama-adhikaris as well, and their disciples can serve these greatest of all teachers through them, again creating a transparent medium-type apparatus. However, it is important to understand that all three categories are gurus in their own right, and can guide disciples according to their means.

Thus, some gurus are close cousins to those who function comfortably in the material world, while others are coming directly from the spiritual kingdom, just to help others out of a sense of compassion. Their respective qualities are described in scripture, and well-meaning spiritual aspirants, who study scripture closely, can save themselves from becoming victims of wolves in sheep's clothing—or from being exploited by false gurus. Indeed, the scriptures do not speak in terms of "good" and "bad" gurus—only "real" and "false" ones. Accordingly, all three legitimate types of gurus described above are real and should be accepted by aspiring devotees.

The guru is an "unalloyed" servant of the Lord. An alloy is a metal that is mixed with other metals. But a guru is unmixed; he is focused on God because of his purity of heart. This sense of purity again feeds into the transparency metaphor—when something is pure, or unalloyed, it is clear, or uncontaminated by extraneous elements.

JUST WHAT IS A GURU?

The idea of a guru goes back to the earliest of Vedic texts:

tad-vijnanartham sa gurum evabhigacchet
samit-panih shrotriyam brahma-nishtham.

In order to obtain knowledge of the Absolute Truth, one should, or must (*evabhi-gacchet*), approach a true guru, carrying firewood for sacrifice. The qualification of such a guru is that he is well-versed in the Vedas (*shrotriyam*) and absorbed in the Absolute Truth (*brahma-jnana*).—*Mundaka Upanisad* (1.2.12)

This Vedic verse tells us much about the bona fide spiritual master. First of all, by using the word *evabhigacchet*, which is in the imperative case, we are told that it is mandatory to accept a guru. That is to say, acceptance of a bona fide perfected master is not optional but rather an essential part of spiritual life.

In Vedic times, the disciple would assist the guru in performing Vedic rituals and complex fire *yajnas*, and so the verse mentions "carrying wood for sacrifice." In modern times, such sacrifices are no longer the prescribed means of self-realization. Rather, the Sankirtana-yajna, or congregational chanting and spreading the word of Krishna, has replaced Vedic rituals, and a true disciple thus aids his guru in the Sankirtana mission.

But the most important part of the Upanishadic verse quoted above is that it reveals two defining characteristics of the bona fide spiritual master: *shrotriyam* and *brahma-nishtham. Shrotriyam* refers to being accomplished in the chanting of Vedic mantras, or *shruti.* In ancient times, one became accomplished in this art by sitting at the feet of a master. There was no other way to properly learn Vedic mantras. In other words, *shrotriyam* refers to the principle of disciplic succession—one learns spiritual science at the feet of a master, who necessarily learned at the feet of his own master, ad infinitum. Thus, one practices Vedic spirituality as part of a lineage, not independently. This is the true implication of the Gita verse referred to above (4.2): "This supreme science was thus received through the chain of disciplic succession (*parampara*)." It is no wonder, therefore, that those who truly know the teachings of the Gita say, "One who claims to be one's own guru has a fool for a disciple."

The other quality is *brahma-nishtham*, or one who is absorbed in the Absolute Truth. The operative word here is "absorbed." Clearly, a guru is not someone who has a part-time interest in spirituality. God engulfs his life, and because of this total immersion, he is brimming with the spiritual world; his very being is an effusion of Krishna Consciousness, enabling him to convey or communicate transcendental subjects by his teaching but no less by his presence and example.

Just as the true guru is someone whose essence reverberates spiritual science, there are those who should *not* be honored as guru, even if they represent themselves as such. The scriptures are clear on this, warning fledgling devotees who might easily be deceived by such persons. Actually, the preponderance of false gurus, especially in India, has led to a certain apathy in regard to guru-disciple relationships. Even so, the logic behind such apathy is clearly wanting. To reject gurus as a category, or as a philosophical necessity, because of impostors, is tantamount to rejecting money because of the circulation of counterfeit bills. Not all bills are really money—not everyone who claims to be a guru is actually a spiritual master. But that doesn't mean that there aren't any real spiritual masters. Only those who belong to the proper lineages and who are totally immersed in God—as mentioned above—are genuine spiritual masters. These are people through whom one can actually see God and learn about Him.

What is a disciple's duty to such a guru? While the Bhagavad Gita gives certain rudimentary instructions in this regard, other texts serve to augment them. For example, the traditional *Manu-samhita* tells us that the disciple should revere and serve the bona fide teacher with heart and soul (12.83). In addition, he should not argue with him (4.179–180) and always occupy a lower seat (2.198). He should never mock his teacher, nor should he abandon him, unless there is an extreme situation wherein the guru himself abandons his spiritual practices (2.199 and 11.60). A true disciple will not associate with his teacher's opponents (3.153) and quickly dismiss himself from the company of those who mock him (2.200). Finally, *Manu* tells us that the guru is responsible for his disciples' *karma*, meaning that all reactions to their disciples' previous activities are absorbed by them and burned to ashes (8.316–318).

CONCLUSION

To return to our metaphor of transparency: A guru is a medium through which we view reality. We want the medium to be transparent so that we can accurately view what is on the other side. This metaphor assumes a couple of things: (1) That the medium is conceptually separate from the object on the other side; and (2) that the process of seeing through the medium does not substantially alter the nature of the object viewed. These two points are central to the Gita's teaching on Guru Tattva, that is, the guru is not God Himself but only His pure representative and that the guru gives us God as He is, without alteration or deviation.

Just as a defective eye cannot see without the "medium" of glasses, so, according to the Gita, one cannot approach the Supreme Lord without the transparent medium of the spiritual master. "Transparent" means that the person who gives you divine vision must be free of contamination. If it is transparent, one can see through it. In the material world, we always see through a glass at least a little bit darkly; there is never a truly transparent medium, however subtle the cloudiness might be. But Guru Tattva is from another plane altogether, where perfect transparency exists in all its glory.

— 8 —

The Demigods:
Exalted Servants
of Krishna

Hinduism, as commonly understood, boasts almost as many gods as it does practitioners. And, because of this, it is often described as polytheistic. Fact is, the religion recognizes roughly thirty-three million divine beings (*devas*), or, according to some, 330 million. So Hindu leaders might easily claim, "Guilty as charged!"

But if one looks a little beneath the surface, monotheism peeks out with marked enthusiasm. This is nowhere as clear as in the Bhagavad Gita, where Lord Krishna is viewed as the one and only Supreme Lord, and India's many other "gods" are relegated to subservient status. Indeed, Vedic texts often refer to "devas" in the plural, indicating that while there are many "gods," there is only one Supreme Godhead.

Still, India's multitude of divine beings, with their many exotic names and supernatural powers, naturally makes one think of the polytheism of ancient Greece, for example. In fact, it has long been known that the Greek pantheon derives from ancient Sanskrit sources. The Vedic gods were clearly prototypes for those that eventually emerged in Greek mythology. One wonders if there might be a unified origin for the world's many mythological tales, an underlying reality for the wondrous myths that have captured our collective imagination for millennia.

The sages who give us the Gita aver that Vedic culture is that fountain, that source, from which all mythological truth originates. Interestingly, many of the names of the Greek gods do not have clear etymological origins in Greek sources. Rather, one must trace them to Sanskrit texts instead. For example, the name of the primary Greek god, Zeus, is mysterious in origin, unless one looks to India's Vedic literature. There, one finds the sky-god Dyaus, a name derived from a root *dyu*, meaning "to shine." Zeus, it is now known, connects to Dyaus, and there are other such linguistic and cultural parallels as well.[1]

In Greece, the gods were known as "demigods," meaning "half-gods"—from the Latin *dimidius*, or "half," which comes to us as the prefix *demi*. This intriguing term referred to special beings born to "mixed" couples: one divine parent and the other, human. Variations on this phenomenon occur in a number of ancient cultures. The biblical Nephilim, for example, were descendants of fallen angels who had had relations with mortal women.

A similar idea is found in the *Mahabharata*, where heavenly gods are said to have mated with earthly queens, in this case Kunti and Madri, to produce the Pandavas. Yudhishthira, the eldest Pandava prince, is thus the son of Dharma, the god of righteousness; Bhima is the child of the wind-god, Vayu; Arjuna is born of Indra, king of the demigods; and the twins, Nakula and Sahadeva, are the offspring of the Ashvins.

Vaishnavas refer to these divine paternal beings as demigods, too. Again, as with the Greek gods, they are seen as "half-gods." But the idea of pairing mortal with god to produce "demigod" progeny is only part of the reason. Ultimately, Vaishnavas call them demigods because—regardless of their parentage, partially divine or not—no living being can ever be equal to or independent of the Supreme Lord, who is here identified as Krishna or His other manifestations as Vishnu and His incarnations. In other words, the "demigods" are not considered God but rather highly empowered beings—and that's it. Not divine, only empowered. Not God, but His servants. Consequently, worship of the demigods is considered inappropriate, for worship is reserved for the Supreme alone.

Echoing these ideas, *Merriam-Webster's Online Dictionary* tells us that demigods are (1) a mythological being with more power than a mortal but less than a god; and (2) a person so outstanding as to seem to approach the divine. . . . " Both definitions would sit well with the teachings of the Bhagavad Gita.

By way of evidence, we might first look to the Gita's ninth chapter, where Krishna says, "Those who are devotees of other gods [demigods] and worship them with faith, actually worship only Me, O son of Kunti [Arjuna], but they do so without complete understanding" (9.23). The exact Sanskrit words Krishna uses for "without complete understanding" are *avidhi-purvakam*—"in an inappropriate, unauthorized way." He further states, "Men in this world desire success in self-centered activities, and therefore they worship the demigods . . . " (4.12). In other words, demigod worship is materially motivated.

Vaishnava commentators have asserted that material gain can never truly satisfy the soul, for all living beings are essentially spiritual. Matter works with matter, and spirit with spirit. How could spiritual beings ever really enjoy material delights? Keeping this in focus, the commentators further state that if one prays to demigods at all, one should do so for spiritual reasons. For example, the elephant-headed god Ganesh is traditionally venerated as "the remover of obstacles." For this reason, he is often called upon when trying to secure a good job, maintain bodily health, or in pursuit of a spouse. More properly, however, he can be asked to remove hindrances on the path to God realization. This would be a more spiritual reason for praying to Ganesh. But Vaishnavism stresses that even this is unnecessary, because all benedictions ultimately come from Krishna.

To highlight Krishna's supremacy and to indicate the secondary status of the demigods, Lord Brahma (who, in the Vaishnava scheme of things, creates the material cosmos on behalf of God) composed the treatise known as the *Brahma-samhita*. The Gaudiya Vaishnava saint Bhaktisiddhanta Sarasvati Thakur writes in his commentary to this great work as follows:

> The *Brahma-samhita* has refuted Panchopasana [Hinduism's traditional worship of five main gods: Vishnu, Surya, Ganesh, Durga, and Shiva].... The worship of Vishnu as found in Panchopasana does not please Vishnu; it is heterodox and highly improper.... The worship of Vishnu as one of the five deities makes His highest dignity, which is without any equal, similar to that of the other deities, and [in that system] His Lordship is counted as one of several deities, which is a great spiritual offense.... It is the eternal duty of all *jivas* [living beings] to serve [only] Krishna [or His alternate form as Vishnu], the Lord of all Lords. All other deities are His servitors. Their function is only to carry out His commands. They will never acquire liberation who conceive of the deities as the different names and bodies of Vishnu instead of knowing them as His servitors. Thus, five *shlokas* of the *Brahma-samhita* have described the natures of the five deities ... (1) "I (that is, Brahma) adore the primeval Lord Govinda [also known as Krishna], in pursuance of whose order the Sun-god [Surya], the king of the planets and the eye of this world, performs his journey mounting the wheel of time. (2) I adore the primeval Lord Govinda, whose lotus-like feet are always held by Ganesh on his head in order to obtain power for his function of destroying all the obstacles of the three worlds. (3) I adore the primeval Lord Govinda, in accordance with whose will Durga, His external potency, conducts her function as the creating, preserving, and destroying agent of the world. (4) I adore the primeval Lord Govinda, who transforms Himself as Shambhu [Shiva] for performing the work of destruction, just as milk is transformed into curd, which is neither the same as, nor different from, milk. (5) I adore the primeval Lord Govinda, who manifests Himself as Vishnu in the same manner as one burning candle communicates its light to another candle which, though existing separately, is of the same quality as the first."[2]

This is the ultimate conclusion of the Bhagavad Gita as well: There is one Supreme Godhead, known as Krishna, and if one worships "lesser" gods (to use the familiar terminology of the Bible) as opposed to worshipping Him, this is known as compromised religion.

What does "compromised religion" actually mean? Krishna answers in the Gita (7.20) by explaining that such religion stems from materialistic desires (*kamaih*), not from genuine spiritual concerns. Moreover, He says that those who surrender to other gods (*anya-devatah*) are, ultimately, bereft of intelligence (*hrita-jnanah*). The intelligent, Lord Krishna says (7.19), surrender to Him only (*mam prapadyante*), knowing Him to be the source of everything. He is the complete whole, the Absolute Truth, of whom all other living beings—even divine, heavenly beings—are a part.

The Gita therefore teaches that by worshiping Krishna one automatically worships all other deities, just as by watering the root of a tree one waters all its leaves and branches or by putting food in the stomach one feeds the entire body. How-ever, if one tries to nourish a tree by watering its leaves and branches only, or feed himself or herself by applying food directly to his or her thighs, for example, the process simply won't work. A comparable result awaits those who favor demigod worship.

Why then would Hinduism evolve as a religion in which numerous gods are worshiped?

Again, people have material desires, and they naturally look for a form of religion, and a deity, who speaks to the particular kinds of desires they have. Krishna, in fact, sets up reality in such a way that all living beings can approach Him according to their particular level of spiritual evolution, or devolution. That is, if one wants to approach God to satisfy his or her material desires, He allows it. He accepts it as a first step on the path to God-realization.

Krishna actually encourages this by setting up systems of religion, that is, demigod worship, whereby one can gain faith and gradually advance to more sophisticated levels of spirituality.

However, the Gita is clear that the benefits one gets from worshiping other gods are temporary (*anta-vat*), and that those who perform such worship are *alpa-medhasa*, "meager in intelligence" (7.23), as stated above. While the devotees of this "compromised religion" may attain higher material planets in the next life, they do not achieve the ultimate spiritual destination, known as the abode of Krishna. This is reserved for devotees of the Supreme Lord.

There are, indeed, Hindus who argue that "Krishna is not the only manifestation of the Supreme"—they say that all the gods should be considered equal. But the Bhagavad Gita disagrees. In 11.43, for example, Arjuna confirms that Lord Krishna stands alone: "No one is equal to You, so who could think that anyone is greater?"

Perhaps the idea that all gods are equal originates in Chapter Ten of the Bhagavad Gita (10.23), where Krishna identifies Himself with Lord Shiva, the demigod of destruction. Such quotes, it might be noted, hearken back to Rig Vedic texts, which tell us that, "Truth is one, even if sages call it by many names." The idea here is that diverse understandings of God are reflected in His many names and forms, and that they should all be accommodated within the framework of a tolerant religious system.

This is certainly true, but it doesn't mean that all names and forms represent the Supreme Absolute Truth. If we carefully look at Krishna's identification with Shiva in the Gita's tenth chapter, for example, we see that this identification has certain limitations. In that same chapter, Krishna identifies Himself with the lion, at least as far as beasts go (10.30); among fishes He is the shark (10.31); among seasons He is spring (10.35); and among cheaters He is gambling (10.36). Clearly, the lion is not God, the shark is not God, spring is not God, and—without doubt—gambling is not God. The point is that each of these, in their respective categories, is at the top of the list, and by thinking of what is best in all possible categories, one can ultimately learn to think of the Supreme Lord, Krishna. It is this realization that the Gita hopes to give its readers. Krishna concludes this section, in fact, by saying,

"Know that all these beautiful, glorious, and mighty creations spring from but a spark of My splendor."

Ultimately, then, *devas*, demigods, angels—or whatever one prefers to call them—are celestial beings, highly empowered souls, or just extraordinary individuals who assist God in universal affairs. This can range from controlling forces of nature, such as fire, air, wind, etc., services the Vedas and other sacred literature attribute to semidivine beings, to managing temples, or favorably guiding people to progressively higher levels of reality. Whatever their service, they are not to be confused with the Supreme Lord, either in His personal form as Krishna or as Brahman, the impersonal aspect of the Absolute. In actuality, there is only one God, and all demigods are, at best, simply mundane manifestations of His grace.

NOTES

1. For more on the Greek/Vedic connections, see Alexander Murray, "Mythology and Religion of the Hindoos," online at http://library.flawlesslogic.com/ved_rel.htm.

2. Bhaktisiddhanta Sarasvati, *Shri Chaitanya's Teachings* (Madras, India: Shree Gaudiya Math, 1934), pp. 309–311.

— 9 —

A Banyan Tree Grows in Brooklyn

A group of friends had long wanted me to join them for a trip to the Botanical Garden in Brooklyn, with its lush foliage, shrubbery, and assorted exotica. One day, I decided to take them up on their offer.

Founded in 1910, the Brooklyn Botanical Garden is a rich experience for all who venture in. Its "Many Gardens within a Garden" include the Children's Garden, tended each year by hundreds of kids; The Cranford Rose Garden, boasting more than 5,000 bushes of nearly 1,200 species; The Herb Garden, with more than 300 varieties, helps visitors rediscover the medicinal, culinary, and other uses of herbs; and The Japanese Hill-and-Pond Garden, is a beautiful creation featuring a Viewing Pavilion, Waiting House, Torri, shrines, bridges, stone lanterns, waterfalls, pond, and a miniaturized landscape.

The Steinhardt Conservatory, my personal favorite, is a $25 million complex housing the Garden's extensive indoor collection in realistic environments. Here the Garden simulates a range of global habitats. For example, The Tropical Pavilion, which is sixty-five feet high, recreates a rain forest complete with waterfall and streams. Flora from the Amazon Basin, African Rain Forest, and tropical eastern Asia thrive in this setting.

And it was there that we saw it. It looked like a banyan tree, but was it? My mind immediately raced to specific verses in the Bhagavad Gita, which introduces its readers to a very special banyan, a tree I would soon discuss with my friends.

A BANYAN BY ANY OTHER NAME

But first, our tour guide told us about banyans in general, confirming that the huge woody perennial in front of us was indeed a banyan: "The banyan tree is named after 'banyans' or 'banians,'" she told us, "the Hindu traders who would often rest or carry out their business under these very distinct trees." She went on to explain that the "roots" of the banyan are most unusual. Their seeds are carried by birds, who sometimes drop them on top of tall palm trees. Those seeds, nourished by the moisture and warmth within the host tree, quickly sprout and grow small branches. These branches grow long aerial roots that eagerly reach downwards toward the ground. Once these grasping roots reach their goal and get a firm grip in the earth, they enlarge to become strong trunks that wrap themselves firmly around the trunk of the host tree. These roots hang down and act as props over an ever-widening circle, which is why these particular trees are known in Sanskrit as *bahupada*, meaning "one with many feet."

"Banyan trees are considered sacred in much of South Asia," our well-trained guide continued, "particularly to Hindus and Buddhists, who refer to it as the Asvattha tree."

"Yes, it's a special tree," I thought to myself. Krishna, the Supreme Person, tells us in the Bhagavad Gita (10.26) that of all trees, He can be identified with the banyan. Our guide continued: "It is known as a tree that represents cosmic reality," she said, obviously attempting to invoke truths she had read in the Bhagavad Gita, "but it is really just a type of fig tree, or *peepul*, as figs are known in India."

At this point, one of my Christian friends spoke up, reminding us of a famous episode in the Bible: Jesus' cursing of a fig tree (Mark 11:12–14). One of the Bible's more debated passages, Jesus mysteriously curses the tree for not bearing any fruit, despite the fact that it wasn't even fruit season. Biblical critics have wondered why such a saintly person would evoke such a gratuitous, seemingly arbitrary curse. For many, it remains one of Jesus' most vexing actions. Some say that, in reality, the incident is meant as a metaphor for something larger. Was his cursing of the fig tree a statement about the material world—a world that does not deliver all that it promises? Indeed, this has been the reading of generations of Christian philosophers. An alternate reading suggests that Jesus was making a point about the Jewish leaders of his time, the curse symbolically indicating that it was they who were not "bearing fruit," and that therefore they would be cursed by God to never bear fruit again.

Since my friend was waxing philosophical, I thought it was high time to join in myself. I decided to begin with her own tradition. "You know," I began, "in Medieval Christianity, the cross was a symbol for 'the Tree of Life,' because various legends had traced the wood of the cross to the tree that sustained Adam and Eve in the Garden of Eden." We all looked at the Botanical Garden around us, recognizing how, glorious though it was, it would definitely pale in the face of Eden.

THE GITA AND THE BANYAN

At that point, the floor was mine, and I went on for a considerable amount of time about the banyan tree mentioned in the Gita. The "tree of life," I started, is a tree that somehow represents cosmic reality, and a similar metaphor is found in the Bhagavad Gita, particularly in its fifteenth chapter. And just as Jesus had cursed the fig tree in the Gospels, Krishna advises us to cut down the "fig tree" of cosmic

> Its roots above, it branches below, this is the eternal banyan tree (*ashvattha*). That alone is the brightness of Brahman! That alone is called the Immortal! On it, all the worlds rest!

But the full sprouting of this tree is found in the Gita (15.1):

> The Supreme Person utters the following words: It is said that there is an imperishable banyan tree that has its roots upward and its branches down and whose leaves are the Vedic hymns. One who knows this tree is the knower of the Vedas (15.1).

When Krishna says, "It is said," He is obviously referring to both the Rig Vedic and Upanishadic verses mentioned above, with which Arjuna, to whom Krishna was speaking, would have been familiar.

I read to my friends from my teacher's explanation, as presented in his book, *The Bhagavad Gita As It Is*:

> The entanglement of this material world is compared here to a banyan tree. For one who is engaged in fruitive activities, there is no end to the banyan tree. He wanders from one branch to another, to another, to another. The tree of this material world has no end, and for one who is attached to this tree, there is no possibility of liberation. The Vedic hymns, meant for elevating oneself, are called the leaves of this tree. This tree's roots grow upward because they begin from where Brahma is located, the topmost planet of this universe. If one can understand this indestructible tree of illusion, then one can get out of it.
>
> This process of extrication should be understood. In the previous chapters it has been explained that there are many processes by which to get out of the material entanglement. And, up to the thirteenth chapter, we have seen that devotional service to the Supreme Lord is the best way. Now, the basic principle of devotional service is detachment from material activities and attachment to the transcendental service of the Lord. The process of breaking attachment to the material world is discussed in the beginning of this chapter. The root of this material existence grows upward. This means that it begins from the total material substance, from the topmost planet of the universe. From there, the whole universe is expanded, with so many branches, representing the various planetary systems. The fruits represent the results of the living entities' activities, namely, religion, economic development, sense gratification and liberation.

While the great teachers in disciplic succession were well aware of banyan trees' peculiar nature—with roots coming from above and branches spreading out below—they prefer, instead, to focus on another dimension of the trees' inversion. The Gita's traditional commentators, including my own teacher, Srila Prabhupada, point out that inverted trees can be found beside any reservoir of natural water. On all water banks that have trees, we can see a reflection in rippled liquid—and there one notices branches that appear down, at the bottom, and roots that go way up to the top. Symbolically, this indicates that the tree of this material world is only a reflection of the real tree, which is the spiritual world—a topsy-turvy reflection at that.

This material reflection of the spiritual world, say Vedic texts, is based on each living entity's desire. In other words, desire that does not correlate with God's desire brings us to the material world, and establishes us in a quagmire of illusion. One who wants to get out of this material existence must know the original "tree" through analytical study and devotional practice. Then he can cut off his relationship with its unworthy reflection, that is, the material world, with the sword of knowledge. This is the process of Krishna Consciousness.

Bhagavad Gita (15.2–4) tells us that, "The branches of this tree, that is, the material world, extend downward and upward, nourished by the three modes of material nature (goodness, passion, and ignorance). The twigs are the objects of the senses. This tree also has roots going down, and these are bound to the fruitive actions of human society. The real form of this tree cannot be perceived in this world. No one can understand where it ends, where it begins, or where its foundation is. But with determination one must cut down this strongly rooted tree with the weapon of detachment. Thereafter, one must seek that place from which, having gone, one never returns, and there surrender to that Supreme Personality of Godhead from whom everything began and from whom everything has extended since time immemorial." Srila Prabhupada comments:

> The description of the banyan tree is further explained here. Its branches spread in all directions. In the lower parts, there are variegated manifestations of living entities—human beings, animals, horses, cows, dogs, cats, etc. These are situated on the lower parts of the branches, whereas on the upper parts are higher forms of living entities: the demigods, Gandharvas and many other higher species of life. As a tree is nourished by water, so this tree is nourished by the three modes of material nature. Sometimes we find that a tract of land is barren for want of sufficient water, and sometimes a tract is very green; similarly, where particular modes of material nature are proportionately greater in quantity, the different species of life are manifested accordingly.
>
> The twigs of the tree are considered to be the sense objects. By development of the different modes of nature we develop different senses, and by the senses we enjoy different varieties of sense objects. The tips of the branches are the senses—the ears, nose, eyes, etc.—which are attached to the enjoyment of different sense objects. The twigs are sound, form, touch, and so on—the sense objects. The subsidiary roots are attachments and aversions, which are byproducts of different varieties of suffering and sense enjoyment. The tendencies toward piety and impiety are considered to develop from these secondary roots, which spread in all directions. The real root is from Brahmaloka, and the other roots are in the human planetary systems. After one enjoys the results of virtuous activities in the upper planetary systems, he comes

down to this earth [in a subsequent birth] and renews his karma or fruitive activities for promotion. This planet of human beings is considered the field of activities.

CONCLUSION

Prabhupada makes it clear that our material sojourn could be understood—really understood—by studying the Bhagavad Gita. He explains that deep meaning is encoded in the Sanskrit words themselves, and that that meaning can be uncovered by studying the text under a bona fide spiritual master. I explained all this to my friends under a Brooklyn banyan.

Still, by the time we left the Botanical Garden, banyan trees mattered little. We were more concerned about our stay in the material world—we agreed that the important thing was to get our business done and to get out, that is, to become a bit more serious about spiritual life and to return to God's kingdom. (Since there were Jews and Christians present [along with devotees of Krishna] that kingdom is envisioned in diverse ways.) In fact, we wanted to bid adieu to banyan trees altogether—especially the one described in the Bhagavad Gita—and go back to our source, where the wish-fulfilling trees are eternal and exist merely to facilitate one's service to God.

— 10 —

Nothing Personal, Part I:
The Gita's Refutation of Advaita Vedanta

In the Gita, God is, first and foremost, a person. And I say this knowing full well that many Gita commentators would have it otherwise.

Krishna says to Arjuna, "Never was there a time when I did not exist, nor you, nor all these kings; nor in the future shall any of us cease to be" (2.12). He is talking here of eternal individuality—not in regard to the body, obviously, but to the soul, the actual spiritual entity within. He goes on to explain the distinction between body and self, and we will look at His teaching on this elsewhere. But for the purposes of this section, let it be underlined that Krishna teaches eternal individuality: it is not that He and Arjuna were at one time one, and that, due to illusion, they are now separated, and that the goal of yoga is to somehow coalesce once again. No. He is quite clear that they were always individuals, and that they will continue to be so.

This is especially emphasized in the Gita's fifteenth chapter, verses sixteen to nineteen. Here, Krishna tells Arjuna that, in reality, there are two kinds of living beings—the fallible and the infallible—and that the former are residents of the material world, while the latter are found in the spiritual realm. Initially, this seems to account for all existing classes of living entities. However, Krishna quickly adds that, besides these two, there is a third kind of living being: the greatest among all, God, or Krishna Himself. He says that He is the Supreme Person. The implications here are considerable—Krishna is perpetually distinct from all other living beings, material or spiritual, and it is for this reason that He is glorified in Vedic texts. He further says that people who know this truth engage in His service, which is the highest form of yoga. Thus, the goal of the Gita is not ultimately seen as merging in the Supreme or somehow becoming one with God but rather learning the art of serving Him with love and devotion. The practitioner seeks to become one with God in purpose, not in terms of morphology or ontology.

WHY IS THIS A CONCERN?

Most systems of Indian philosophy endorse the notion that, in some sense, all living beings are one with God. Some would say that spiritual philosophy in general—East *and* West—is based on the premise of oneness, suggesting an ontological unity for all that is. The reasoning is straightforward: since everything emanates from God, and since God is absolute, then His emanations partake of His essential nature, even if they exist in temporary forgetfulness.[1] Thus, ultimate spiritual vision, according to this line of thought, breaks down all barriers and allows us to see the truth of our essential oneness with God.

But how far can one take this truth? Is it "ultimate reality," or merely an aspect of reality, eclipsed by higher realizations marked by a transcendental form of dualism? This latter perspective is the view of most Vaishnavas, the devotees of God who claim that the dualities of the material world are indeed surpassed by the "oneness" propounded by Advaita Vedanta, as philosophical monism is technically called. But Vaishnavas go further, stating that to come full circle, spiritually, one must become aware of transcendental dualism—wherein a practitioner's enhanced sense of oneness is exceeded by relationship with God. Implicitly, say the Vaishnavas, a relationship requires two, not one.

The key here is relationship. Logic, religion, and philosophy have no meaning without it. In fact, the things most precious to us—love, compassion, and friendship—fall into oblivion if there is no relationship, if everything is ultimately one.

For example, if we are all one, who is relating to whom? Human nature itself thus instigates the urge to understand the relation of substance and attribute, cause and effect, subject and predicate. We naturally want to know God's relationship to the world, to other individuals. Vaishnava Vedanta supplies satisfying answers to these questions; Advaita Vedanta does not. This is because relationship presupposes two entities that interact—Advaita Vedanta presupposes no "other," no entity with whom one might enter relationship. In other words, to interact, two entities must be different, even if they are, in some abstract sense, one.

By the same token, however, total otherness also precludes relationship. If we disregard the essential oneness that exists between each of us, we are destined to extreme isolation. Differences are important but should not be overemphasized. There exists a genetic and spiritual bonding between all living beings as children of God. There is also a fundamental connection between all living beings and the rest of the visible world, which is also an emanation of the Divine. Thus, the concept of "difference," while revealing truths that are absent in Advaita Vedanta, should not be taken too far either, for it too has limitations.

UNITY IN DIVERSITY

Clearly, then, spiritual philosophy reaches its most complete form in the *achintya-bhedabheda* school of Sri Chaitanya (1486–1533), which is considered the cap on the Vaishnava tradition, for here we see both monism and dualism fully actualized as complementary aspects of the same truth. The phrase *achintya-bhedabheda* means "the inconceivable oneness and difference between God and the living being." It encompasses both the essential truths of Advaita Vedanta as well as the sense of "difference" found in earlier Vaishnava traditions. Here we see the idea of the "unity of opposites" in its most developed form. Mature religious understanding, Sri Chaitanya argues, is a constant dialogue between One and Zero, form and formlessness, feasting and fasting, and yes and no—seeing harmony in the obvious differences of diametrically opposed phenomena. And yet "harmony" presupposes an interaction of different elements working together. In the Gita, this has been analyzed as the paradox of the One and the Many—a paradox that has been resolved by monists in one way, as we have seen, and by Vaishnavas in quite another.

In the West, we tend to think about the One and the Many by looking at the phrase "E Pluribus Unum," which was a motto that originally meant "out of many colonies, one nation." Eventually, the phrase grew to encompass ethnic and European national dimensions: "out of many peoples, one people." Indic traditions, however, go further, using the principle to expound on religious pluralism, for it recognizes the great variety of human perceptions in relation to God. All of this is implied by the Rig Vedic verse, "Truth is one, though the wise refer to it by various names."

Western mystics have also taken E Pluribus Unum in more metaphysical directions, even to the point of unity among opposites, that is, among the One and the Many. "The fundamental law of the universe," it is said, "is the law of the unity of opposites."

The idea is usually traced to the Greek philosopher Heraclitus and, later, it is again seen in Plato's *Symposium*. Even in logic, the Greek writers tell us, the unity of opposites is a way of understanding something in its entirety. Instead of just taking one aspect or one part of a given phenomenon, seeing something in terms of a unity of opposites is recognizing the complete dialectical composition of that thing. Because everything has its opposite, to fully understand it one must not only understand its present form and its opposite form, but the unity of those two forms, or what they mean in relation to each other.

All of this is implied in Sri Chaitanya's idea of *achintya-bhedabheda*, the inconceivable oneness and difference between God and the living being. The simple yet profound philosophy at its base is explained as follows: Living beings are one with God and yet also different from Him in the same way that a drop of water, chemically analyzed, is one with an ocean but simultaneously different from it. That is to say, a drop of water may be one with an ocean in terms of quality, but it is different in terms of quantity. So, too, is the living being one and different from God in these same ways.

God, by definition, has all auspicious qualities in full: He is a virtual storehouse of strength, beauty, wealth, fame, knowledge, and renunciation. Ordinary living beings might have these qualities as well, but only in minute proportions. Again, quality but not quantity. Thus, India's Vaishnava sages teach that our oneness with God has certain limitations, and while a fledgling practitioner would do well to realize his or her oneness with all that exists, that is, with God, it behooves them to go further, to reach for the culmination of the spiritual pursuit, wherein they go beyond this sense of spiritual oneness and situate themselves in a loving relationship with the Lord, the reservoir of all transcendental qualities. This is the ultimate perfection to which the Gita hopes to bring its readers.

THE TEACHINGS OF SHANKARA

The person responsible for popularizing Advaita Vedanta—to the exclusion of Vaishnava Vedanta—was known as Shankaracharya (ninth century CE), whose "nondual" philosophy had roots in the Upanishads. He taught that absolute monism is the highest truth, and that Brahman, as the Divine was known in the Vedas, is ultimately impersonal, with incarnations that are only lesser manifestations. He also taught that the world is an illusion (*maya*) created by an all-pervasive ignorance (*avidya*), and that when this ignorance is dispelled, one realizes one's inherent divinity or identity with the Supreme. Although there has been some heated discussion about what Shankara actually taught, and, indeed, what he actually meant, the above is clearly the essence of his teaching. A famous quote from his very own work, the *Vivekachudamani*, succinctly summarizes his philosophy: *Brahma satyam jagat mithya, jivo brahmaiva naparah*—"Brahman is the only truth, the world is unreal, and there is ultimately no difference between Brahman and individual self." Noted scholar Georg Feuerstein summarizes the Advaita realization as follows: "The manifold universe is, in truth, a Single Reality. There is only one Great Being, which the sages call Brahman, in which all the countless forms of existence reside. That Great Being is utter Consciousness, and It is the very Essence, or Self (Atman) of all beings."[2] Impersonal God, complete oneness, all relationship is illusion. Though admittedly simplified, this is a summary of Shankara's beliefs, making it clear why Vaishnavas came to see his doctrine as an anathema. Vaishnavas look not so much for *fusion* but rather *communion* with the Divine.

Indeed, Vaishnava schools of thought were formalized as a response to Shankara: Ramanuja's Vishishtadvaita ("Qualified Nondualism"), Madhva's Dvaita ("Dualism"), Vallabha's Shuddhadvaita ("Pure Nondualism"), among others. These even have the "advaita" nomenclature as part of their official titles, but even the other Vaishnava schools, without such obvious titles, were clearly reactions to Shankara. He had touched a nerve, depersonalizing the cherished God whom Vaishnavas had come to know and love. His clinical, philosophical stance had become offensive to devotional hearts.

To be fair, Shankara acknowledges both personal and impersonal features of the Supreme. In his work, he describes two levels of Brahman: *saguna* ("with qualities") and *nirguna* ("without qualities"). The *saguna* Absolute is a personal God, with attributes and characteristics, whereas the *nirguna* Absolute is without qualities and impersonal. Vaishnavas also acknowledge both dimension of the Supreme. The difference here is that Shankara gives priority to the impersonal aspect, claiming it is the source of God and His manifold incarnations. Vaishnavas debate this claim with scripture and logic—with special attention to the Bhagavad Gita.

Shankara's position might also be questioned in terms of the three levels of God-realization outlined in the Gita: Brahman, Paramatma, and Bhagavan. Brahman is considered the rudimentary level, wherein one realizes the truths of Advaita Vedanta and the glory of merging into an impersonal Absolute; it is said to give practitioners an overwhelming sense of eternality. Paramatma is realization of a more localized aspect of God—evoking a type of panentheism in which God exists within and in between every atom; it affords practitioners a sense of eternality and divine knowledge as well. Finally, Bhagavan realization is considered the zenith of spiritual attainment, wherein one develops a loving relationship with God; here one achieves inner awareness of both eternality and knowledge, as in Brahman and Paramatma, and a profound sense of bliss, too. These levels of God-realization are depicted as hierarchical, with progressively greater dimensions of insight accruing for practitioners of each. Additionally, as one graduates from Brahman to Paramatma to Bhagavan, one finds that each level contains or encompasses the prior one, so that the third and final level, Bhagavan realization, is the most comprehensive of the three.

Generally, these three successive platforms of realization correspond to India's three major paths: Jnana-marga ("The Path of Knowledge"), which brings one to Brahman; Karma-marga ("The Path of Work"), leading to realization of Paramatma; and Bhakti-marga ("The Path of Devotion"), which establishes devotees in loving relationship to the Supreme Person, Bhagavan.[3]

In Western philosophy, we might refer to these as cognitive, conative, and affective ways of being, respectively. To expand on this correlation, consider the following: There are basically three sets of relations between consciousness and its content—thinking, willing, and feeling (again, cognitive, conative, and affective). "Thinking" is abstract, removed—witness the austere meditator, indifferent to the world around him. "Willing" is the urge to act, to "make manifest," to use the body in its most appropriate way for the best possible action. But "feeling" surpasses all the rest. The heart envelops our actions and our thoughts, making us whole as human beings. One can utilize one's ability to think and act, but if done without feeling, aren't we merely automata? The sages of ancient India have thus analyzed these three functions as a detailed science, developing them into spiritual practices known as Jnana-marga, Karma-marga, and Bhakti-marga. Shrivatsa Goswami, a contemporary Vaishnava scholar, puts it like this:

> If one's point of departure is cognitive or indifferent, the Ultimate Reality of the absolute is undifferentiated consciousness. The cognitive path is recognized by the Advaita Vedanta of Shankara, where we are Ultimate Reality, Brahman. If one's approach is conative, then the end to be attained subjectively is Paramatma, the

supreme innermost being of all beings. . . . But if one's approach is affective, reality
becomes manifest in the fullest form of all, as Bhagavan, the Supreme Godhead.[4]

Thus, Vaishnavas argue that the notion of oneness with God is only preliminary,
subservient to Paramatma and Bhagavan realization, and that, ultimately, one
must realize the virtue of devotion to the personal Godhead. In the words of
Madhvacharya (1118–1238 CE), one of the world's most renowned Vaishnavas:

> The Supreme Person is the foundation upon which everything rests. O individual
> spirit-soul, you are simply a reflection of that Godhead. Only one moon shines in
> the sky, although innumerable reflections of that moon may appear in the water
> or in other places. O individual spirit soul, the Supreme Person is like that single,
> original moon, and the individual spirit souls are like innumerable reflections of
> Him. Just as the reflections remain always distinct from the moon itself, in the same
> way the individual spirit souls remain eternally different from their original source,
> the Supreme Personality of Godhead. O individual spirit soul, this is the eternal
> distinction between you and the Supreme [*Sri Tattva-muktavali*, Text 12].

These words merely echo those of the Gita, which in turn echo the Upanishads. *Ni-
tyo nityanam chetanas chetananam*, says the *Katha Upanishad* (2.2.13): "Although
there are innumerable eternal beings, there is one Supreme eternal amongst all
these eternals. According to the Gita, that Supreme eternal being is Krishna, the
Personality of Godhead.

NOTES

   1. This forgetfulness, of course, is the first philosophical problem in Advaita Vedanta.
If Brahman is Ultimate reality, and if it is One without a second, how does one account for
illusion (*maya*) and ignorance (*avidya*), which suggests duality in Brahman? Advaitins are
void of an answer.
   2. Quoted in Samuel Birchwood, *Monism East and West* (New York: Shalley Press, 2001),
p. 7.
   3. Alternatively, these successive stages are sometimes expressed as follows: While Jnana-
marga is always associated with Brahman, Karma-marga is sometimes aligned with svargaloka, that is, by practicing Karma Yoga one can attain the heavenly regions or the astral plane.
And, in this schema, it is Ashtanga Yoga, or the Eightfold Path (systematized by Patanjali),
that is associated with Paramatma realization. In other words, there are diverse ways in
which the scriptures view its numerous yoga systems, ascribing alternate conceptions of
Godhead and hierarchical considerations as a result of this variance.
   4. Shrivatsa Goswami, "Radha: The Play and Perfection of Rasa," in John Stratton
Hawley and Donna Marie Wulff, eds., *The Divine Consort: Radha and the Goddesses of India*
(Berkeley, CA: The Graduate Theological Union, 1982), pp. 73–74.

— 11 —

Nothing Personal, Part II:
God Is True to Form

"God exists, and God is light
    for those poor souls who dwell in night.
But doth a human form display
    To those who dwell in realms of day."
                —William Blake

A major publisher recently approached me to write a book comparing over a hundred English translations of the Bhagavad Gita. I told them I would consider their offer, and within a week I received at my door, special delivery, a box full of the decade's most prominent Gita translations. Looking through each one carefully, I was surprised that the majority of translators misunderstood the basic teaching of this seminal text—that God is a person, Krishna, and that the goal of life is to develop love for Him. Instead, these "Gitas" claimed that God is an abstract force, an impersonal entity that lies beyond the purview of the senses—the commentators squeezed this out of the Sanskrit itself and often made it the focus of their analyses.

To be sure, Vaishnava stalwarts had many times written that nondevotees tend to misunderstand Lord Krishna's words. The sacred text, according to Vaishnavas, must be understood from the lips of a pure devotee and by engaging in devotional service under his or her direction. Otherwise, if one is pursuing the Gita in terms of mere scholarship—or even for the purposes of realizing Brahman or Paramatma—its ultimate conclusion, in terms of Bhagavan realization, will remain far, far away. It should be clear: The impersonal or monistic conception of the Supreme—wherein one envisions God as an inconceivable force, without form—is a legitimate part of what the Bhagavad Gita teaches. But it is only a part, and it is eclipsed by the idea of God as the Supreme Person. As Krishna Himself says in the Gita, "Uninformed people, who do not know Me perfectly, think that I, the Supreme Lord, Krishna, was impersonal before and have now assumed this personality. Due to their poor fund of knowledge, they do not know My higher nature, which is imperishable and supreme" (7.24).

And yet, despite the Gita's emphasis on God's personhood, its impersonalistic dimension has become more popular. There are many reasons why this might be so. Teachers in the Vaishnava tradition suggest that the desire to depersonalize God comes, on a subliminal level, from the desire to avoid surrender: After all, if God is a person, then questions of submission and subservience come into play. If He is a formless abstraction, we can philosophize about Him without a sense of commitment, without the fear of having to acknowledge our duty to a higher being. Then again, maybe the popularity of the impersonal conception, at least in relation to the Gita, can be traced to inadequate knowledge of Sanskrit. Plain and simple.

WHY IMPERSONALISM?

Think about it: Form is everywhere, from mountain to snowflake. Everything has form. Even when things are invisible, they have shape. Consider the atom: Though we don't see it, we know it occupies definite space and, with the proper equipment, it can be perceived. Deep down, we know that, in this world, a thing and its form are inseparable.

And this, of course, is where impersonalism comes in. If everything in this world has form, everything in "that" world must be formless, for matter and spirit are seen as diametrically opposed. While the premise here may be true, the conclusion is all but logical. Rather, it is like the conditioned thinking of a cow that runs from a burning barn. If a barn catches fire, the cows running for their lives will naturally be afraid, and it is likely that whenever they subsequently see red, or something resembling fire, they will fear another blaze. Similarly, everyone in this world knows that material forms are temporary and limited—even the greatest of forms, like planets, deteriorate and eventually disappear, nothing escaping impermanence. This truth is embedded in our consciousness, and we naturally (if sometimes subliminally) apply it to all form—never imagining that spiritual form may have different characteristics altogether. We consequently foist formlessness on God and on all spiritual phenomena, following Shankara like a cow running from a burning barn.

If one studies the Gita as an aspiring devotee of God, however, it becomes clear that it is the person Krishna, also known as Bhagavan (the Lord), who reigns Supreme. It is service to Him that is emphasized in nearly every verse. Again, the Gita itself supports the personalistic doctrine: Krishna says, "I am at the basis of the impersonal Brahman [that is, the formless Absolute]" (14.27). And, when discussing the comparative value of the impersonal and the personal, He says, "Those who focus their minds on My personal form, always engaged in worshiping Me with intense spiritual faith, are considered by Me to be most perfect" (12.2). In other words, the conception of God as a person, to Whom one may become devoted, is prior and superior to the conception of God as an impersonal force, into which one may merge. At least according to the Gita.

And what exactly does "merging" mean, anyway? Vaishnavas, worshipers of Krishna, shun this idea of becoming "one with God," saying it is almost as abominable as gross materialism. His Divine Grace A. C. Bhaktivedanta Swami Prabhupada, one of the world's foremost authorities on the Bhagavad Gita, says that it is motivated by fear. In his Gita commentary (4.10) he writes:

> It is difficult for a person who is too materially affected to understand the personal nature of the Supreme Absolute Truth. Generally, people who are attached to the bodily conception of life are so absorbed in materialism that it is almost impossible for them to understand how the Supreme can be a person. Such materialists cannot even imagine that there is a transcendental body that is imperishable, full of knowledge and eternally blissful. In the materialistic concept, the body is perishable, full of ignorance and completely miserable. Therefore, people in general keep this same bodily idea in mind when they are informed of the personal form of the Lord. For such materialistic men, the form of the gigantic material manifestation is supreme. Consequently, they consider the Supreme to be impersonal. And because they are too materially absorbed, the conception of retaining the personality after liberation from matter frightens them. When they are informed that spiritual life is also individual and personal, they become afraid of becoming persons again, and so they naturally prefer a kind of merging into the impersonal void.[1]

So just as impersonalism stems from the fear that one will have to submit to a higher entity, as stated earlier, we now see that its concomitant "merging" is also a product of fear—the fear that one's individual existence, with all its imperfections, will continue into eternity. But Vaishnavas promote a philosophy of fearlessness, for they know that spiritual personality is not beleaguered by the limitations of matter. There are scholars who are wise to this, too. For example, Professor Huston Smith, a prominent author and teacher in the field of comparative religion, eloquently expresses the distaste that Vaishnavas have for merging with the Supreme. He does this with the help of a traditional *bhakti* poem written in Medieval India:

> As healthy love is out-going, the *bhakta* [devotee] will reject all suggestions that the God one loves is oneself, even one's deepest Self, and insist on God's otherness. As a ... devotional classic puts the point, "I want to *taste* sugar; I don't want to *be* sugar."

> Can water quaff itself?
> Can trees taste of the fruit they bear?
> He who worships God must stand distinct from Him,
> So only shall he know the joyful love of God;
> For if he say that God and he are one,
> That joy, that love, shall vanish instantly away.

> Pray no more for utter oneness with God:
> Where were the beauty if jewel and setting were one?
> The heat and the shade are two,

If not, where were the comfort of shade?
Mother and child are two,
If not, where were the love?
When after being sundered, they meet,
What joy do they feel, the mother and child!
Where were joy, if the two were one?
Pray, then, no more for utter oneness with God. (A poem by Tukaram)[2]

BUT IS GOD REALLY A PERSON?

Seeing the many impersonal translations and commentaries really got my ire. I decided to find arguments supporting the idea that God is indeed a person, for if I were to make a comparative study of existing Gita translations, as I was asked to do, I would want to emphasize the conclusion of the great masters. I would, as a student of Vaishnavism, want to follow the lead of Vaishnava luminaries and present Bhagavad Gita as it is—showing that God is, at least as far as the Gita is concerned, a person. *As It Is*, in fact, is the name of Prabhupada's translation and commentary, which gives a lot of ammunition for the argument of personalism.

Prabhupada is clear about the primacy of personalism in his own Gita commentary, incredulous that anyone could accept the impersonal idea of the Absolute:

> We cannot understand how the Supreme Personality of Godhead could be impersonal; the imposition theory of the impersonalist monist is false as far as the statements of the Gita are concerned. It is clear herein that the Supreme Absolute Truth, Lord Krsna, has both form and personality (7.24, purport).

When Prabhupada mentions the "imposition theory," he refers to a particular group of impersonalists who claim that God's impersonal feature is superior to His form. This group further says that God's form is an "artificial imposition" created by the illusory energy. However, they don't explain why or how God's energy, which is subservient to Him, is able to obscure His form, nor are they able to reconcile their position with scriptural statements.

This personalistic view is not only supported by scripture but, at times, it is also given play by modern scientists. Though I have now come across many such statements, here is a particularly powerful one by Dr. John C. Cotran, who, before he retired, was Professor of Chemistry and the Chairman of the Science and Mathematics Division at the University of Minnesota. He was known for his penetrating logical abilities and insightful perceptions:

> Chemistry discloses that matter is ceasing to exist, some varieties exceedingly slowly, others exceedingly swiftly. Therefore, the existence of matter is not eternal. Consequently, matter must have had a beginning. Evidence from Chemistry and other sciences indicates that this beginning was not slow and gradual; on the contrary, it was sudden, and the evidence even indicates the approximate time when it occurred. Thus at some rather definite time the material world was created and ever since has

been obeying law, not the dictates of chance. Now, the material realm not being able to create itself and its governing laws, the act of creation must have been performed by some nonmaterial agent. The stupendous marvels accomplished in that act show that this agent must possess superlative intelligence, an attribute of mind. But to bring mind into action in the material realm as, for example, in the practice of medicine and the field of parapsychology, the exercise of will is required, and this can be exerted only by a person. Hence our logical and inescapable conclusion is not only that creation occurred but that it was brought about according to the plan and will of a person endowed with supreme intelligence and knowledge (omniscience), and the power to bring it about and keep it running according to plan (omnipotence) always and everywhere throughout the universe (omnipresence). That is to say, we accept unhesitatingly the fact of the existence of "the supreme spiritual being, God, the creator and director of the universe."[3]

Seems obvious. And this is what Vaishnava teachers have been saying for millennia. But (with due respect to Dr. Cotran) for those who have a personal relationship with the Lord, like Prabhupada and other great devotees, it is not some removed philosophical outlook. Vaishnava devotees feel personally offended when their beautiful Lord is described as having no eyes, no mouth, no hair, no form, and, as a result, no love. To deny God these distinct personal characteristics, they say, is the height of arrogance. Do humans have something that God does not? Would this not make us greater than Him? Especially when it comes to loving exchange. We can love, but God cannot? To say God is unlimited and then to say that He cannot have a form is contradictory. If He is unlimited, He can do whatever He likes. And if loving exchange is the highest activity, as most will admit, then God would most definitely deign to be a person—for loving exchange loses meaning without personhood; it can only exist between people.

WHAT THE TRADITION TEACHES

Ultimately, Vaishnava philosophy says that all conceptions of God are included in the personal form of Sri Krishna. The impersonal Brahman, according to the tenets of Vaishnavism, is but an aspect of the Absolute, which by its very nature is endlessly qualified and perfect in unlimited ways. The concept of the Absolute as *merely* impersonal, beyond all thought and speech, is dismissed by Vaishnavas as meaningless and absurd. Such an Absolute cannot stand, for it would cancel itself out. Our very language disallows it: even to say that Brahman is inexpressible or unthinkable is to say or think something about it. This is the argument that Jiva Gosvami (a great Vaishnava teacher and philosophical commentator) poses in his classic work, *Sarva-samvadini*, and it is certainly a powerful one. He points out that the whole proposition of Brahman as an independent Absolute, without being counterbalanced by a Personal Absolute, is full of inherent contradictions.

Jiva Gosvami cites the teachings of Shankaracharya, the ninth-century philosopher mentioned above, who was among the first to emphasize the impersonal Absolute. Having accepted the undifferentiated Brahman as the sole category of existence, Jiva tells us, Shankara fails to give a satisfactory explanation of the world of appearance, which necessarily implies qualities (*vishesha*) in Brahman. In other words, how can a variegated world, with such diverse attributes, come from an undifferentiated Absolute? There is something unnatural about it. In India, impersonalist philosophers say that all variety in the material world is false, and that only the Supreme Brahman, or Spirit, is real. But if Brahman is real, as they say, how can the world and its varieties, which they admit emanate from Brahman, be false? If Brahman is real, its emanations must be real. For example, if a tree bears many fruits, can anyone realistically claim that the tree is real but its fruits are not? No. Brahman is real and so are the variegated emanations that come from it.

To be sure, it's not just the followers of Shankara who are given to this impersonalistic madness. Such via negativa philosophy is commonly identified with the Buddhistic thought of Nagarjuna as well. And philosophers in the West haven't shown immunity, either: impersonalism is seen in Jewish thinkers, such as Maimonides, and in the Christian mysticism of Pseudo-Dionysius and Meister Eckhart, among others. It's being carried on today by Matthew Fox, and even Fritjof Capra, and Gary Zukav, to name a few.

Ultimately, however, the Absolute is positive, and since nothing positive is without attributes, the Absolute must embody divine qualities (*savishesha*). Not only must it be determined by certain qualities or attributes, but also because it is infinite, it must be determined or qualified in endless ways. There should be nothing in which it is wanting. If there is anything that in some form does not belong to it, then in so far as it is lacking in that, it is imperfect and cannot, properly speaking, be called Absolute. This means that the Absolute must be personal, beginningless, and the origin or the ground of everything else. Thus, the notion of personality is not only consistent with the infinite Godhead but also essential to it. As if to sum up, the *Brahma-samhita* (5.1), one of India's most ancient religious texts, says: *ishvarah paramah krishnah, sat-chid-ananda-vigrahah, anadir adir govindah, sarva-karana-karanam*—"Krishna, or Govinda, the Supreme Godhead, who has an eternal, blissful, spiritual body, is the prime cause of all causes." It is this same Krishna who speaks the Bhagavad Gita.

But even without scripture, if we think about it, the whole impersonalistic enterprise just doesn't make sense: I'm a person. If my source is impersonal, then where do I come from and *what am I* in an ultimate sense? If my source is impersonal, how can I, a person, relate to it? Moreover, even if some kind of impersonal experience exists, such an experience always occurs to a person—it's you and I, people, who have the "impersonal" exchange with God! In other words, even if you call it "impersonal," because it happens to a person it must be considered a variety of personal experience.

Impersonalistic philosophers, however, argue that a qualified and personal Absolute must be limited, because to attribute certain qualities to it is to deny certain others, which are opposed to them. But impersonalists must understand that it is not personification or attribution of character or qualities to the infinite that puts limitation upon it, but it's these things not carried to their fullest extent.

The *Chandogya Upanishad* (7.14.4) describes Brahman as *sarva-karma sarvakamah sarvagandhah sarvarasah*, which indicates that Brahman is not only endowed with characteristics, but that it also displays such characteristics in endless ways. The Vedic texts frequently describe Brahman as *vijnana-ghana* and *ananda-ghana* as in verse seventy-nine of the *Gopala Tapani Upanishad*. In texts such as this, the word *ghana* implies that Brahman is knowledge (*vijnana*) and bliss (*ananda*) personified. There are innumerable other verses that support this view.

Thus, Sri Chaitanya (1486–1533), the incarnation of Krishna who appeared in Bengal, India, some five centuries ago, argued that the impersonalistic view of unqualified Brahman is based mainly on the indirect meaning of Sanskrit words. The argument is elaborate, but to summarize: The indirect meaning of words (*lakshana vritti*) is justified only where the direct meaning (*mukhya vritti*) does not make any sense. Shankara's exclusive emphasis on unqualified Brahman makes him conceal the direct and real meaning of the scriptures, which more often than not describes Brahman as qualified.

Srila Madhvacarya, one of the original systematizers of the Vaishnava tradition, gives an example of how Mayavadi philosophers (as a particular school of impersonalists in India are known) conceal the direct meaning of Sanskrit words:

> The Mayavadi commentator on the Vedanta claimed that the words *tat tvam asi* are among the most important statements in the Vedas. And according to his explanation, *tat* means "the Suprme," *tvam* means "you," and *asi* means "are." He therefore interpreted the phrase to mean "You are the Supreme," and he claimed that there is no difference between the Supreme and the individual spirit soul.

> The Vaishnava commentator interpreted these words in a different way, saying that *tat-tvam* is a possessive compound word. According to his explanation, *tat* means "of the Supreme," and the entire phrase means, "You are the servant of the Supreme." In this way, the proper meaning was revealed by Vaisnava commentators (Madhvacarya, *Tattva-muktavali*, Text 6).

Madhva further argues that the Puranas unambiguously describe how the entire universe came into existence from a lotus that sprouted from the Lord's navel. This leads him to a natural question: Are we then to conclude that the Supreme has only a disembodied navel and not a complete body? If the Supreme Lord has a navel, he says, then He must also have a body, complete with limbs and senses—*though they are not like our limbs and senses* (see *Sri Tattva-muktavali*, text 45, emphasis added). As outlandish as this argument might appear, it nonetheless carries weight for those who accept Puranic stories as divine revelation. Since both Vaishnavas and Advaitins give them such credence, the disembodied lotus polemic is more sensible than it might sound to Western ears. Further, it might additionally be argued that Vishnu and His lotus-bearing navel are to be seen as merely metaphorical—but the Puranas are quite clear that the story be taken literally, and Vaishnava and Advaitain sages from the earliest epochs of history have understood it in this way.

One wonders, therefore, how impersonalists, especially those who follow India's sacred texts, can make any case at all for a formless Absolute. To be fair to them, then, it must be admitted that there are also many texts that describe Brahman as unqualified. *Katha Upanisad* (1.3.15), for example, describes Brahman as *ashabdam, asparsham,* and *arupam,* which means that Brahman has neither sound, nor touch, nor form. This idea is echoed in the *Brihadaranyaka Upanisad* (1.4.10), wherein Brahman is described as *achakshushkam, asrotram, avak, amanah,* etc., meaning that Brahman has neither eyes, nor ears, nor speech, nor mouth, nor mind.

Jiva Gosvami resolves the issue by explaining that the scriptures often use the word "*nirvishesha* (without qualities)," for example, to deny all *prakrita,* or "material," qualities of Brahman and not to deny qualities as such. If it were used to deny qualities as such it would not be possible to attribute to Brahman the qualities of *nityatva* (eternity) and *vibhutva* (all-pervasiveness), which are accepted by even the followers of Shankara themselves as undeniable qualities of the Absolute. Jiva Gosvami also quotes from the *Vishnu Purana* to prove that although Brahman does not have any ordinary or material qualities, it has infinite transcendental qualities.

Thus, Brahman, or God, cannot be described as *merely* unqualified. Jiva Gosvami writes that such a "Brahman" is like the subject of predication apart from its predicates, or the substance apart from its attributes. Since the complete (*samyak*) form of an object includes both its substance and its attributes, the unqualified Brahman is only an incomplete (*asamyak*) manifestation of the Absolute. Jiva Gosvami insists that the personal Brahman includes the impersonal Brahman as the formless luster of His divine form (*anga-kanti*). In Prabhupada's words, the impersonal Brahman is merely "Krishna's effulgence."

Implicit in these arguments is the understanding that God is inconceivable, and that He is, ultimately, both personal and impersonal. It is further understood, as stated, that His impersonal aspect is dependent upon His personal form, which is prior. The arguments are logical enough, and yet our minds revolt against the idea of an Absolute being at once personal and impersonal. We want to choose one or the other. This is because we are inclined to think of the Absolute in human terms. For this reason, it must be reiterated that the form of the Absolute is different from our own. We have to be careful not to limit the infinite with our human thoughts and terms, which would be the fallacy that impersonalists attribute to the doctrine of a personal God. When dealing with any problem relating to the infinite, we have to use normal logical laws with reservation and necessary caution, not allowing them to impair the perfection of the infinite or impoverish our notion of divinity.

Henry L. Mansel, a nineteenth-century English philosopher, who was Professor of Moral and Metaphysical Philosophy at Oxford, expressed the same idea in this way:

> It is our duty, then, to think of God as personal; and it is our duty to believe that He is infinite. It is true that we cannot reconcile these two representations with each other, as our conception of personality involves attributes apparently contradictory to the

notion of infinity. But it does not follow that this contradiction exists anywhere but in our own minds; it does not follow that it implies any impossibility in the absolute nature of God. The apparent contradiction, in this case, as in those previously noticed, is the necessary consequence of an attempt on the part of the human thinker to transcend the boundaries of his own consciousness. It proves that there are limits to man's power of thought, and it proves no more.[4]

CONCLUSION

To describe the Absolute as merely *nirvishesha*, or without quality and attributes, is to make Him imperfect by amputating, as it were, the auspicious limbs of His divine personality. Once the absolute, complete, and perfect nature of the Divine Being is recognized, the philosophy of impersonalism cannot consistently be maintained. The Bhagavad Gita clearly describes the Absolute as both personal and impersonal, or rather as possessing infinite attributes and forms, including an impersonal dimension. When this is properly understood, the conflicting statements of the Vedas and the Puranas can easily be reconciled. But according to the primary and general sense of the scriptures, the Absolute is essentially personal, because only in a personal Absolute, possessing infinite and inconceivable potencies, can the manifold forms of Godhead, including the impersonal Brahman, have their place.

In fact, complete monism, or Advaita Vedanta, would inadvertently obliterate the entire spiritual quest as we know it—for how can one worship oneself? On a practical level, it is simply not possible, leading to frustration and the abandonment of spirituality in general. But more to the point is this: If one is, in the ultimate sense, God, there is no need for submission to a superior spirit. There is no I and Thou, no relationship, and no love. Believers in Advaita Vedanta might call this mystical exaltation or a higher sort of divine union, but, looked at objectively, it is simply unabashed egotism, the ultimate illusion—the desire to be God.

Will I write the requested book about the many existing editions of the Gita? Probably not. Vaishnava editions are clear enough about what the Gita teaches and include the best of all the versions I looked through. So I may just have to send all those books back to that publisher. But if they would like me to do a book on personalism versus impersonalism, I might just go for it. Nothing personal, of course.

NOTES

1. His Divine Grace A. C. Bhaktivedanta Swami Prabhupada, *Bhagavad Gita As It Is* (New York: Collier Books, 1972), purport, p. 230.

2. Quoted in Huston Smith, *The World's Religions* (New York: HarperCollins, 1991, reprint), p. 33.

3. Quoted in Bruce Satfield, *New Frontiers: The Meeting of Science and Religion* (Los Angeles, CA: Netshed Publishers, 1995), p. 7.

4. Quoted in S. Caldecott and M. Mackintosh, eds., *Selections from the Literature of Theism* (Britain: H & L Publishers, 1975, reprint), p. 64.

—12—

Explosive Devotion: Robert Oppenheimer and the Universal Form

For some, the recent nuclear testing in Pokhran, Rajasthan (part of the Thar Desert in India), was reminiscent of an earlier time, in 1974, when India first experimented with nuclear weapons. Right there, in the same area (though many miles underground), the country's first bomb succeeded in shocking the scientists who built it: elaborate monitors revealed that the blast generated enough heat to compete with the sun. Huge rocks, the size of mountains, vaporized on the spot, and immense shockwaves tossed mounds of earth the size of football fields from one region to another. It was later documented that some of the scientists, watching closely, compared the local devastation to the work of Shiva, the god of destruction, and also to that of Krishna, the Supreme Person, who manifested the awe-inspiring Universal Form (*virat-rupa*) mentioned in the Bhagavad Gita.

The nuclear tests in India bring to my mind a much earlier experiment—also with atomic energy—but this one was in America. It was the very first nuclear test at the Trinity Site in New Mexico on July 16, 1945. J. Robert Oppenheimer (1904–1967), head of the Manhattan Project, witnessed the explosion, and because of its enormity, he was reminded of a passage from one of his favorite texts, the Bhagavad Gita's eleventh chapter. He later recalled the incident and translated the verses in question for a news broadcast:

> If the radiance of a thousand suns
> were to burst into the sky,
> that would be like
> the splendor of the Mighty One.

During that same seminal detonation, as a mushroom cloud overtook the once-clear Los Alamos sky, he remembered another line from the same chapter. Again in his translation:

I am become Death, the shatterer of worlds.

Having studied Sanskrit under Arthur Ryder at Berkeley—specifically to learn the Gita—he knew the book well. It is thus likely that, when witnessing that first atomic blast, he remembered the verses in the original language, as opposed to the loose translations mentioned above. (For example, the word rendered as "death," in the verse already quoted, is more strictly translated as "time." But, following his teacher, Ryder, he opted for the former, which is not wrong but simply less accurate.)[1]

Elaborating on Oppenheimer's reaction to the blast in *Brighter than a Thousand Suns*, author Robert Jungk goes on to say, "Sri Krishna, the Exalted One, lord of the fate of mortals, had [originally] uttered the phrase. But Robert Oppenheimer was only a man, into whose hands a mighty, a far too mighty, instrument of power had been given."[2]

OPPENHEIMER'S GITA

Contrary to popular belief, Oppenheimer's familiarity with the Gita was profound, and the verses he recalled on that eventful day were anything but haphazard. "It is the most beautiful philosophical song existing in any known tongue,"[3] he once said of the 700-verse devotional poem. Reading it for the first time while at Harvard, he learned Sanskrit at Berkeley, as already mentioned, to enter into it more fully. Even though he was well on his way to becoming a renowned physicist, which requires a good deal of work in and of itself, the Gita occupied a special place in his day-to-day life. He prepared his own translation for regular use and studied the *Mahabharata*, the larger epic of which the Gita is one small section, just so he could understand its context.[4] It is said that he always kept a worn pink copy—his own edition of the Gita—on the bookshelf closest to his desk.[5]

The book meant so much to him that he just had to share it with others, and when it wasn't dominating his conversation, he was purchasing copies and sending it out to people he knew. "Oppie" wrote biographers Bird and Sherwin, "took to passing out copies of the Gita as gifts to his friends."[6] Although he wasn't living the life of a conventional devotee, the Gita and the culture from which it comes became a central concern for him. As one small indicator of this, in 1933, when his father bought him a Chrysler, he named it "the Garuda," after Vishnu's divine eagle carrier.[7] Such Krishna-centered enthusiasm led one biographer to speculate, "Had Oppenheimer been a child of the '60s, he would have likely joined the Hare Krishna movement!"[8]

Well, maybe not. His Divine Grace A. C. Bhaktivedanta Swami Prabhupada, the movement's founder, was outspoken regarding his disapproval of atomic energy and the bomb. Indeed, the ninth verse of the Gita's sixteenth chapter tells us, "Following such [atheistic] conclusions, the demoniac, who are lost to themselves and have no real intelligence, engage in unbeneficial, horrible works meant to destroy the world." One can only wonder if Oppenheimer thought of this verse in terms of his own work with nuclear weaponry. But Prabhupada certainly made the connection. In his commentary, he writes, "Indirectly, this verse anticipates the invention of nuclear weapons, of which the whole world is today very proud. At any moment . . . war may take place, and these atomic weapons may create havoc. Such things are created solely for the destruction of the world, and this is indicated here. Due to godlessness, such weapons are invented in human society; they are not meant for the peace and prosperity of the world."[9]

How would Oppenheimer view such a quote? We will never know for sure. We do know that his relationship with the Bhagavad Gita ran deep, and that it allowed him to continue his work. He found solace in the fact that Lord Sri Krishna encouraged His devotee and friend Arjuna to participate in the Kurukshetra battle—which resulted in the death of innumerable soldiers. Oppenheimer realized that he, too, was engaged in work that could cause the deaths of millions, even if this was, clearly, not what he wanted. His nuclear experiments were initially meant to avert disaster, not cause it, and to better the world—as was Arjuna's war—and he continued to work with this in mind.

"Surely," he wrote in his journal, "Krishna would approve that I am doing my work well."[10] In fact, one of the Gita's main teachings, Oppenheimer later wrote to his brother, was that of doing one's duty, whatever the result. The well-meaning scientist, of course, didn't have the benefit of a spiritual master, and so his "duty," to him, merely meant doing his job, even though he had to do it without the direction and guidance of a bona fide guru. As we have seen, at least one such guru would have disagreed with him, or at least set him in a different direction.

The results of his work, he knew, could be devastating, and they were. Nonetheless, he had faith in God and hoped that his preoccupation with the bomb could be used for positive ends, even if, as time went on, he realized that this was quite unlikely.

"Mr. President," he wrote to Harry Truman, in 1947, "I feel I have blood on my hands."[11] In other words, he was keenly aware that the bomb would be used to ill effect. "It is a profound and necessary truth," he told a Canadian audience in 1962, "that the deep things in science are not necessarily found because they are useful; they are found because it was possible to find them."[12] In this case, he wanted the United States to find them first, because he truly believed that it was the one country that would build nuclear weapons with the idea of forestalling their use.

Still, history leaves no doubt that he acquiesced to the bombing of Hiroshima and Nagasaki.[13] He attended the meetings where it was concluded that the bombs would be used against Japanese civilians; and with little prodding, he assented to the devastation. Thus, in due course, the uranium bomb, nicknamed "Little Boy," was sent untested to Tinian for the Japan drop, which was followed by "Fat Man" at Trinity. He was forthright enough after the war, openly stating that he was glad the bomb was used, its destructive force demonstrated for all to see. "I am glad," he went on, "that all of us knew, as a few of us already did, what was up and what readjustments in human life and in political institutions would be called for."[14]

Despite Oppenheimer's peculiar understanding of his own situation in relation to the Gita, his now famous recollection of the eleventh chapter should be understood in terms of the original. The historic detonation of the first atom bomb was a mere firecracker when compared to Krishna's Universal Form, and Oppenheimer was aware of this. Without any further ado, then, let us briefly glimpse the form that is only hinted at by a devastating atomic blast.

THE UNIVERSAL FORM

In the eleventh chapter of the Gita, Krishna directly reveals His "universal form"—a mystical image in which all of creation appears. This is the revelation by which Krishna "shows" His Godhood to Arjuna. The chapter begins with Arjuna's declaration that he is now freed from illusion. He attributes this to Krishna's mercy, to everything the Lord had explained to him and shown him. He knows Krishna is Supreme, and he knows what he now must do on the battlefield. However, despite his certainty of Krishna's divinity and his confidence about his own course of action, he fears that others, in the future, might misunderstand. He therefore requests Krishna: "O greatest of all beings, O supreme person, though I see You here before me in Your actual form, I wish to see You as this cosmic manifestation. I wish to see that form of Yours" (11.3). To establish that Krishna is God beyond the shadow of a doubt, Arjuna requests Him to reveal His gigantic form of everything in existence (11.2–4). Krishna agrees to do this and grants Arjuna divine vision, enabling him to see it (11.5–8).

Krishna then reveals the spectacular, inconceivable form (11.9–49). Viewing it with astonishment, Arjuna sees that "everything—moving and nonmoving—is here completely, all in one place (11.7). . . . the unlimited expansions of the uni-7break; verse, all at once, although divided into many, untold thousands" (11.13). He sees "unlimited mouths, eyes, and wonderful visions . . . All are inconceivable, brilliant, and ever-expanding" (11.11). Arjuna, his hairs standing on end, describes the vast and effulgent form and offers prayers of glorification (11.14–25).

CONCLUSION

To sum up, Robert Oppenheimer also felt his hair stand on end, if not as an ecstatic symptom then in cold, stark fear. For him, the first atomic blast was reminiscent of Krishna's universal form. As a prominent figure in the development of atomic power and an important beneficiary of its success, he waited with bated breath for the testing of the first nuclear blast. An observer who watched him that morning was quoted in Ted Single's book, *The Ultimate Moment*:

> He grew tenser as the seconds ticked off. He scarcely breathed. He held on to a post to steady himself. . . . When the announcer shouted 'Now!' and there came this tremendous burst of light, followed . . . by the deep-growling roar of the explosion, his face relaxed in an expression of tremendous relief.[15]

Devastated by the sheer power of this event, Oppenheimer sat back in a stupor as he remembered the two Gita verses quoted at the beginning of this essay. He was deeply disturbed by the evil potential of his accomplishments. But the atomic age was not to be held back, and it was now underway with full force. Arjuna, too, was disturbed by the magnitude of Krishna's universal image, and he anxiously asked Krishna to return to His more familiar form (11.45–46). But, unlike Arjuna, Oppenheimer could not go back.

After informing Arjuna that he was the first person to have ever seen this particular manifestation of the universal form (11.47–48), Krishna resumed first His four-armed Vishnu form and then finally His original two-armed form, thus pacifying Arjuna, His devotee and friend (11.49–51).

Krishna then explains that His beautiful two-armed form is His most confidential feature, His original aspect, and inconceivable even to the demigods. It is beyond understanding by Vedic study, penance, charity, and worship (11.52–53). Krishna concludes the chapter by declaring that His transcendental, humanlike form can be directly understood only by pure devotional service (*bhakti*) and that pure devotees, who are "friendly to every living entity," attain His eternal association (11.54–55). Ah, if only Oppenheimer had had the virtue of Srila Prabhupada's translation along with a society of devotees with which to develop his devotional sentiments.

NOTES

1. For more on the various uses of the Sanskrit word *kala*, see M. V. Ramana, "The Bomb of the Blue God," online at http://www.samarmagazine.org/archive/article.php?id=36.

2. Robert Jungk, *Brighter than a Thousand Suns: A Personal History of the Atomic Scientists* (New York: Harcourt Brace, 1958), p. 22. See also Peter Goodchild, *J. Robert Oppenheimer: Shatterer of Worlds* (New York: Fromm International, 1985); and Richard Rhodes, "'I am Become Death': The Agony of J. Robert Oppenheimer," in *American Heritage* 28(6) (October 1977), pp. 70–83.

3. See James A. Hijiya, "The Gita of J. Robert Oppenheimer," in *Proceedings of the American Philosophical Society* 144(2) (June 2000), p. 130. This is easily the most informative overall article on Robert Oppenheimer and his connection to the Bhagavad Gita.

4. Ibid., p. 131.

5. Denise Royal, *The Story of J. Robert Oppenheimer* (New York: St. Martin's Press, 1969), p. 64.

6. Ibid.

7. Kai Bird and Martin J. Sherwin, *American Prometheus: The Triumph and Tragedy of J. Robert Oppenheimer* (New York: Vintage Books, 2006), p. 100.

8. Michael Hodes, *J. Robert Oppenheimer and the Manhattan Project* (Los Angeles, CA: Merchant Press, 1998), p. 6.

9. His Divine Grace A. C. Bhaktivedanta Swami Prabhupada, *Bhagavad Gita As It Is* (New York: Collier Books, 1972), 16.9, pp. 734–735.

10. See Hijiya, op. cit.

11. Quoted in Peter Goodchild, op. cit., p. 180. See also Hijiya, op. cit., p. 158.

    12. Quoted in Sharon Kramer, *The Politics of J. Robert Oppenheimer* (San Francisco, CA:
Cruz Press, 2000), p. 16.
    13. Ibid., p. 18.
    14. Ibid.
    15. Quoted in Ted Single, *The Ultimate Moment* (New York: Rider Books, 1990), p. 24.

—13—

Dante's Song: Was the Famous Italian Epic Influenced by the Bhagavad Gita?

I recently sat in on a course on "Western Epic Literature" at a local college. As a writer—and particularly as one who focuses on epics of the East—I wanted to know something about the Occident's contribution to this particular genre. Today's subject: Dante's *The Divine Comedy*.

As the professor began her discourse, she told us a little about the author and the purpose of his work. Dante Alighieri (1265–1321) wrote his epic poem, *The Divine Comedy*, toward the end of his life, while in exile from his native Florence. There are three parts to this massive work: *Inferno*, *Purgatory*, and *Paradise*. In each section Dante recounts the travels of the Pilgrim—his alter ego—through hell, purgatory, and heaven, where he meets God face to face.

"Who knows any other epic poems?" our professor asked the class. I raised my hand: "The *Ramayana* and the *Mahabharata* are India's great epics." She acknowledged by nodding her head but added that those poems were quite different than Dante's. Since her focus was Western texts, I wondered if she had actually read either of the Indian epics.

She told us more about *The Divine Comedy*: Dante relates in the first person his travel through the three realms of the dead. His guide through Hell and Purgatory is the Latin poet Virgil, author of *The Aeneid*, and the guide through Paradise is Beatrice, Dante's ideal of a perfect woman. In real life, Beatrice was a childhood crush, and so he used her in his work.

Dante constructed both his work and his Pilgrim as models for the reader. He hoped to lead that reader to a greater understanding of his place in the universe and to prepare him for the next life, for the life that begins after death. The poet begins by saying, "Midway in the journey of 'our' life," deepening the significance of what happens to him by suggesting that it is, in a sense, what happens to all of us.

At that point, our professor looked around the room—"So the Pilgrim's journey is *our* journey." This reminded me of Arjuna in the Bhagavad Gita, which is part of the *Mahabharata*. Among its many definitions, Arjuna can mean "Everyman," and, along these lines, Srila Prabhupada, one of the greatest Gita commentators of modern times, often told his disciples that Arjuna's plight was meant to inform and instruct us all.

The first section of *The Divine Comedy*, as our professor told us, portrays the spiritual dejection of Dante the Wayfarer. He goes through a crisis of faith, not knowing what to do, and the reader becomes concerned with his personal struggle. As the Gita opens, Arjuna, too, is bewildered about his duty, experiencing existential angst. The Gita's first chapter, in fact, is called *Vishadayoga*, or "the Yoga of Dejection." So both books are set up in the same way. And there are other parallels that are even more engaging.

In looking at the protagonists of both the Gita and *The Divine Comedy*, it becomes clear that their more subtle enemies are perceived in the same way. For Dante, his paralyzing fear in the "dark wood" is traceable to three "beasts" that terrorize him from all sides. First, the leopard, a symbol of luxury, attacks, and renders him senseless. Next a lion approaches, raging with hunger, symbolizing pride and leading to human weakness. And then a she-wolf, representing avarice and sexual appetite, engulfs his soul, and this is described as the most ferocious of his attackers. The English professor concluded this segment of her talk: These are the enemies of the soul—selfish desire, the frustration that comes from not being able to fulfill these desires, and irrational passions that grow ever stronger.

I just had to raise my hand again: In the Gita's third chapter, and in its sixteenth as well, these enemies are identified as lust (*kama*), anger (*krodha*), and greed (*lobha*). Lust, here, is not merely sexual desire but rather all selfish craving, me-centered acts that disqualify us from making spiritual advancement. It's basically the same thing described by Dante. Arjuna is told that his inner turmoil stems from these iniquities, these animalistic urges, and that these iniquities, too, are what separates him from God, who stands before him on the battlefield of Kurukshetra. But the class was over, and it wouldn't resume until a week later.

As I walked out, I started to wonder if there wasn't more than mere coincidence here. The opening of the Gita is all-too-reminiscent of *The Divine Comedy*. That being said, Dante was probably unaware of India's sacred text, since, according to modern historians, fourteenth-century Italy was neither home to Sanskritists nor were there Italian translations of the Gita at that time. Yet the parallels are so compelling that one would think otherwise, indicating that perhaps, just maybe, unbeknownst to historians, there was an edition of the Gita floating around in Dante's time, or, more likely still, that he was tapping into the fount of knowledge known as the *philosophia perennis*, that is, into universal truths that transcend time and space, which are found in everyone's heart of hearts. Whatever the case—we will never know for sure.

As these thoughts raced through my mind, the professor caught up to me, asking, anxiously, how the Gita resolves Arjuna's problem. I asked her to tell me, first, how Dante resolved his.

Dante, she said, is described as being surrounded by the very forces of Hell, which prevent him from acting righteously, as he knows he should. In the midst of these three beasts, mentioned earlier, he sees Virgil, the light of reason, in the distance. Virgil is his savior, carrying him out of his sloth, his ambivalence, and his inaction. Reason helps him through the terrible oceans of Hell. But Dante's ultimate liberation comes from Beatrice in Heaven. Beatrice represents love and devotion, and it is here that Dante finds the ultimate goal of life.

I enjoyed my professor's description of *The Divine Comedy*. But before offering my analysis in terms of the Gita, I told her that the conversation between Krishna and Arjuna actually occurred, whereas Dante's epic is fictitious, even if it certainly has a real message. This is an important distinction between the two books. The Gita is part of a literary genre known as *itihasa*, which means "that which actually happened," that is, history. At least this is how the tradition sees itself. Interestingly, the Sanskrit word *ithasa* can also mean, "the ultimate humor, or comedy," which, of course, resonates with the title of *The Divine Comedy*.

What Dante suggests in his epic poem, I began, was earlier described as a science in the Bhagavad Gita. Krishna first enlightens Arjuna with knowledge, helping him to conquer the universal beasts: lust, anger, and greed. The Lord identifies the main culprit as lust itself: "A person's pure consciousness is covered by his eternal enemy in the form of lust, which is never satisfied and which burns like fire." Krishna further tells Arjuna that this lust is the destroyer of knowledge and self-realization. And that by learning how to realize one's inner nature as a spirit-soul, different from the body, one can control the lower self by the higher self, thus conquering the insatiable enemy known as lust. The whole of the Gita consists of Krishna's instructions on how to accomplish this—how to identify the enemy in one's day-to-day life, and how to overcome it. This, according to the Gita, is true knowledge.

But Krishna continues from there. Just as resolution to Dante's pain only begins with Virgil, and needs Beatrice before bringing him true "succor," as most translations of the Comedy put it, Arjuna needs to go beyond knowledge to love and devotion, to *bhakti*, which is the real teaching of the Gita. In other words, in *The Divine Comedy*, Beatrice corresponds to *bhakti*. That is to say, Dante comes to understand the importance of proper work, proper knowledge, and so on. But it is not until he fully appreciates Beatrice—that is, his relationship with God and the importance of devotion—that he really embraces the ultimate goal of life. So, in the same way that Krishna lifts Arjuna out of "the sea of death" (*mrityu-samsara-sagara*)—a phrase, sans Sanskrit, which occurs throughout *The Divine Comedy*—Beatrice offers Dante a similar opportunity.

My professor, now a friend, was anxious to read the Gita. She had always heard of it, and meant to read it, but this conversation had renewed her interest. She was a specialist on epic literature, but she had neglected one of the world's most important epics, the *Mahabharata*, whose section known as the Bhagavad Gita was more interesting than she had at first suspected.

—14—

Grandfather Bhishma and the
Vegetarian Alternative

Diet does not play a major role in the Gita's teachings. That being said, Krishna does insist that all food should first be offered to Him in sacrifice (9.27). In addition, He specifically asks for simple, natural products (9.26), which, if considered in conjunction with other proclamations in the *Mahabharata*, clearly lead to vegetarianism, and that's the focus of this article.

Those familiar with the Krishna Consciousness movement—a movement that bases its teachings on the Bhagavad Gita—are aware of its penchant for vegetarianism, with cookbooks, restaurants, and "Sunday Love Feasts" deliciously advertising their harmless way of life. Cow protection, farm communities, and a philosophy that emphasizes the soul (as opposed to its bodily covering) effectively bring the teaching home.

It should be known, however, that, for devotees of Krishna, vegetarianism is not merely a dietary preference, nor is it like the meatless cuisine of materialistic food faddists. Rather, their emphasis is *prasadam*, that is, food offered to Krishna in sacrifice. In fact, Krishna says that eating such food frees one from sin (3.13). In other words, devotees are vegetarians because they eat only food that is holy, and, as the *Mahabharata* will make clear, such edibles are necessarily vegetarian.

But the *prasadam* factor is not the only reason for Hare Krishna vegetarianism—they see the diet as more desirable on a number of levels. While *prasadam* is the *spiritual* reason for their vegetarianism, there are also health reasons for the diet and even subtle psychological advantages to it. The evidence for this is found in many good books now on the market, with scientists, over the last thirty years or so, endorsing the truthfulness of these claims.

Devotees of Krishna, however, are more interested in scriptural support for their practices, and they heed the voices of sages whose time-tested proclamations might just be worth listening to. In the present context, Grandfather Bhishma, a leading patriarch in the Krishna tradition, states that vegetarianism is a virtue, in and of itself. But before recounting his sagacious words on the matter, it would be wise to look at just who Bhishmadeva was as well as the circumstances surrounding his endorsement of the vegetarian diet.

GRANDFATHER BHISHMA

The *Bhagavata Purana* (6.3.20), known to devotees as the ripened fruit of the Vedic tree of knowledge, lists twelve Mahajanas, or "great devotees of Vishnu (Krishna)," who are praised as ultimate authorities on Absolute Truth. These twelve luminaries are Brahma, Narada, Shiva, the four Kumaras, Kapila (the son of Devahuti), Svayambhuva Manu, Prahlada Maharaja, Janaka Maharaja, Bali Maharaja, Shukadeva Goswami, Yamaraja, and, yes, Bhishmadeva. For those who know the Vedic literature, this list reads like a "who's who" of transcendence. These are revered historical personages whose teachings are to be heard, and whose examples are to be followed.

Bhishma was the son of Shantanu and the river goddess, Ganges. His mother Ganges left Shantanu after giving birth to this special soul; Bhishma was thus raised by his stepmother Satyavati, a virtuous woman whose life was steeped in God consciousness.

In his youth, he had given his word of honor to his stepmother that he would remain celibate throughout his life. He was so true to his word that he never even entertained the *thought* of marriage, not even for a moment, and sensual desire never arose in his mind. He was thus a great yogi, adept at self-control and true to his vows.

In due course, he became the most respected person in the kingdom of Hastinapura, reverentially referred to "Bhishma Pitamaha," or Grandsire Bhishma.

Naturally, then, when the great battle of Kurukshetra broke out between the Pandavas and the Kauravas—with Krishna in the center—Bhishma was called upon as one of the leading generals of the time. Unfortunately, due to a complex series of events, he fought on the side of the Kauravas, who were the adversaries of the righteous Pandavas, led by Arjuna. As most readers of this article will by now know, Krishna drove Arjuna's chariot.

The battle lasted for eighteen devastating days, but the tenth was marked by a consequential event—the downing of Grandfather Bhishma. As a highly qualified general, he was naturally one of the most feared men on the battlefield. Arjuna faced him and fought with both determination and caution, aware that he was battling with one who was worthy of his veneration. As the fight progressed, Shikhandi appeared before Bhishma ready to fight with him as well. This Shikhandi was a warrior who had previously been female in his former life, and Bhishma had vowed never to strike a woman. Thus, all at once, the esteemed Grandsire threw down his bow and arrows, and Arjuna's arrows completed the task.

Falling to the ground, the great Bhishma was defeated the only way possible—by his own surrender.

But his body did not in fact touch the ground. Arjuna's many arrows had formed a bed for him. And in this regard, Bhishma thanked Arjuna for allowing him a hero's end. All the fighting temporarily stopped, as warriors from all over came to witness Bhishma's auspicious passing away. Even Duryodhana, Karna, Kripa, and other leaders of the Kaurava army ran to the spot where Bhishma lay. Yudhishthira, Bhima, and others too numerous to mention, watched on.

Bhishma was parched and asked for water.

Even evil Duryodhana was ready to comply. But Bhishma smiled as he lay dying: "My son, the water I seek is not the water you can offer."

He then looked at Arjuna, who understood his mind. The young Pandava Prince shot an arrow piercing deep into the ground, and crystal clear waters shot up in fountains that fell straight into Bhishma's open mouth. The stream of water welling up from the earth was none other than Mother Ganga, returning to quench her son's thirst.

Bhishma then turned toward Duryodhana and said, "My son, give up your obstinacy. Make peace with Yudhishthira. Live happily with the Pandavas as brothers— they are devotees of Krishna and should thus be honored."

Bhishma, as an accomplished yogi, could die at will. So he waited for Uttarayana Punyakala, an auspicious time when, it is said, the doors of Vaikuntha, the ultimate spiritual realm, are thrown open for souls to enter. In the meantime, he proceeded to lecture all present, with his final words to Yudhishthira, the eldest Pandava Prince, being, "Protect Dharma. Punish the wicked. Do not give up Truth. Give up egoism. Rule in the interest of the subjects. May you all prosper!"

At that point, Bhishma gazed upon Krishna, who was also at his side, with great joy.

He said, "Where there is Lord Krishna, there is Dharma (right conduct) and where there is Dharma, there is victory. I bow to you, my Master. You are the Lord of all the worlds. I am tired of material existence. Dharma has triumphed and I am happy. So now I take my leave of this earth."

VEGETARIAN DHARMA

What does Bhishma's life have to do with vegetarianism? For the most part, very little. But in those last days, speaking from his heart to all who approached his arrow-made bed, he revealed a great deal about the diet and its implications. Preserved in the *Anushashana-parvan* (Chapter 116) of the *Mahabharata*, we are privy to this Mahajana's words about a very important diet.

Bhishma in fact advocates various degrees of vegetarianism, for various people, according to their capacity. Overall, he condemns eating meat, saying that it is like eating the flesh of one's own son. Yudhishthira raises the objection that the rules of Vedic sacrifices sometimes mandate the eating of meat. In reply, Bhishma refers to Manu, who states that the vegetarian is the "friend of all living beings." He cites the sage Narada, too, who praised restraint from devouring animals. Yudhishthira responds by reminding him that Manu did sanction the use of meat for certain ceremonies. Still, Bhishma tells him, such sanctioning was exceptional and not the usual state of affairs, nor should it be embraced by the mass of people.

Bhishma then says that, if one cannot give up meat in toto, then one should abstain for selected periods, particularly when the moon is waxing in the month spanning September and October—the benefits of vegetarianism, he says, are particularly efficacious at this time. He notes that numerous warriors from the Kurukshetra battle, in his own time, some 5,000 years ago, refrained from meat during this auspicious period, indicating that if they could do it—for many of them had become accustomed to meat while preparing for battle while in the forest—then others could perform the austerity as well.

Bhishma further notes that vegetarianism spares one from rebirth as an animal, and states that it is a diet that suits both renunciants and those who are active in the world.

His words are poignant:

> Meat is not born of grass, wood or rock.
> Meat arises from killing a living being.
> Thus, in the enjoyment of meat there is fault.
> The beloved, sincere, truthful gods
> have in hand (for nourishment)
> oblations, sacrificial offerings, and nectar.
> (By contrast), consider the tortuous,
> unrighteous ways of flesh-eating demons.
> O King, in not eating meat
> one goes without fear in moonlight
> or in the dreadful, dangerous darkness
> or in the twilight approach of night
> or at the crossroads or in the assemblies of people.
> If there were no meat-eaters,
> there would be no killers.
> A meat-eating man is a killer indeed,
> causing death for the purpose of food.
> If meat were considered not to be food,
> there would be no violence.
> Violence is done to animals
> for the sake of the meat-eater only.
> Because the life of violent ones
> is shortened as well (due to their deeds),
> the one who wishes long life for himself
> should refuse meat, O splendid one.
> Those fierce ones who do violence to life
> are not able to go for protection (when they need it).
> They are to be feared by beings as beasts of prey [26–32].[1]

Bhishma also recognizes the subtle anxieties of those who eat meat, affirming, too, that abstaining from flesh foods and adhering to nonviolence advances one toward a heavenly realm:

The one who desires to increase
his flesh with the flesh of another
lives in entrenched anxiety
and is born here and there.
Those great vow-keeping seers have said
that those who do not eat meat are great,
are progressing to heaven,
and are bringing good fortune, renown, and long life [34–35].

Bhishma states that vegetarians are able to live without fear and that the practice of nonviolence results in "beauty, perfection of limbs, long life, intelligence, lightness, accomplishment, and memory"[8].

CONCLUSION

Thus, while the Krishna movement generally promotes vegetarianism only within the context of *prasadam*, it is clear that the tradition acknowledges the benefits of a vegetarian diet as a stepping stone to spiritual perfection. In the Bhagavad Gita (Chapter Seventeen), Lord Krishna Himself acknowledges that food can be divided into three categories: that of goodness, passion, and ignorance. Clearly, the effect of eating food in passion and ignorance, which includes the eating of meat, has adverse affects on the human condition. This is supported by Bhishmadeva in the above verses. Conversely, eating food in goodness—fruits, nuts, vegetables, whole grains, milk, and so on—sets the stage for transcendence, wherein one has the opportunity to become more appreciative of spirituality in general.

True, until a devotee comes along and offers the food to Krishna, making it *prasadam*, one is likely to have a set stage with no actors and no performance. That is, vegetarianism may position us for higher material aspirations and predispose us to Krishna consciousness, but without the touch of God, through the agency of His devotees, we are likely to not get all that can be gotten from a vegetarian diet. Why not, suggests the Bhagavad Gita, get the most out of our vegetarianism by offering our food to God? This might be called "Complete Vegetarianism," for it takes Bhishmadeva's words into account and augments it by recognizing the importance of offering our food as a sacrifice. Who would deny that it is important to do so? We need merely ask ourselves, given a choice between vegetarian foods and vegetarian foods offered to Krishna, which would Grandfather Bhishma prefer?

NOTES

1. All *Mahabharata* translations are by Christopher Key Chapple, in *Nonviolence to Animals, Earth, and Self in Asian Traditions* (Albany, NY: State University of New York Press, 1993).

—15—

Kierkegaard and the Three Modes of Material Nature

Danish philosopher Soren Kierkegaard (1813–1855) is perhaps best-known for his theory of the three stages of human existence: the aesthetic stage, the ethical stage, and the religious stage.[1]

The aesthetic stage is not about being an aesthete, as one might suspect. Rather, a person in the aesthetic stage pursues pleasure and avoids commitment. This stage, says Kierkegaard, begins and ends with despair.

A person in the ethical stage is committed. He or she has a sense of duty, labors for family and society, and pursues universal goals. In this stage the feverish worker usually loses his or her individuality, becoming a cog in the work-a-day machine of life.

The religious stage, according to Kierkegaard, generally comes after repeated frustration with working hard for society, the rewards seeming limited and meager. At this point, says our Danish philosopher, a person moves beyond the universal to the specific and starts to worship God.

Not all people go through all three stages. Kierkegaard says that in a person's life, one stage will predominate and usually engulf a person until the day he dies.

Anyone who is familiar with the Bhagavad Gita and the philosophy at its core will notice how Kierkegaard's three stages correspond to the three modes of material nature. These three modes—*sattva* (goodness, virtue), *rajas* (energy, passion, and turbulence), and *tamas* (inertia, ignorance)—are an integral part of the Gita's worldview.

Mode is a loose translation of the Sanskrit word *guna,* which literally means "thread" or "rope," implying that goodness, passion, and ignorance are the ropes that bind one to the material world. According to the Gita, these three modes, or qualities, underlie everything we see, hear, taste, touch, and smell. Permutations of these qualities make up the world, mixing like the primary colors to produce countless variations.

Sattva controls virtues and qualities such as joy, wisdom, and altruism; *rajas* controls greed, anger, ambition, and frustration; *tamas* controls sloth, delusion, and idleness. *Sattva* clarifies and pacifies; *rajas* confuses and impels; *tamas* obscures and impedes.

According to traditional Hindu theology, Lord Vishnu, the supreme Godhead who maintains the cosmic manifestation, is naturally the master of the mode of goodness; Brahma, the creator, controls passion; and Shiva, the destroyer, presides over ignorance.

As in Kierkegaard's system, the Gita explains that a particular mode will predominate in a person's life, influencing the way he or she behaves. And while we might achieve relative happiness by understanding how the modes condition us and interact with our consciousness, we should aspire to become detached from all three modes, even goodness, which embodies finer material qualities. Such qualities are still material and can serve as "the last infirmity of a noble mind," as Indologist A. L. Basham has articulated it, "causing the soul to cling to wisdom and joy as opposed to God consciousness proper."[2]

The Gita devotes 100 of its 700 verses to a systematic analysis of the modes of nature. According to the Gita, God, as the creator of the modes, is naturally above them (7.13); but the modes bind the ordinary soul to the body through conditioning (14.5); once we understand how the modes work and discover what lies beyond them, we can become free of conditioning and devote our pure mind to the service of God (14.19).

The Fourteenth Chapter of the Gita outlines the general characteristics of the modes, and the Seventeenth Chapter teaches how to perceive the modes in various types of worship, food, sacrifice, austerities, and even charity. By analyzing how the modes affect people, the Bhagavad Gita helps us understand distinct personality types.

The Gita mainly discusses how the modes influence a person's character, behavior, and approach to life. For example, if goodness predominates, one will aspire for (and generally achieve) long-term happiness, even if one must accept temporary inconveniences. The person overtaken by passion is usually satisfied by short-term happiness and doesn't expect much more out of life. And the person dominated by ignorance rarely achieves happiness at all.

In applying the three modes to food, the Gita says that a person in the mode of goodness leans toward healthy and nutritious food, which increases strength and longevity. Persons in passion like overly spiced foods with powerful flavors, temporarily enjoying tasty cuisine that brings on sickness and disease. A person in ignorance has little taste left and tends to eat rotten food that quickly causes ill health.

The Gita summarizes: Goodness leads to lasting happiness that begins by tasting like poison but ends by tasting like nectar. Passion leads to short-term happiness that begins like nectar but ends like poison. And ignorance (at best) leads to happiness that is illusory in both the long- and the short-term, being the result of sleep, idleness, and negligence. In this way the Gita analyzes various aspects of life and shows how the modes influence all living beings and the world.

OTHER TRADITIONS

Other traditions have elaborated on three-part processes that correspond to personality types. Plato, for example, discusses the rational soul, the spirited soul, and the appetitive soul. These refer, respectively, to the intellectual, contemplative person; the pugnacious, overly active person; and the self-centered braggadocio. Plato acknowledges that all three personality types can be found in everyone but inevitably (as with the three modes of nature) one personality type will predominate.

Modern psychology acknowledges three somatotypes, or body types, namely ectomorphy (thin), mesomorphy (muscular), and endomorphy (fat). These are said to correspond to certain mental dispositions: cerebrotonia (brain-oriented), somatotonia (muscle-oriented), and viscerotonia (stomach-heart-oriented). Scholars of Indian religion, such as A. L. Herman, professor of philosophy at the University of Wisconsin-Stevens Point, have noted that while this classification does not directly correspond to the three modes of material nature, the similarity warrants further research.[3] Nonetheless, as Herman acknowledges, the Gita provides one of the most consistent and far-reaching psychological analyses of people and their conditioned responses to the material world. Therefore the Gita, with its in-depth study of the three modes of material nature, offers us indispensable clues about the true nature of the world around us. Taking these clues to heart may enable us to become happy in this life and in the next one as well.

A STEP FURTHER

Kierkegaard would probably have appreciated the analysis of the modes set down in the Gita. In fact, after reading the Gita he could conceivably have added a fourth stage to his three stages of life: the transcendental stage. The Gita explains goodness, the highest mode, in about the same way that Kierkegaard explains his religious stage. But what exists beyond the religious stage? What does one do after going through the despair associated with the mode of ignorance (the aesthetic stage), the work ethic associated with the mode of passion (the ethical stage), and the abandonment of all prior conceptions to come to the mode of goodness (the religious stage), where one lives happily and begins to serve God?

According to the Gita, when one meets a pure devotee of Krishna, one moves beyond religious generality and becomes absorbed in true transcendence. Vaishnava texts speak about this often: ordinary religiosity versus transcendental religiosity. The science of how to transcend the three modes, and thus to transcend Kierkegaard's three stages of life, is thus found within the sacred pages of the Bhagavad Gita.

NOTES

1. See Soren Kierkegaard's *Stages on Life's Way*, vol. 11 (paperback), ed., and trans., Howard V. Hong and Edna H. Hong (Princeton, NJ: Princeton University Press, new edition, 1988).

2. A. L. Basham, *The Sacred Cow: The Evolution of Classical Hinduism* (Boston, MA: Beacon Press, 1989, reprint), p. 87.

3. A. L. Herman, *A Brief Introduction to Hinduism* (Boulder, CO: Westview Press, 1991), pp. 123–128.

— 16 —

Social Classification in Gandhi, Plato, and the Vaishnava Masters

In a recent conversation with a well-to-do Hindu gentleman in New York City, I happened to mention that I was "twice-initiated"—which means that I am a Brahmin priest who regularly chanted the confidential Gayatri mantra and sometimes officiated at Vedic ceremonies. He was taken aback. "How is that possible?" he asked. "You're not born Indian or to Brahmin parents."

My Hindu friend—his name, I soon came to learn, was Amarnath—obviously believed that Brahminhood is related to birthright, a common misconception in India. Wanting to set things straight, I decided to fill him in on the ancient Varnashrama system as it was originally espoused in Vedic texts, millennia ago. This system is described in the earliest portions of the Vedic literature (*Rig Veda* 10.90.12), where the various classes of society are compared to the human body. One part may be positioned higher than the other, but all parts are necessary for the body's proper functioning. Varnashrama is further delineated in *the Vishnu Purana* (3.8.9) and in the Bhagavad Gita (4.13), where it is described as a natural component of any well-established society.

Briefly, the Varnashrama system comprises four basic material occupations or duties (*varnas*) and four spiritual stages (*ashramas*). The *varnas* are (1) Brahmins (intellectuals and priests); (2) Kshatriyas (warriors and administrators); (3) Vaishyas (farmers and business people); and (4) Shudras (manual laborers and general assistants). Most people exhibit qualities that reflect an overlapping of these categories, but one occupational inclination will eventually predominate.

The four spiritual stages (*ashramas*) are: (1) Brahmacharya (celibate student life); (2) Grihastha (married life); (3) Vanaprastha (retired life); and (4) Sannyasa (renunciation and complete dedication to the Absolute). But we will not concern ourselves in this short article with these spiritual stages of life, both because of limited space and because it was not what Amarnath and I spoke about.

BIRTHRIGHT OR BIRTH-WRONG?

I pointed out to Amarnath that Vedic culture takes into account the psychophysical nature of individuals before assigning a place for them in the Varnashrama system. Unfortunately, this system has devolved into the modern-day caste system, where people are classified according to birth. If one is born into a Brahmin family, for example, one is automatically considered a Brahmin, regardless of that person's skill sets and vocational aptitudes. This superficial reading of *varna* has led to the *jati* system, with its innumerable subcastes and variations on the original four *varnas*.

This system has caused considerable confusion, civil strife, and social unrest in Indian society.

In the early 1970s, His Divine Grace A. C. Bhaktivedanta Swami Prabhupada, the founder and spiritual preceptor of the International Society for Krishna Consciousness, discussed this topic with a prominent Indologist in Moscow:

Prof. Kotovsky: According to the scriptures—the Puranas, etc.—every member of one of these four classes of *varnas* has to be born within it.
Prabhupada: No, no, no, no.
Prof. Kotovsky: That is the foundation of all the *varnas*.
Prabhupada: You have spoken incorrectly. With great respect I beg to submit that you are not speaking correctly. In the Bhagavad Gita [4.13] it is stated, *chatur-varnyam maya shrishtam guna-karma-vibhagashaha*: "These four orders of *brahmanas, kshatriyas, vaishyas,* and *shudras* were created by Me according to quality and work." There is no mention of birth.
Prof. Kotovsky: I agree with you that this is the addition of later *brahmanas* who tried to perpetuate these qualities.
Prabhupada: That has killed the Indian culture.[1]

THE *VARNA* SYSTEM ACCORDING TO GANDHI

While birth may point one in a particular direction or help in other ways, it is never the sole factor in determining one's lifelong occupation. For example, birth in a judge's family may afford one a good education and provide one's vocational inclination early in life, but it doesn't guarantee judgeship. Again, this "quality and work" criterion in relation to *varna* is clear from the Gita itself, though few modern Indians are aware of this.

Amarnath, for instance, insisted that while ancient Vedic texts, and thus Prabhupada, as a modern representative of these texts, may endorse the idea that *varna* is about quality and work, "modern Hinduism," as he called it, has another story to tell. He pointed out that most Indians today say that *varna* refers to birthright. We both wondered aloud: What, if anything, do they base this on? Apparently, not much. While the scriptures, to be sure, sometimes relate incidents that appear to subscribe to *varna* birthright, overall, and studied in context, the virtues of personal skill and individual aptitude rise to the fore.

Even Gandhi, considered by many to be the father of "modern India," totes the "quality and work" line:

> Varna is generally determined by birth, but can be retained only by observing its obligations. One born of Brahmana parents will be called a Brahmana, but if his life fails to reveal the attributes of a Brahmana when he comes of age, he cannot be called a Brahmana. He will have fallen from Brahmanahood. On the other hand, one who is born not a Brahmana but reveals in his conduct the attributes of a Brahmana should be regarded as a Brahmana.[2]

If even the father of modern India rejects the birthright polemic, why should it be given any credence? Whatever the answer, the birth oriented caste system is deeply embedded in the Indian psyche and it is likely that it is here to stay.

A FEW WORDS FROM BHAKTIVINODA THAKURA

Social stratification occurs naturally, and it cannot be dictated by birthright. Bhaktivinoda Thakura (1838–1914), a great scholar and saint in the Gaudiya Vaishnava tradition, observes how the *varna* system naturally occurs in all societies:

> When we consider the modern societies of Europe, whatever beauty exists in these societies depends upon the natural *varnashrama* that exists within them. In Europe, those who have the nature of traders are fond of trading and thereby advance them-selves by trade. Those who have the nature of *khatriyas* adopt the military life, and those who have the nature of *shudras* love doing menial service.[3]

But Bhaktivinoda is critical of the prevailing caste system, specifically because it points to birth as the deciding criterion of one's *varna*.[4] He writes that the original *varna* system was pure and based on "scientific" (*vaijnanika*) principles.[5] He further writes that from the time of the *Mahabharata* (roughly 5,000 years ago) the system had become corrupt and deviated from its original purpose, that is, to help people gradually develop love of God. Bhaktivinoda called the original system, which centered on spiritual principles, Daivi-varnashrama ("divine" Varnashrama)— which is a far cry, he says, from the current-day caste system.[6] If social stratification is not applied in order to get closer to God, wrote Bhaktivinoda, then it is a useless waste of time.

As for the societies of the Western world, while Bhaktivinoda recognizes a natural *varna* system within these societies, he stops short of calling them scientific (*vaijnanika*) Varnashrama: "Though the nations of Europe follow the *varna* system to some extent, it is not scientific . . . . In Europe, and, for that matter, in all countries except India, it is the nonscientific *varna* system that guides them."[7] Bhaktivinoda is here expressing his appreciation for the system as it is elucidated in Vedic texts, which elaborate on specific principles for determining the part of society in which a particular individual may belong.

Briefly, Bhaktivinoda summarizes the Vedic perspective:

1. Varna should be determined by studying the nature of a child after examining a child's associations and tendency toward learning during childhood.
2. At the time of selecting *varna* there should also be some consideration of the *varna* of the mother and the father.
3. *Varna* should be determined, at the time of education, by the family priest, father, respectable seniors, and spiritual preceptor.
4. In case of dispute, there should be a two-year trial period and a review committee to examine the case after that time.[8]

Bhaktivinoda goes on to write of an unscrupulous class of Brahmins and Kshatriyas who, to establish authority over others, rewrote books like the *Manu-samhita* and other *dharma-shastras* so that these respected texts appear to endorse birthright as a preeminent qualification for Brahminhood. This, he writes, contributed to the fall of a once glorious society in the Indian world.

DOES PLATO HAVE CLASS?

The Greek philosopher Plato—though most probably unaware of Vedic texts—recognized social divisions that are strikingly similar to those of the *varna* system. In his *Republic*, he argues that social classes correspond to a hierarchy of personality types. The class predominated by the philosophical intellect, he says, is the highest; after that come those dominated by the emotions; and finally we find those in whom "the appetites" (sensual desires) predominate. Further, says Plato, one finds that society is naturally divided in a similar way. On top are the philosopher-kings, who rule; below them are the warriors, whom he refers to as "auxiliaries," since they assist the king; and finally we have the merchants and workers, whom Plato combines into one distinct category.[9]

He compares rulers to gold, auxiliaries to silver, and those in the third class to brass and iron. According to Plato, golden parents will tend to have golden children, as silver parents will naturally have silver children, and so on. But sometimes, he admits, golden parents may have silver, brass, or iron children, and the reverse is also true. When this occurs, says Plato, one must be flexible enough to acknowledge that a golden child born to an iron parent, for example, is indeed golden—his birthright should be disregarded in favor of his natural quality.[10]

The Gita's teachings, particularly as expressed by Prabhupada, concur with Plato's. Both say that birth is not the sole criterion but can afford one a better chance in a particular area of endeavor. Prabhupada says: "It is not that one automatically becomes a *brahmana* because he is born in a *brahmana* family. Rather, he has a better chance of being trained as a *brahmana* if his father is a *brahmana*, just as one has a better chance of being trained as a musician or a cobbler if those are his father's occupations. However, it is not that a cobbler cannot become a *brahmana*. If he acquires the qualifications, he should be considered a *brahmana*."[11]

ALL VARNAS FOR KRISHNA

Amarnath accepted the point: Vedic texts and their modern-day representatives, like Bhaktivinoda Thakura and Srila Prabhupada, endorse the *varna* system as natural and beneficial, and as an asset in developing love for God. Further, Gandhi and Plato accept the basic premises of the *varna* system—even down to the fact that it should be based on inherent quality and natural inclination rather than family status and birthright. Still, Amarnath and I agreed, being born in a particular family may help because if one is educated from birth in the duties of a specific occupation, then one will more likely develop expertise in that particular field.

As we reviewed one of the other central points of our discussion, Amarnath was disturbed, but he had to admit that it rang true: In the present epoch of world history (Kali, the age of quarrel and hypocrisy), the actual *varna* system has degraded into what is now known as the caste system, so much a part of modern India. As many have suggested, this is because unqualified Brahmins and Kshatriyas, in particular, wanted to maintain their status without developing the necessary education and characteristic to legitimately do so. They deceptively emphasized birthright and powerfully enforced their position among the common people, creating the oppressive atmosphere now associated with the Indian social system.

"What to do?" Amarnath asked.

In response, I presented the basic message of the Bhagavad Gita: By proper work, according to one's inclination, one can gradually advance in one's pursuit of God. Anyone properly engaged can rise to the level of a Brahmin and, further, to that of a Vaishnava, or a pure devotee of Krishna. Vaishnavas both embrace and transcend the *varna* system. They engage their God-given talents in Krishna's service—this is the essence of the *varna* system—but accept all classes equally, for all are directing their endeavors in the service of Krishna. This, as Bhaktivinoda tells us, is the *daivi*, or divine, *varna* system.

To sum up, I told Amarnath a story from the *Mahabharata* known as "The Enchanted Pool." King Yudhishthira, eldest of the Pandava princes, was once called upon to answer questions before being allowed to drink deeply from a pool of beautiful, clear water. One of the questions was "What makes a true Brahmin? Is it birth, learning, or good conduct?" Yudhishthira replied, "Birth and superior learning do not make one a Brahmin. Good conduct alone does." Thus, by action anyone can rise to a higher spiritual level. In this context, birthright is never mentioned, and it is merely a peripheral consideration.

Amarnath, among all-too-few of his Indian brethren, was convinced.

NOTES

1. See "Spiritual Communism" in His Divine Grace A. C. Bhaktivedanta Swami Prabhupada, *The Science of Self-Realization* (Los Angeles, CA: Bhaktivedanta Book Trust, 1977), p. 206.

2. M. K. Gandhi, "In Search of the Supreme," in *Harijan* (September 28, 1934), p. 260.

3. Bhaktivinoda Thakura, *Caitanya-shikshamrita*, Bengali edition, V, 61 (Mayapura, India: Chaitanya Math, 1974, reprint), p. 107. See also Sree Gaudiya Math translation of the same text, Chapter 2, entitled "Competence of Karma and Caste Distinctions," pp. 76–83.

4. Ibid., Appendix V, p. 58.

5. Ibid., p. 59.

6. Ibid., p. 60. See also Shukavak N. Dasa, *Hindu Encounter with Modernity* (Los Angeles, CA: Sri Publications, 1999), p. 212.

7. Ibid., pp. 107–108.

8. Ibid., part 1, p. 113. See also *Sajjana-toshani*, vol. 2 (1885), p. 123.

9. The *Rig Veda*, too, initially divides the *varnas* into three classes, but later Hindu tradition split the final class into two: the Vaishyas and the Shudras.

10. See "Plato's Republic" in *The Dialogues of Plato*, trans., B. Jowett (New York: Random House, 1965, reprint), vol. 1, p. 415.

11. His Divine Grace A. C. Bhaktivedanta Swami Prabhupada, *Dialectic Spiritualism: A Vedic View of Western Philosophy* (Moundsville, WV: Prabhupada Books, 1985), p. 287.

—— 17 ——

Spirituality in the Workplace

On October 30, 2006, *BusinessWeek* ran a feature, entitled, "Karma Capitalism." The tagline said it all: "Times have changed since Gordon Gekko quoted Sun Tzu in the 1987 movie *Wall Street*. Has the *Bhagavad Gita* replaced *The Art of War* as the hip new ancient Eastern management text?"[1]

Some would say that it has. Indeed, until recently, three exceptional strategy manuals—*The Art of War* by Sun Tzu, *The Prince* by Machiavelli, and *Go Rin No Sho* ("The Book of Five Rings") by Miyamoto Mushasi—have dominated the new trend of spirituality in the workplace. But the Gita is now taking their place. Earlier this year, in fact, a manager at Sprint Nextel Corporation, Pujan Roka, wrote what is sure to become the business yogis' "how-to" guide: *Bhagavad Gita on Effective Leadership: Timeless Wisdom for Leaders.*[2]

Roka advises businessmen to take certain principles, as articulated in the Gita, and apply them advantageously in the workplace. His book is one among many on this subject, though he's getting quite a bit of publicity these days. Without doubt, there is value and benefit to this modern application of the Gita's teachings, even if it doesn't focus on the text's ultimate message of love of God.

When the Gita was originally enunciated, was it to make Arjuna more effective in his work environment? In a sense, yes. He was a warrior, and Krishna's teachings led him to do his duty with greater enthusiasm and determination. But the personal characteristics and qualities one acquires from implementing these teachings are subservient to the text's main message. That is, such qualities are merely by-products of learning how to love God. With that reservation in place—and with the caveat that one learn the Gita from a teacher who really knows the meaning behind Krishna's words—any exposure to the text is a good thing, and it might even encourage those who are ready to take the next step, to nurture their relationship with the divine. For those who aren't ready, there are always the Gita's secondary teachings, and these are the focus of Gita in the workplace.

Spirituality—the kind found in abundance in the Gita—offers certain advantages over the usual materialistic approach to life and business. It fosters a holistic lifestyle, with benefits for family, neighbors, and community, and certainly for the individual. Along similar lines, it would have value in the modern workplace venue as well. It was just a matter of time before high-powered executives and their coworkers became aware of this. According to Roka and others, that time is now.

Roka, in particular, points his readers to Arjuna's dilemma on the battlefield. The great archer found himself in the midst of a war in which he was called upon to kill teachers, relatives, and friends. Not an easy call. But Roka shows us that all conflicts and adverse situations, if not as serious as Arjuna's, can lead to maturation and growth, just as it did on the battlefield of Kurukshetra. He uses this to enthuse young leaders and those who want to get ahead in business.

Self-awareness, too, is of paramount importance in the work-a-day world, as it is in all spheres of life, and Arjuna is taught the difference between his apparent self (the body) and his real self (the soul within). Understanding this distinction allowed him to do his duty more effectively. And—or so the argument goes—it will allow workers in modern offices to do their duties more effectively, too.

Using ideas such as these, Roka and others are showing the Gita's value in high-pressure work situations. In fact, the recent spate of professional presentations, journal articles, books, and conferences seems to indicate that there is no other book quite like the Gita to accomplish this end. Consequently, business people of all stripes are now touting the glories of the Gita. This includes a newfound appreciation for God, the importance of prayer, the well-being of other people, and environmental ethics.

Of course, this workplace spirituality is rarely taken to the point of religious practice as such, nor do its advocates generally recommend a "Bhagavad Gita Study Group," as Christians do with the Bible. Rather, it is merely a stark recognition of the Gita's universality and wide-range applicability. The text is nonsectarian in scope and goes far beyond ordinary religious mores. Its uses go well beyond its central concern of love of God.

The Gita speaks of individual aptitudes and the psychology of transformation—and this is at the heart of why it has value in the workplace. It includes a systematic approach to developing a peaceful mind, with a concomitant alleviation of suffering. Its teachings breaks down the underlying causes of conditioning, along with its anger, fear, greed, jealousy, confusion, worry, attachment, selfishness, pride, expectations, and desire, affording its readers deeper awareness of what makes them tick, and of what makes others tick as well.

Naturally, this is useful when dealing with administrative and trade opposition.

SOME BACKGROUND

The Gita's penetration into the workplace is a growing phenomenon, with precedents in all major religious traditions. There are numerous books and DVDs now showing how principles found in Judaism, Christianity, Islam, Buddhism, and Hinduism might also be effectively used in work environments. The Gita, supported by both its Hindu and non-Hindu following, is the latest in this series, and many claim it will be the most effective of them all. The Spirit in Business Institute (SBI) and the Association of Spirituality at Work (ASAW) are just two of many active groups now gaining momentum throughout the world, and the Gita occupies a prominent place in their presentation and agenda. But the point is this: Gita in the workplace is symptomatic of something larger.

Ian Mitroff and Elizabeth Denton,[3] who authored a more generic book on spirituality in the workplace, tell us that modern assumptions about the separation of work and faith are now profitably being reconsidered. The two researchers systematically surveyed the beliefs and practices of high-level managers and executives about spirituality in the boardroom, now that it has become something of a fad. After analyzing exhaustive data from in-depth interviews, they concluded that many of today's most important organizational problems are due to spiritual penury.

Mitroff and Denton conclude that companies offering spiritual counseling tend to have employees who are more creative, loyal, productive, and adaptive to change. Overall, the two authors write, workers with a spiritual sense—and managers who foster this—tend to bring their whole being to their work, with a sense of integration not found in more materialistic settings.

For both organizations and individuals, then, this new workplace spirituality waves good-bye to the usual "me-centered" sensibility, so common in today's culture, and this is particularly meaningful for Baby-Boomers and Generation X. For such people, concepts such as "employee welfare" and "servant leadership" are bandied about with increasing frequency and sincerity. Where corporate philanthropy and coworker consideration were once begrudgingly engaged in big business milieus, they're now becoming competitive advantages for attracting and retaining desirable work partners.

BACK TO THE GITA

Why is the Gita, in particular, being called upon as a spiritual text with a corporate message? Many of those now writing on the subject note that Arjuna was, first and foremost, a man of integrity. He was encouraged to do his duty as if his life depended on it—and with love and devotion. The Gita teaches that enlightened souls should master their senses, their impulses or emotions, which, if not controlled, will often blur sound judgment. Arjuna shows us that good leaders are selfless, take initiative, and focus on their duty, rather than obsessing over outcomes or financial gain. "The key point," says Ram Charan, a coach to CEOs such as General Electric Company's Jeffrey R. Immelt, "is to put purpose before self. This is absolutely applicable to corporate leadership today and is a teaching found in the Bhagavad Gita."[4]

Of course, Indian-born thinkers—and the Bhagavad Gita—didn't invent all these concepts. But they're clearly playing a big role in pushing them into the

modern work environment. "Marketing has tended to use the language of con-
quest," says Kellogg professor Mohanbir S. Sawhney, a major proponent of the
Bhagavad Gita in the workplace. "Now the focus is on using customer input to
dream up new products," Sawhney writes, "which requires a symbiotic relationship
with those around us. [This is taught in the Bhagavad Gita.]"[5]

Modern business concepts, even in the West, value visionary thinking, leadership models, motivational skills, excellence in work, goal oriented action, informed
decision-making, and procedure that considers a large number of people—all these
and more are discussed in the Bhagavad Gita. But with one major difference. While
Western management tends to deal with these phenomena on material, external
levels, the Gita hones in on the underlying psychology, and on the spiritual reasons behind human thinking. Some of the people now bringing the Gita into the
workplace are aware of this.

As M. P. Bhattathiri writes in his article, "Bhagavad Gita and Management,"
ancient India's sacred scriptures have much to offer the world, especially today.[6] In
this modern world, Bhattathiri tells us, the art of management has become a part
of everyday life, whether at home, in the office, or in government. In all spheres
of human existence, where people assemble for a common purpose, management
principles come into play through the proper use of resources, finance, planning,
priorities, policies, and practice. The science of management is a systematic way
of carrying out activities in any field of human effort.

But Bhattathiri is clear: While Western management philosophy may have
created prosperity—for some—it has failed in the overarching goal of ensuring a
better life, both for individuals and for the world at large. It has remained by and
large a soulless edifice, he writes, and an oasis of plenty for precious few, offering
only a poor quality of life for the vast majority.

Hence, there is an urgent need to reexamine prevailing management dis-
ciplines—their objectives, scope, and content. The Bhagavad Gita, says Bhattathiri,
offers a needed corrective to this mundane worldview.

As interesting as this is, we need not here go into detail about how the Gita puts
such qualities in place. Suffice it to say that the spiritual path propounded by Lord
Krishna involves renouncing egoism, putting others before oneself, emphasizing
the association of progressive individuals, cooperation (team playing), integrity,
nonaggression, and trust—and, indeed, sacrificing lower desires for higher goals,
which is often the opposite of what one finds in the modern workplace.

"Work must be done with detachment," teaches the Gita.

In essence, Lord Krishna discloses leadership techniques based on those of
the Vedic literature, harkening back to the principle-centered models of God-
conscious kings, such as Maharaja Yudhishthira and Lord Rama. Basically, the
techniques focus on ethics and morals, about putting the other person first, and
about humility. Overall, it is leadership with God in the center, showing how to
manage one's kingdom, work environment, family, and life from a spiritual point of
view. Since these principles were already found in the Vedic literature, what these

modern writers really offer are "modern technologies," or practical applicative methods that modern workers could use in their daily lives.

MOVING TOWARD THE FUTURE

Earlier, we cited a dichotomy between using only certain of the Gita's teachings to get ahead in a business environment and the Gita's ultimate theological principle, which is to develop love for God. It is critical that students of the Gita understand this dichotomy, especially if they are to use this sacred text in the workplace. Along these lines, there are two overarching dimensions of Lord Krishna's teachings that might help.

First, as human beings, we have two kinds of duties: the duties related to our life in this world, as in our vocation or employment, and the duties of the spirit soul, in which we nurture our eternal relationship with God. Of the two, the second is more important. What the Gita does, in effect, is to show us how to use the former to accomplish the latter. That is, by focusing on the social system known as Varnashrama, wherein all souls are engaged according to their natural work tastes and psychophysical inclinations, Krishna explains how one might serve Him in this world. By exercising one's natural capacity for work, and one's proclivity to work in a particular way, it is possible to achieve spiritual perfection—but it must be guided and directed by a self-realized soul, one who knows Krishna in truth. In this way, even business can be converted to spiritual duty.

And this leads us to the second point: The main challenge in advisers teaching the Gita to business executives is the advisers themselves: Because they generally don't know the real inner teachings of the Gita—to develop love for Krishna, or God—they tend to give half-truths or inadequate guidance. Indeed, the Gita is properly taught in traditional lineages, and few in the modern workplace would have had the advantage of learning it in this way. If they did, they could then teach it more effectively.

CONCLUSION

Can the Gita be useful in a business environment? Sure. Following its principles can lead to an increase in productivity and reduce stress—it can even help one become a more "mindful" businessperson. Properly taught, the Gita will indeed create these qualities in prospective candidates. But there's the rub. Who out there is qualified to properly teach the Gita? According to the Gita itself, it should be heard from the lips of a pure devotee, from one who is not envious of the Lord.

If such a one were to go into the business world to help people, his priority would be to help them realize their inner spiritual nature, and to become better devotees of the Lord. The other qualities would naturally rise to the fore, too, but merely asincidental developments to the main effect: deepening devotion for God. But that would hold true in any sphere: temple services, family relationships, or whatever. What's needed, in other words, is not "Gita in the boardroom" but simply "Gita." Indeed, only this one-pointed approach to Lord Krishna and His teachings will have the desired effect.

The sad part is that, like everything else in the twenty-first century, the Gita has been commodified, prepackaged, and stripped down for fast, easy consumption. We've become expert at feeding the gaping maw of the Internet and other information technologies with the equivalent of spiritual junk food. Wisdom, like everything else, has been sacrificed for commerce. We prefer to learn history from a ninety-minute film, because then we can fool ourselves into thinking, "now I know about an ancient spiritual text," for example, and avoid the hard work of having to actually read it and study it with anything resembling seriousness. Why actually study the Bhagavad Gita when you can hire a business consultant to tell you everything the Gita has to say about business success in a one-hour session? The answer to this, of course, can be found in the Gita itself. Or in the book you now hold in your hands.

NOTES

1. See online at http://www.businessweek.com/magazine/content/06_44/b4007091.htm.

2. Pujan Roka, *Bhagavad Gita on Effective Leadership: Timeless Wisdom for Leaders* (Lincoln, NE: iUniverse, 2006). See also Meera Uberoi, *Leadership Secrets from the Mahabharata* (New Delhi, India: Penguin Books, 2003).

3. Ian Mitroff and Elizabeth Denton, *A Spiritual Audit of Corporate America: A Hard Look at Spirituality, Religion, and Values in the Workplace* (San Francisco, CA: Jossey-Bass, 1999).

4. Quoted in Roka, op. cit.

5. Quoted in *BusinessWeek* article, op. cit. In regard to Sawhney's use of the word "symbiosis": Symbiotic means, "any interdependent or mutually beneficial relationship between two persons, groups, etc." Thus, symbiosis is all over the Gita—in Krishna's relationship with Arjuna, in the Pandavas fighting the battle according to the rules of Kshatriya warfare, and even among the Kauravas—in the way they worked together to oppose their enemies (though it can be argued that this was not "mutually beneficial" in the larger sense of the phrase).

6. See http://www.refresher.com/ampbgita.html.

—18—

The Mystery of Madhusudana

Madhusudana. The name always seemed curious to me. Where did it come from? It appears in the Bhagavad Gita no less than five times (1.35, 2.1, 2.4, 6.33, and 8.2): Krishna is referred to as Madhusudana, or "the killer of the Madhu demon." And yet, Krishna didn't kill a demon named Madhu. I looked through the vast storehouse of Krishna's pastimes over and over again. No Madhu, at least not in the form of a demon.

Most commentators, including Srila Prabhupada, tell us that by referring to Krishna in this way, Arjuna, the hero of the Gita, is poetically indicating that Krishna should now slay his (Arjuna's) doubts, just as He had slain the three-dimensional foe of His past. But, again, where does such slaying take place? When did Krishna kill a Madhu demon?

Baladeva Vidyabhusana, an eighteenth-century Vaishnava commentator, writes that the Gita's use of the name Madhusudana implies that Krishna can kill the grief (*shokam*) of Arjuna just as He had killed Madhu in the past (*madhusudana iti tasya sokam api madhuvan nihanisyatiti bhavah*). And by now, I'm not only wondering just where this Madhu demon is to be found, but why refer to Madhu at all? By the time of the Kurukshetra war, Krishna had killed many demons, and Arjuna could have referred to any one of them—"O slayer of Putana, conqueror of Kamsa," and so on. So, to me, it was obvious that the Gita was pointing to something else.

With a little digging, I found that, sure enough, Madhu was not killed by Krishna at all, at least not by Krishna in His original form. Rather, it was Vishnu—Krishna's expansion—who did away with the Madhu-Kaitabha threat (a story I will discuss in detail below). More specifically, Vishnu killed Madhu through His Hayagriva incarnation, which has a horse-like body and is celebrated in the sacred texts known as the *puranas*. In identifying Krishna as Madhusudana, then, the Gita is making a somewhat covert connection between Krishna and Vishnu, thus offering readers a glimpse of Krishna's divinity.

In fact, whenever India's sacred texts relate a story wherein Krishna's divinity might be questioned, as in His birth and death pastimes (for one might wonder why God is "born" or "dies" at all), the name Madhusudana shows up yet again. The name may or may not appear in other parts of the Krishna story, but it always makes its appearance in these more controversial segments: To see the name in Krishna's birth story, one need look no further than the *Bhagavata Purana* 10.3.29 and for His disappearance story, one might look to 11.30.35. It's as if Vyasa, the author, is saying, "Don't doubt it for a second—Krishna is indeed nondifferent from Vishnu, God."

This is not to say that Krishna's divinity is somehow dependent on His identity with Vishnu. Actually, according to the most esoteric Vaishnava traditions, it is the other way around, for Krishna is the source of all divine forms and incarnations (see the *Bhagavata Purana* 1.3.28). But the common conception of God—that He is all-powerful and awe-inspiring, embodying grandeur rather than simplicity, invoking praise instead of intimacy—is more in line with Vishnu. And so, even in Vedic times, the word "Vaishnavism," or "the worship of Vishnu" (as opposed to Krishnaism), was the preferred name for Sanatana Dharma, or the eternal religion of the soul. Indeed, many scholars of the Gita—traditionalists and Western academics as well—tend to see the "great revelation" in the Gita's eleventh chapter, wherein Krishna majestically shows His all-encompassing "Universal Form" to Arjuna, as the text's climax. Their assumption stems from the sheer magnificence and opulence of the revelation. But Gaudiya Vaishnavism's great teachers, in their wisdom, place more emphasis on Arjuna's humble request that Krishna again show His more intimate—though superior—two-armed form. And they prefer, instead, to focus on the instruction at the Gita's end: to abandon all varieties of religion and simply surrender unto God, that is, Krishna (18.66), with a faithful heart of love and devotion.

WHAT'S IN A NAME?

The Madhusudana appellation first appears in the Gita's first chapter, before Krishna reveals to Arjuna that both He and His loving devotee had taken many births in the past (4.5), and before He shows His divinity to Arjuna in any conclusive way (Chapter 11). The implications are significant: It means that Arjuna's illusion is just *lila* (transcendental, playful pastime, arranged by the Lord). That is to say, he is placed in a temporary state of forgetfulness so that Krishna might speak the Gita, to instruct Arjuna and, through him, each and every one of us. Otherwise, how does Arjuna know, right from the beginning, that Krishna is indeed Vishnu, who incarnated previously to kill the Madhu demon?

Of course, followers of Srila Prabhupada knew this all along. In the Introduction to his translation and commentary of the Bhagavad Gita, Prabhupada writes: "Being an associate of Lord Krishna, Arjuna was above all ignorance, but Arjuna was put into ignorance on the Battlefield of Kuruksetra just to question Lord Krsna about the problems of life so that the Lord could explain them for the benefit of future generations of human beings . . . "

Yet it's interesting to see how this plays out in the *Mahabharata*, of which the Gita is a small section: Arjuna had been told something about his divine partnership as Nara with Narayana, by Shiva (*Mahabharata*, 3.41:1–4), and by Yamaraja, the lord of death (3.42:17–23). Yama even says, " . . . with Vishnu you will lighten the burden of the earth." This all occurs prior to the Sixth Book, in which the Gita appears. Krishna also reveals His divine form to those assembled in the Kaurava court while He is on his "peace mission" for the Pandavas, and when these same heroes choose Him instead of His armed forces. Thus, by the time of the Bhagavad Gita everyone involved clearly understood Krishna's divinity. Arjuna certainly knew it, and yet he knew it not. Like Mother Yashoda, who saw the entire universe in baby Krishna's mouth.

The epithet Madhusudana is specifically used before the Gita, in the larger Epic, too, usually by Vaishampayana, but also, notably, within his narration, from the mouth of Shishupala (2.34:10, 11, 21; 2.42:19), who, as a demon, is one of Krishna's mortal enemies, and from that of Draupadi (3.13:44, 52, 56, 69, 71, 103, 108, 112). Arjuna, as might be expected, calls Him this as well, even prior to the Bhagavad Gita (*Mahabharata*, 1.214:15; 3.13:12, 32, 34). So Krishna's identity as the Supreme Lord, as Vishnu, is clear from early in the *Mahabharata*, and from early in the Gita, too. And Arjuna himself, though ostensibly in illusion, tells us that it is so—simply by using the name Madhusudana.

THE STORY OF MADHU

The story of the Madhu demon is revealed in the *Kalika Purana*, the *Devi Bhagavata*, and also in the *Mahabharata* (3.194–195). It is this latter version to which we refer. Srila Prabhupada, too, briefly mentions the story in *Krsna Book* ("Prayers of Akrura") and in the *Srimad Bhagavatam* (7.9.37, purport), and his words will naturally guide us in our own retelling.

At the beginning of time, there was only the causal ocean, as the spiritual world brought forth the material spheres. Lord Vishnu lay on Shesha, His serpent bedstead, in deep cosmic slumber. While He slept, a lotus stalk arose from His navel. At the upper end of the stalk was a lotus flower, on which Brahma, the first created being, appeared. He was given the charge of creation, and he meditated on how he would accomplish his God-given task. As Brahma sat in deep meditation, "ear wax" (*karnasrotodbhava*), it is said, flowed from Vishnu's ears.

Two ferocious demons, Madhu and Kaitabha, were born out of this wax. They performed great penance for thousands of years, and so, the Lord's consort, Lakshmi, pleased with their devotion, appeared before them and granted them the boon that they would only die when they so desired. Proud of their newly acquired asset, the demons became outrageously arrogant. They attacked Brahma, who was still meditating on his lotus stem, and stole from him the four Vedas. Brahma, though furious, was helpless in the presence of such powerful adversaries. Thus, he rushed to his one and only shelter, Vishnu, asking for help.

Vishnu, however, was in deep sleep—the yogic trance, or cosmic slumber, mentioned previously—and did not wake up, even though Brahma tried his best to awaken Him. Realizing that the Lord slept for reasons of His own, Brahma decided to pray to Yoga-nidra, who is none other than the goddess herself in a special form that facilitates the Lord's yogic sleep. As Brahma had hoped, she showed mercy on him and awakened the Lord.

Brahma immediately told him about the nefarious deeds of Madhu and Kaitabha and begged Him to destroy them. Thus Lord Vishnu manifested as Hayagriva, the beautiful horse incarnation, and engaged in direct battle with Madhu and Kaitabha, ultimately retrieving the Vedic scriptures. But they could only die when they wanted to, as their boon had stated. And so Vishnu cleverly told them that just as they were given a boon by the goddess, His consort, they should allow Him a boon as well. After all, He told them, they were so powerful that they should show Him the same courtesy that His feminine half, the embodied form of His mystic energy, showed them.

In their arrogance, they fell for His ruse, asking Him, "What boon do you want from us? We will give you anything You want." To this, the Lord replied, "I want your death!" And so it was—Hayagriva put an end to their menace once and for all.

As Srila Prabhupada writes in the *Srimad-Bhagavatam* (7:9:37, purport): "The Supreme Personality of Godhead in His transcendental form is always ready to give protection to His devotees. As mentioned herein, the Lord in the form of Hayagriva killed two demons named Madhu and Kaitabha when they attacked Lord Brahma. Modern demons think that there was no life in the beginning of creation, but from *Srimad-Bhagavatam* we understand that the first living creature created by the Supreme Personality of Godhead was Lord Brahma, who is full of Vedic understanding. Unfortunately, those entrusted with distributing Vedic knowledge, such as the devotees engaged in spreading Krsna consciousness, may sometimes be attacked by demons, but they must rest assured that demoniac attacks will not be able to harm them, for the Lord is always prepared to give them protection."

MADHUSUDANA REVISITED

There is one final consideration when discussing "Madhusudana," and it may be the most esoteric dimension of the name. Not only does it mean "He who defeated the Madhu-demon"—it also means "He who defeats honey in sweetness." Thus, the great commentator Shridhar Swami defines the name as follows, "False ego is as sweet as honey and resides in the heart of everyone, making one forget his own true identity. It intoxicates everyone. He who destroys false ego with the torchlight of knowledge is called Madhusudana." By extension, the word *madhu* has come to refer to both the bumblebee and also to Krishna. That is to say, just as bees tend to enjoy the honey of the lotus, Krishna enjoys the honey of His devotees' love. Thus, Rupa Goswami, the great Vaishnava saint of sixteenth-century India, uses this dual meaning of Madhusudana in Act Five of his devotional drama, *Vidagdha Madhava*:

Once, when Radha and Krishna were sitting together, a bee was disturbing Radharani by flying near her. Krishna requested a friend who was nearby to chase away the bee, and after finishing the task the friend came back proclaiming that *madhu* was gone. As the word can refer to both the bee and to Krishna, Radharani "mistakenly" took it in the latter sense and began to cry, thinking Krishna was now gone. Seeing Radharani's tears of love, Krishna also began to cry, and their tears mingled together to become the now sacred pond known as Prema Sarovara in present-day Braja.

Of course, Krishna's friend was referring to the fact that the bee had left, but when Radha considered the other meaning—that Krishna was gone—she was totally gripped by *vipralambha-bhava*, or the loving mood of divine separation, a level of enhanced mysticism aspired for by advanced Vaishnavas, even though she was right there in Krishna's arms.

In this way, the name Madhusudana, as mentioned in the Bhagavad Gita, conjures up the most intimate aspects of divine knowledge, from the Lord's earliest manifestation of Vishnu to His most ecstatic exchanges with Radharani, His divine pleasure potency and feminine counterpart. It was she, in her expansion as Lakshmi and Yoga-nidra, who bestowed mercy on the Madhu-Kaitabha demons, and thus allowed Krishna to become Madhusudana.

—19—

Arjuna's Yogic Preference*

Traditionally, the Bhagavad Gita is seen as a *yoga-sutra*, or a treatise on yoga. The entire purpose of *yoga* is to "link with God," as the word itself indicates—and the Gita has often been honored as the clearest and most thorough text on how such "linking" takes place. And yet, it is not uncommon, at least in Western countries, for aspiring yogis to be intimidated by its technical Sanskrit jargon, setting it aside as something "to be studied later." While such a response is certainly understandable, one who is serious about yoga would take the time to closely peruse this work. Indeed, only by such study will it become clear why this most sacred of scriptures is, and for centuries has been, one of India's most important textbooks on yoga and all related subjects.

CONTEMPLATIVE AND ACTIVE FORMS OF SPIRITUALITY

The Gita's third chapter introduces its readers to two forms of spirituality: the contemplative and the active. At the time, in India, the majority of yoga practitioners were inclined to extreme acts of asceticism and renunciation, believing this to be the only way they could get close to God. But the Gita seeks to correct this misperception—it takes the doctrine of *nivriitti*, negation, so dominant in ancient India, and augments it with *pravriitti*, or positive spiritual action. Thus, Krishna teaches Arjuna not so much about "renunciation *of* action" but rather about "renunciation *in* action." In later Vaishnava terminology, this is the preferred *yukta vairagya*, or "renouncing the world by acting for the Supreme," as opposed to *phalgu vairagya*, or "renouncing the world by refusing to act." Both forms of renunciation are accepted by the Gita, but Krishna prefers the "active" form, saying that it is more practical and more effective as well.

---

*A Lecture Given at the Institute for Advanced Yogic Studies, San Francisco, California.

Whichever approach one happens to adopt, says Krishna, detachment from sense objects is compulsory. Thus, whether one is inclined to be a renunciant in the usual sense or if one chooses to take up the Gita on its teaching of yogic action—the difference lies only in how one uses or participates in the external world. Along these lines, Krishna asserts that contemplative, inactive yoga is difficult, for the mind often becomes restless or distracted. Rather, as already stated, He recommends the active form of yoga, which He calls Karma Yoga. This is more to the point, He says, for one still strives to focus the mind, using various techniques of contemplative meditation, as in the inactive, more traditional form of yoga, but augments this endeavor with practical engagement in the world of three dimensions.

Krishna makes all of this quite clear in the Gita's fifth chapter (in my own translation):

> Both renunciation, or the contemplative approach, and the yoga of work, or Karma Yoga, can bring about the desired goal. But of the two, Karma Yoga is better. The real renunciant neither hates nor hankers; being without duality, O mighty-armed one [Arjuna], he easily frees himself from bondage—for he is a true philosopher. The inexperienced person—as opposed to those who are learned—talks of philosophy and yoga as being different. But listen: if either approach is practiced in a proper and thorough way, one attains the same result. The state attained by philosophers is reached by yogis, too: Thus, he who sees philosophy and yoga as one, truly sees. But renunciation is difficult to attain without yoga, O mighty-armed one, whereas the sage endowed with yoga attains the Supreme soon enough (5.2–6).

MEDITATION: RESTRAINING THE MIND

Krishna explains that both processes of yoga, the contemplative and the active, begin with learning the art of controlling the mind. In the modern world, this is often referred to as "meditation."

> By meditation (*dhyana*), one can learn to behold the Lord in his own heart. This can be achieved by the yoga of philosophy and by the yoga of works (Karma Yoga) (13.25).

Earlier in the Gita, Krishna refers to this same process, explaining the virtues of a controlled mind:

> When the yogi, by practice of yoga, disciplines his mental activities and becomes situated in true spirituality—devoid of material desires—he is said to be fully established in yoga. As a fire in a place that is devoid of wind does not waver, so the true spiritualist, whose mind is controlled, remains steady in meditation on the transcendental self (6.19–23).

Such meditation, Krishna admits, is difficult, but it can be achieved through arduous effort:

Of course...the mind is fickle and difficult to restrain. But by practice and a renounced mood... it can be attained. For one lacking in self-control, yoga is nearly
unachievable. But one who strives with self-control may eventually attain it by the
correct means (6.35–36).

In verses ten through fourteen of the Gita's sixth chapter, Krishna elaborates on
what He means by the "correct means." Here, one begins to see how truly difficult
it is to perform this kind of meditation: The yogi must learn to properly meditate
without interruption, in perfect solitude. He must fully restrain his mind and
desires, letting go of both wants and possessions. And that's the easy part.

He must prepare a seat for himself in a clean place, neither too high nor too low,
covered with cloth, antelope-skin, or *kusha* [grass,] and he must sit in this specially
prepared place, says the Gita, learning to make his mind "one-pointed"—which
means utterly focused. He should practice such meditation for his own purification
only, without any ulterior motive. Firmly holding the base of his body, neck, and
head straight and in one place, looking only at the tip of his own nose, he must be
peaceful, without fear, and above any prurient interest.

With this as a starting point, the aspiring yogi is ready to control his breathing
(*pranayama*), which serves to manipulate the energy in the body (*prana*) in a
positive way. This, along with intricate sitting postures (*asana*), enables one to
control body and mind and is considered an effective means for further quieting
one's passions, controlling material desires, and focusing on God.

The yogi must engage in this practice, Krishna says, while fully devoted to the
Supreme. Or else it just won't work.

Krishna calls this method Raja Yoga, because it was successfully employed by
great kings (*raja*) in ancient times. But times have changed, and this mechanical,
contemplative form of yoga—which was eventually systematized in Patanjali's
Yoga-sutras and now popular in the West as Hatha Yoga—is too difficult for most
people, at least if they are going to do it properly, and Krishna says as much by the
end of the Gita's sixth chapter.

Still, He is careful not to throw the baby out with the rice water, recommending
elements of contemplative yoga along with the yoga of action, or Karma Yoga.

It is no wonder, therefore, that Arjuna expressed confusion—just which form
of yoga is Krishna really recommending? Does He prefer this austere form of
disciplined sitting and meditation, as described above, or action in perfect consciousness? Does the Gita recommend Hatha Yoga, or does it recommend work
in proper consciousness? Although Krishna certainly answered these questions
earlier in the Gita, Arjuna wants Him to articulate it in such a way that there can
be no mistake.

Ultimately, the Gita reveals a sort of hierarchy, a "yoga ladder," in which one
begins by studying the subject of yoga with some serious interest—this is called
Abhyasa Yoga—and ends up, if successful, by graduating to Bhakti Yoga, or the path
of devotion. All the stages in-between—and there are many—are quite complex,
and it is at this point that most modern Western practitioners become daunted in

their study of the Gita. Our next section, therefore, will analyze only those concepts central to understanding this yoga ladder, and, in so doing, bypass much of the Gita's intimidating language.

STAGES OF YOGA

One may wonder why the two basic approaches to yoga, the contemplative and the active, and their many variations, seem to be interchangeable in one section of the Gita, while they clearly manifest as a hierarchy in another. The answer lies in the Gita's use of yoga terminology, a glossary that, again, can be somewhat off-putting. Suffice it to say, the different words used in this connection actually refer, in a sense, to the same thing: the various yoga systems are all forms of Bhakti Yoga. The differences are mainly in emphasis.

It is called Karma Yoga, for example, when, in the practitioner's mind, the particular type of yoga, in this case "Karma," takes precedence—not just in the physical placement of the word, but conceptually. For instance, in Karma Yoga, one wants to perform work (*karma*) and is attached to a particular kind of work, but he wants to do it for Krishna—which is what makes it yoga. In this scenario, *karma* is primary and yoga is secondary. But since it is directed to God, it can be called Karma Yoga instead of just *karma*. The same principle can be applied to all other yoga systems.

Of all yogas, however, the Gita teaches that Bhakti Yoga is the highest. This is because the first word in this yogic phrase is *bhakti*, or devotional love. In the purest form of love, one becomes selfless, and thus, instead of giving a prominent place to one's own desire, one considers the beloved first. Thus, the second part of the phrase (yoga) becomes prominent—linking with God takes precedence over the practitioner's personal desires or wants. In fact, the first and second words of this particular phrase become one. The devotee wants to love (*bhakti*), but he considers Krishna's desire before his own. This makes Bhakti Yoga the perfection of the yoga process.

In other words, the many types of "yoga" found in the Gita are in some ways merely stepping-stones to Bhakti Yoga. But, more directly, they are all *variations* on Bhakti Yoga, with specific *emphases* meant to gradually take practitioners to perfection. Karma Yoga emphasizes "working" for the Supreme; Jnana Yoga emphasizes "focusing one's knowledge" on the Supreme; Dhyana Yoga involves "contemplating" the Supreme; Buddhi Yoga is about directing the "intellect" toward the Supreme; and Bhakti Yoga, the perfection of all yogas, occurs when "devotion" is emphasized in relation to the Supreme. Again, the main principle of yoga, in whatever form, is to direct your activity toward linking with God.

CONCLUSION

We may first of all, then, observe that the Gita accepts all traditional forms of yoga as legitimate and claims that they are merely variations on a theme—they all focus on linking with the Supreme. However, the Gita also creates a hierarchy of sorts. Indulging some of the text's terminology, the hierarchy runs something like this: First there is study (Abhyasa Yoga), understanding (Jnana Yoga), and meditation (Dhyana Yoga) on the meaning of scripture. This leads to the contemplation of philosophy and eventually wisdom (Sankhya or Jnana Yoga), culminating in renunciation (Sannyasa Yoga). This, in turn, leads to the proper use of intelligence (Buddhi Yoga). When engaged practically, this is called Karma Yoga, and, when imbued with devotion, Bhakti Yoga.

All of this involves a complex inner development, beginning with an understanding of the temporary nature of the material world and the nature of duality. Realizing that the world of matter eventually ceases to exist and that birth will no doubt lead us to death, the aspiring yogi begins to practice external renunciation and gradually *internal renunciation*, which, ultimately, comprises giving up the fruits of one's work (*karma-phala-tyaga*) and performing the work itself as an offering to God (*bhagavad-artha-karman*). This method of detached action (Karma Yoga) leads to the "perfection of inaction" (*naishkarmya-siddhi*), that is, freedom from the bondage of works. One becomes free from such bondage because one learns to work as an "agent" rather than as an "enjoyer"—one learns to work for God, on His behalf. This is the essential teaching of the Gita, and in its pages Krishna methodically takes Arjuna (and each of us) through each step of the yoga process to get us there.

The Gita's entire sixth chapter, however, is about Arjuna's rejection of conventional yoga; he describes it as impractical and "too difficult to perform" in our current age of distraction and degradation (known as Kali Yuga). Does Krishna castigate Arjuna for expressing this problematic view of conventional yoga or, further, for declining to practice it?

Not at all. Rather, Krishna says, "Of all yogis—including Hatha Yogis, Jnana Yogis, Dhyana Yogis, and Karma Yogis—you are the best." Why is Arjuna the best? Because he is a devotee, willing to work on Krishna's behalf. This is Bhakti Yoga, which is the best way to link with God most effectively.

Krishna explains the essential element of Bhakti Yoga that distinguishes it from all the rest: "Of all yogis, the one who is constantly thinking of Me within himself, meditating on Me within the heart, is the first-class yogi." This, again, is because the goal of yoga is to relink with God, as the word itself indicates. *Yoga* comes from the Sanskrit root *yuj*, which means "to link up with, to combine." It is similar to *religio*, the Latin root of the word "religion," which means, "to bind together." Interestingly, religion and yoga do, indeed, have the same end in mind: combining or linking with God. This is the essential purpose of the yoga process, and the end to which the Gita hopes to bring its readers. Thank you very much.

—20—

Bagger Vance: The Mystical Underpinnings of a Contemporary Golf Tale

By now, the words "Bagger Vance" have become well known in Western pop culture. A good number of people have either read the novel or seen the movie. For those who haven't, "Bagger Vance" may sound as strange as a "bag of ants"—but it is much, much more. The story behind the story? In 1995 William Morrow and Company published *The Legend of Bagger Vance: Golf and the Game of Life*, a novel by Steven Pressfield that explores the spiritual side of golf ala Bhagavad Gita.

Although there have been several other works on golf and mysticism—including Michael Murphy's 1972 classic, *Golf in the Kingdom*, which is considered the forerunner of the genre—Pressfield's book is unique[1]. He creatively restructures the Bhagavad Gita, originally spoken on a battlefield, so that it now takes place on a golf course. In his work, he introduces us to the mysterious caddie known as Bagger Vance (a variation on Bhagavan, "the Holy One," a Sanskrit name for Lord Sri Krishna—God—speaker of Bhagavad Gita), who knows the parallels between the secrets of golf and the secrets of life.

The setting of the novel revolves around a golf tournament at Krewe Island, near Savannah, Georgia's windy Atlantic shore. The year is 1931, and we are transported into a soon-to-come thirty-six-hole match. Bobby Jones and Walter Hagen, well-known golf legends, are joined by a reluctant opponent, the famed but troubled war hero, Rannulph Junah (read: R. Junah, or Arjuna, Krishna's archer-devotee from Bhagavad Gita). The outcome of the game, as we soon see, is more dependent on Bagger Vance, a caddie who carries the secret of "the Authentic Swing," than on the talents of the golfers. His inscrutable wisdom and mysterious powers guide the play and leave a lasting impression, not only on R. Junah but—sixty years later—on a brilliant but discouraged young medical student. The narrator of the story, Dr. Hardison Greaves (who parallels Sanjaya, the narrator of the Gita), was ten-years-old when he witnessed the epic golf battle in 1931. Today, he shares Vance's knowledge with that medical student, and, through him, with each of us.

The implication here is that, like the Gita, the instructions of Bagger Vance are not just for R. Junah but also for Everyman.

Bagger Vance, tall and blackish (like Krishna), turns the game field into something more, into the battlefield of life. He instructs R. Junah in a good deal more than golf, and, by the end of the novel, it becomes clear that Bagger Vance is no ordinary mortal. ("Everything that is," says Vance, "is brought into being and sustained by me" p. 184.) In the movie version, the shaman-like Vance is not overtly Bhagavan, Lord of the Universe, but he is definitely no ordinary Joe, either.

Since the Gita is not mentioned directly (except in one verse, which opens the book), those who are unfamiliar with the ancient classic will not see it in Pressfield's novel. His work stands on its own. But for those who know the Gita, the parallels are interesting and provocative.

What do golf and the ancient Indian classic, Bhagavad Gita, have in common? At first glance, not much. We might philosophize based on the Gita's essential teachings, extrapolating that human life is like a golf ball: Imagine a ball soaring through the sky, seemingly as free as a bird. That freedom, the Gita would remind us, is the freedom to be struck by a golf club, to be smacked from here to there. As the golf ball's freedom is illusory, so is that of the conditioned soul who, thinking himself free, is the victim of his own conditional responses. The Gita teaches how to overcome conditioning and, in so doing, hit a hole in one, as Vance would say.

But our focus here is different. Instead, I look at the parallels between the Gita and a twentieth-century novel. What I do for the remainder of this chapter—as I do in my book, *Gita on the Green: The Mystical Tradition Behind Bagger Vance* (Continuum International, New York, 2000)—is to make explicit that which is only implicit in Pressfield's work. Whether or not one has poured through the Gita or *The Legend of Bagger Vance*, by reading my analysis of both one can enter into an understanding of each of them. Additionally, I will here tell the story of how I came to write *Gita on the Green*.

To put it succinctly, my book (*Gita on the Green*) is about a book (*The Legend of Bagger Vance*), which is itself about a third book (the Bhagavad Gita). One might wonder why Pressfield chose to initiate this process by rewriting the Gita as he did. In fact, I asked him directly, and he told me that he had always been interested in the Gita and appreciated the idea of Bhagavan, God, humbling Himself to become the charioteer of His devotee, Arjuna. In the same way, Pressfield said, a caddie, as qualified as he may be, takes a humble position in assisting his chosen golfer. Pressfield wanted to express this beautiful idea to the people of the modern world.

In an interview published on the Bagger Vance Web site, Pressfield reveals his idea behind the book:

> The idea behind Bagger Vance was to do the Bhagavad Gita contemporarily. In the Gita the troubled warrior Arjuna receives instruction from Krishna, Supreme Lord of the Universe, who has assumed human form as Arjuna's charioteer. Instead of a troubled warrior, it's a troubled golf champion (Rannulph Junah); instead of his charioteer, it's his caddie—Bagger Vance. . . . Golf, as everyone knows who has played

it and loved it, is a very mystical sport. A golf course is like a battlefield. It even looks like a battlefield, with its rolling ramparts and redoubts.

In other words, Pressfield used the Gita as his cue to tell a traditional story in his own way, in a way that would speak to people in his own time, with a similar frame of reference. As it turns out, using a contemporary Western sport—golf—to communicate the teachings of the Gita was a brilliant use of the ancient tale, making it accessible to a new generation of beneficiaries, as sales of his book clearly indicated. As an addendum, it was my hope that by reading *Gita on the Green*, Pressfield's readers—and many others—will come to appreciate the original book upon which *Bagger Vance* is based.

TEEING OFF

How did I come to write *Gita on the Green*? It was late April 2000. Late in the month and late to write such a book. You'll see why in a moment. A good friend had asked me if I had read Pressfield's novel. "I don't usually read novels," I told him. Knowing my lifelong interest in the Gita, he said to me, "This is one novel you'll want to read—it's the Bhagavad Gita on a golf course!" I was intrigued.

The next day I went to Barnes & Noble and secured a copy of the book. Immediately after purchasing it, I sat on a park bench, thinking I would spy a few lines. I was enthralled. I sat for what turned into a couple of hours and devoured the entire novel. Returning home, I decided to track down the author, to congratulate him on a job well done. I managed to locate his phone number and gave him a call. We hit it off straightaway, kindred spirits, spending a couple of hours immersed in conversation.

I told him of parallels between his book and the Gita that hadn't even occurred to him! I had been studying the Gita for nearly thirty years, and he was impressed with my knowledge of the subject. He told me, in that first conversation, that of the many reviews his book had received—and there had been quite a few—only one South Asian scholar mentioned the Gita connection. No one else seemed aware of the parallels. He further told me that his book was being made into a major motion picture. In fact, by the time of my initial conversation with him, the filming had long been completed. It was directed by Robert Redford and was due out by August 2000. It was to be distributed by DreamWorks Pictures and produced by Redford, Jake Eberts, and Michael Nozik, who runs Redford's production company, Wildwood Enterprises. Among the screenwriters is Richard LaGravenese (*Living out Loud*, *The Bridges of Madison County*, *The Fisher King*, and *Unsung Heroes*, etc.). Award-winning actors Will Smith and Matt Damon portray Bagger Vance and R. Junah, respectively. And Hollywood veteran, Jack Lemon, plays the narrator.

When I got off the phone I was vexed. I thought about all the people who will read his novel, or see the movie, and yet remain totally unaware of the great classic upon which the two are based. I decided that I would write a book that illuminated all the connections between *Bagger Vance* and the Bhagavad Gita. With this in mind, I immediately called Pressfield a second time.

He loved the idea. He said, "You write that book, and I'll write the Foreword." Great idea: The author of the original novel writing the Foreword for my book. A great impetus, indeed. But he left me with a serious reservation: "Fact is," he said, "it is unlikely that you'll get it done in time for the movie's release—and that would be the most effective time for such a book to come out." He was right. The movie was supposed to come out on August 4. It was now late April. I had to write a book and get it to a publisher—and they would have to get it printed—all within three months. It was just not physically possible.

I called a few publishers that I had worked with before. They confirmed my worst fears: "No way. It will take at least six months, and that's if you finish it immediately. After you finish it, we have to put it through the reviewing process, which also takes time. Forget it."

Somehow, I decided to start anyway. Day and night I worked. I kept Pressfield's novel and a host of golf books open before me. I brought a string of Gita commentaries into the fray as well. I worked like this for about one month. Inexplicably, I forged ahead, knowing that I would probably never get a publisher. Then, in late June, I received an e-mail message from Pressfield—it was clearly divine intervention: "Hey, guess what? Redford feels the movie is a definite Oscar contender. He's moving the release date to November 3, because movies that are released closer to the date of the Academy Awards are more likely to be nominated. You've got an extra four months!" Unbelievable. I called several publishers and told them the good news. They could relate. Next thing I knew, there was a bidding war, and I couldn't be happier.

I finished the book late that summer, and Continuum agreed to get it out in time for the movie—no small task. But they did it. Pressfield wrote the Foreword and things are going well.

POP GOES THE GITA

"Bhagavad Gita, The Movie?" Well, not exactly. The Gita has been adapted for pop culture over the years—mainly out of India—in terms of popular movies, musicals, and the performing arts. "The Legend of Bagger Vance"—the movie version—doesn't exactly follow in this line. In fact, much if not all of the Gita has been deleted from the film. I was fortunate enough to read an early version of the screenplay in which large portions of the Bhagavad Gita remained intact. Journalist David Orr also noted that the Gita was retained in early versions of the screenplay. His article on the subject was published in a magazine called *Creative Screenwriting*, 7(6), offering a critical assessment of Jeremy Leven's draft from February 28, 1997, which was still Gita-heavy. Somewhere between that version and what ended up in the movie, the Gita disintegrated.

Apparently, Redford decided to go Hollywood, settling for vague innuendoes of spiritual abstraction—"wishy-washy mumbo-jumbo," as one reviewer put it.

Of course, it's all too easy to blame Redford. There are probably many who share responsibility for the film's neglect of the Gita, the source text whose background presence is so abundant in Pressfield's novel.

Wherever the responsibility lies, the movie, in its present form, offers little of substance. This, of course, will lead to speculations about what the film is actually trying to say. Once the intelligentsia discovers that Redford's film is based on a novel that is based on the Gita, they will read into it various ideas that simply don't belong there. For example, David O'Reilly, a staff writer for the *Philadelphia Inquirer*, tries to uncover the Gita's "hidden truths" in an article called "Big-Screen Caddy is Hindu Hero in Disguise" (November 19, 2000). Revealing what the film is "really" all about, he says that "Hagen, symbol of the mind-state of sensuousness, and Jones, symbol of knowledge, and Adele, symbol of devotion, come to admire Junah without ever grasping his enlightenment."

Here, Hagen is supposed to represent *karma*, fruitive activity, and Jones, *jnana*, or knowledge. This seems to work, at least to a certain degree. But then to equate Adele (a love interest who plays a small role in Pressfield's novel but is predictably elevated to center stage in the movie) with *bhakti*, or devotion, simply misses the mark. She has all but forgotten Junah until he works his way back into her life—or, rather, until she works him back in, and with ulterior motive. This is not *bhakti*. Besides, even if one wants to read some sort of devotion into Adele's behavior, it still can't be called *bhakti*. The Gita teaches that *bhakti* is a specific kind of devotion—it is directed toward God. At best, one could say that Junah was supposed to develop *bhakti* toward Vance. But even this is not something that happens in the movie.

The amorphous spiritual message of the film can be cited as among the main reasons for its lukewarm reviews. One wonders if Redford and company had stood their ground—if they had shown Vance display his "Universal Form" or had him articulate the deeper teachings of the Gita—might the film have been a more thorough success? We will never know. As it stands, the film is now (in DVD format) doing moderately well. Despite the well-deserved criticism already mentioned, it received accolades from important reviewers: "I won't soon forget this masterpiece.... A beautiful, dreamlike fable which reaffirms your faith that somewhere out there, great films are being made..." (Jeffrey Lyons, MSNBC); "... Meticulous in its craftsmanship" (*Los Angeles Times*); "Lovely, mythopoetic" (*The Atlanta Constitution*); "There's much to enjoy in *The Legend of Bagger Vance*" (*The Wall Street Journal*). *Rolling Stone* also gave it a great review, even mentioning the connection with Bhagavad Gita (which is naturally absent from most reviews).

The film has increased book sales, too. Two paperback movie tie-in editions of Pressfield's novel were in stores just two months before the release of the movie. In addition, the classic hardcover edition has met with renewed interest, selling over 100,000 copies. Not a bestseller—but if only my book would do as well!

And what about my book? *Gita on the Green*, as the title suggests, elucidates—even emphasizes—the Bhagavad Gita underpinnings of the Bagger Vance story. Drawing on both *Bagger Vance* and on an assortment of studies on the Gita, I show how Pressfield makes good use of the original spiritual classic, and, how, at times, he veers away from its central teachings. Focusing on the popular interest generated by the film, I have structured the book in such a way that it would be of value to golf enthusiasts, spiritual seekers, self-help and new age fans, and students of Indian philosophy. My main interests in this book are the links between *Bagger Vance* and Bhagavad Gita.

BAGGER AND BHAGAVAN: THE LINKS

Imagine, if you will, Junah and Arjuna, meeting at the links, discussing the parallels in their respective books while tackling the green. They might each begin their discussion by relating their most intense moment of turmoil, when they first became aware of the seemingly senseless battle that lay before them. In the Bagger Vance story, for example, the grief-stricken Junah sees the galleries gathering like armies before the match. He becomes overwhelmed with depression, ordering Bagger to drive the Chalmers out onto the dunes between "the armies." Once in that strategic position, he pulls over, lays down his clubs, and refuses to participate in the match.

As elaborated upon in the thirteenth chapter of *Bagger Vance*:

"Put the clubs away . . . ," he [Junah] said in a voice nearly inaudible. "I see no profit in them or this whole fool enterprise."

"Your mind is clearly in torment, Junah," Bagger Vance spoke slowly and evenly. "Tell me please: what is the nature of your complaint?"

Junah glanced up sharply at this word, which seemed to trivialize his emotion. "It couldn't be more obvious, could it?" He gestured toward the multitudes in their bright battle lines, visible across the linksland. "This whole endeavor is a freak show. A joke. What good will any of it do me, or anyone attached to it?" (p. 94).

Junah's hands were trembling. He ran them in pain through his hair, eyes gazing hollowly before him into the dunes. "What is ever gained by 'defeating' others? What can be gained here today? If I win I take no pleasure, and if I lose . . . " (p. 95).

This correlates precisely to the first chapter of the Gita:

Arjuna said: O infallible Krishna, please drive my chariot between the two armies—I wish to see who is present here, who is desirous of fighting, and with whom I must contend in this enormous battle (1.21–22).

Sanjaya, the narrator, said: Being so requested by Arjuna, Lord Krishna brought their magnificent chariot in the midst of both armies (1.24).

At this point Arjuna could see that among the armies were his fathers, grandfathers, teachers, maternal uncles, brothers, sons, grandsons, friends, and also his father-in-law and well-wishers—all were present and ready to do battle (1.26).

Arjuna said: My dear Krishna, seeing my friends and relatives present before me in such a fighting mood, I feel the limbs of my body quivering and my mouth drying up. In fact, my whole body is trembling, and my hair is standing on end. My bow is slipping from my hand, and my skin is now burning (1.28–29).

O Govinda [Krishna], of what avail to us are kingdoms, happiness, or even life itself when all our nearest and dearest are ready to engage in combat with us? O Krishna, seeing all my relatives ready to give up their lives and properties as they stand before me, I become despondent. Why should I wish to kill them, even if I were to survive? O maintainer of all living beings, I am not prepared to fight with them even in exchange for the universe, let alone for this meager earth (1.32–35).

If Junah and Arjuna were to continue their fictitious dialogue, they would inevitably discuss the point in their lives when they desperately sought help from their respective mentors.

For example, while Junah is besieged by what can only be called an existential dilemma, Vance helps him understand his true identity, much as Krishna reminds Arjuna that he is the soul rather than the body:

"Tell me who you are Junah. Who, in your deepest parts, when all that is inauthentic has been stripped away. Are you your name, Rannulph Junah? Will that hit this shot for you? Are you your illustrious forebears? Will they hit it? . . . Are you your roles, Junah? Scion, soldier, Southerner? Husband, father, lover? Slayer of the foe in battle, comforter of the friend at home? Are you your virtues, Junah, or your sins? Your deeds, your feats? Are you your dreams or your nightmares? Tell me, Junah. Can you hit the ball with any of these?" . . . Vance pressed yet harder, "Then who are you? Answer me!" (p. 113).

Bagger Vance elaborates on the spiritual dimension of reality, and that all beings partake of this higher nature. This corresponds to the teachings in the Gita's second chapter.

Gita parallels go further. Though Bagger Vance doesn't use Sanskrit terminology, he offers a brilliant analogy involving the path of discipline (Karma Yoga), the path of knowledge (Jnana Yoga), and the path of devotion (Bhakti Yoga), acknowledging the supremacy of *bhakti* over all others. While explaining how to master the Game, Vance describes three possible approaches:

The first path, I heard him say, was the path of Discipline. It had something to do with beating balls, with endless practice, an utter relentless commitment to achieving physical mastery of the game.

Second was the path of Wisdom. I heard practically nothing of what Vance said here (I was checking yardage to three separate bunkers off the eighteenth) except, I believe, that the process was largely mental—a study of the Swing much like a scientist might undertake: analysis, dissection, and so on.

Third (and this I heard most of) was the path of love.

On this path, Vance said, we learn the Swing the way a child acquires its native tongue. We absorb it through pure love of the game. This is how boys and girls learn, intuitively, through their pores, by total devotion and immersion. Without technically "studying" the swing, they imbibe it by osmosis, from watching accomplished players and from sensing it within their own bones (pp. 73–74).

Vance goes on to explain that the path of love is the most effective of the three. If you love the Game, you have the best chance of being a great player. This directly corresponds to the Gita's teaching on the three paths.

In the Gita, Krishna reveals His Godhood to Arjuna by giving him the ability to see "a cosmic form," or a vision in which the great prince inexplicably sees "everything—moving and nonmoving—completely, in one place" (11.7). Vance also shows Junah a universal form: "Only to you, Junah, will I show myself in all my power. I give you the divine eye with which to see; otherwise the merest fragment of this vision would be your end" (p. 176). He proceeds to show Junah a form that approximates the one seen by Arjuna in the Gita. Arjuna, by the way, is also given "divine eyes" so that he may witness the revelation (11.8).

Vance identifies himself with all-devouring time (p. 186), as Krishna does in the Gita (11.32). And there are several other parallels along these same lines. Finally, Vance says, "I come again in every age, taking on human form to perform the duty I set myself. I return to right the balance of things" (p. 184). This directly correlates with Krishna's revelation in the Gita: "I Myself appear, again and again in every age, to deliver the pious and to annihilate the miscreants, as well as to reestablish the principles of religion" (4.8).

Junah and Arjuna no doubt have a lot in common, and if they were to discuss their stories further, many of the parallels I address in my book would be the subject of their conversation. The differences between our two heroes, of course, are many. For one, Junah is a fictional character, while Arjuna is accepted as an historical personality. Bhagavad Gita is a serious book of spiritual truths, sacred to millions; Bagger Vance is a novel that, while conveying important ideas, skews toward the whimsical. Golf is not war, a caddie is not a charioteer. Junah does not fight for God; Vance is not Supreme. But, when read with the Gita in mind, Bagger Vance can swing with the best of them, illuminating eternal truths that might otherwise fall into the worst of sand traps: oblivion.

NOTES

1. See Steven Pressfield, *The Legend of Bagger Vance: A Novel of Golf and the Game of Life* (New York: Avon Books, 1995, reprint) and Michael Murphy, *Golf in the Kingdom* (New York: The Penguin Group, 1997, reprint).

— 21 —

Yoda and Yoga: *Star Wars* and the Hindu tradition

At first glance, it might seem that *Star Wars* and Hinduism have little in common. *Star Wars* is a modern sci-fi classic, produced for entertainment purposes. It makes use of futuristic spaceships and imaginative weapons that the real world has not yet seen. Hinduism, for its part, is an ancient religious tradition—or, more correctly, a *family* of religious traditions, such as Vaishnavism, Shaivism, and Shaktism—meant for spiritual enhancement and personal fulfillment. What, if anything, does the film have to do with the religion?

My thesis is simple. Lucas, the creator of *Star Wars*, was heavily influenced by Joseph Campbell, the famed mythologist. This he admits openly. Campbell's preferred stock of philosophical stories come from India. This is well known. Campbell explained the *Mahabharata* and the *Ramayana*, the main epics of contemporary Hinduism, to Lucas, who digested their many stories and gave them back to us as *Star Wars*. Lucas himself admits that he was "influenced by Eastern myths." Here's one example I use in my forthcoming book to prove this, drawing on the first episode of the series:

> A beautiful princess is kidnapped by a powerful but evil warlord. With determined urgency, a mysterious non-human entity delivers a distress call to a budding young hero. The youthful hero, a prince, comes to the princess's rescue, aided by a noble creature that is half-man and half-animal. In the end, after a war that epitomizes the perennial battle between good and evil, the beautiful maiden returns home. The valiant efforts of the prince and his comrade, who were assisted by an army of humanlike bears in the fight to return the princess to safety, are duly rewarded, and peace and righteousness once again engulf the kingdom.

> In the eastern part of the world, the story evokes memories of the *Ramayana*, an ancient epic from which many of India's myths and religious traditions originate: The princess is Sita, kidnapped by the power-mad Ravana. Her loving husband Rama,

the archetypal hero who, as the story goes, is Vishnu (God) in human form, soon becomes aware of her plight and anxiously pursues her. How did he learn of Ravana's nefarious deed? The good-hearted Jatayu, a vulture-like creature with the ability to speak, sworn to protect the princess, sees the demon-king forcibly abduct Sita. He attempts to rescue her on his own, but he is mercilessly cut down by Ravana. Luckily, Rama happens upon the dying Jatayu, who reveals all that has taken place. After a period of intense grieving, Rama engages his devoted half-human/half monkey companion, Hanuman, in an elaborate search for the princess and, after a complex series of events, a massive war breaks out to get her back. Aided by an army of Vanaras (bears and monkeys who have humanlike characteristics), Rama rescues Sita from the evil Ravana. The forces of the underworld defeated, Rama-raja (the kingdom of truth and righteousness) reigns supreme.

In Western countries, the story is more reminiscent of the first of the *Star Wars* epics, the film series brought to life by George Lucas, the now multimillion dollar writer/director/filmmaker at its helm. Here, too, the princess—this time, Princess Leia—is kidnapped. In the *Star Wars* universe, evil incarnates as Darth Vader, who holds Leia against her will. Artoo-Deetoo (R2-D2), an android instead of a talking vulture, carries a desperate cry for help. The princess, just prior to being captured, managed to conceal a holographic message in the droid's memory banks. Thus, through this futuristic robot, she asks for the assistance of Obi-Wan Kenobi, a master among the mystical Jedi knights, hoping he would come to her aid. Luke Skywalker, a farm boy from the planet Tatooine, is the one who initially receives this message, however, and it is he who apprises the otherwise retired Obi-Wan about the mission to rescue the princess. Luke is reluctant to travel into unknown territory, into a world of action and intrigue. After all, he knows little beyond his simple farm. But brave Obi-Wan convinces him to go, telling him that "the Force" will protect him. The two team up with Han Solo, a renegade space traveler, and Chewbacca, a "half-man/half-monkey" creature who devotedly assists them. By the end of the original *Star Wars* trilogy, in the company of legions of bear soldiers, they wage a war to end all wars—Darth Vader and his entire evil empire are defeated and the princess is returned to safety.[1]

Is it a stretch to say that Lucas was directly and/or indirectly influenced by the *Ramayana*? You can answer that question with another: Does the above seem like a stretch? This author, obviously, thinks not. If the reader has doubts, let him read my entire book—soon to be published—which offers many such clear-cut parallels and overlapping between the two.

Another glaring example is the relationship between Yoda and Luke—a dead-ringer for the traditional Guru/disciple relationship, especially as depicted in the ancient Hindu text, the Bhagavad Gita. Yoda teaches Luke self-control, the importance of restraining the senses. Every Jedi, he says, must overcome desire and anger. The Gita must have been Yoda's sourcebook: "A faithful man who is dedicated to the pursuit of knowledge—and who subdues his senses—is eligible to achieve such knowledge, and having achieved it he quickly attains the supreme spiritual peace" (4.39). Again, "By the time death arrives, one must be able to tolerate the urges of the material senses and overcome the force of desire and anger. If one does so, he will be well-situated and able to leave his body without regret" (5.23).

It is interesting, too, that Yoda locates the source of the Jedis' strength: It is not accessed independently but rather it flows from "the Force," which he essentially defines as the ground of all being. Indeed, Yoda tells Luke that all ability comes from the Force, but that this is especially true of the Jedis' supernatural powers. The Gita also says that all power flows from the "Force," that is, the metaphysical source of all that is: "Of all that is material and all that is spiritual, know for certain that I am both the origin and dissolution.... Everything rests upon Me, as pearls are strung on a thread.... I am the ability in man" (7.6–8).

Yoda's name is closely linked to the Sanskrit *yuddha*, which means "war." Accordingly, he indeed teaches a chivalrous form of warfare, imbued with ethics and spirituality, to the Jedi knights. The nonaggressive but valiant ways of these knights are exactly like those of Kshatriyas, ancient Indian warriors who emphasized yogic codes and the art of protective combat. In this, Yoda resembles Dronacharya from the *Mahabharata*, who, in the forest (again like Yoda), trains the Pandava heroes to be righteous protectors of the innocent. In the *Ramayana*, another Hindu epic, Vishvamitra Muni, as Rama's spiritual master, teaches the great *avatar* to be adept in the art of war, but he also teaches him that fighting must always be based on yogic principles—he teaches Rama while they are living in the forest as well. Both Dronacharya and Vishvamitra seem like earlier incarnations of Yoda.

In this sense, and in many others, the Hindu scriptures may be the ultimate guidebooks for aspiring Jedis: Consider the Bhagavad Gita yet again: Lust, anger, and greed, the Gita tells us, are deeply embedded in our consciousness. Just ask Anakin. And deep-rooted habits are not always easy to overcome. Nonetheless, in the Gita, Krishna helps us through the darkest of battles by explaining the source of our dilemma, the gradual steps by which we delude ourselves, and by putting us in touch with the spiritual element lying dormant within our hearts. He tells us that those who are enamored by materialistic life begin simply by contemplating the objects of the senses. Again, just ask Anakin. Such contemplation naturally leads to self-interested action and, finally, attachment. This, in turn, gives rise to anger. Why anger? Because everything in the world is temporary, and so we eventually lose the objects of our attachment. Anger, Krishna says, leads to bewilderment, and bewilderment to loss of memory. At this point, intelligence is lost. We can watch this happening to Anakin in "Attack of the Clones" and, further, in "Revenge of the Sith."

According to Krishna, intelligence means good memory and fine discretion—both of which fall away when we adopt a materialistic and self-centered approach to life. This vicious cycle puts us in a nonspiritual frame of mind, in which we forget who we are and what life is really all about. Krishna refers to this as "a material whirlpool," which drags people ever lower; it is a complex downward spiral that begins, as He says in the Gita, simply by one's contemplating the objects of the senses (2.61–64). Krishna thus tells Arjuna not to be fooled by sensual stimulation and, instead, to control his senses for a higher purpose. This, indeed, is the teaching of the Jedi and a lesson that is valuable to each and every one of us.

Can people learn this from a viewing of *Star Wars*? Most likely not. Most likely they'll have to go to established religious texts and the paths traversed by the sages. But something is definitely afoot here. More than 70,000 people in Australia, in a census poll, declared that they are followers of the Jedi faith, the "religion" created by the *Star Wars* films! I discuss this faith and its ramifications throughout my book. Despite the extremism and absurdity of this statistic—of people adhering to a faith concocted in a fictional film series—experts see in it a pointer to the spiritual dimension of the movies themselves, and how fans tend to pull religious themes out of what is otherwise merely a sci-fi epic.

In the light of this enthusiasm, the *Star Wars* universe rages on. Lucas is now remastering the entire series—one by one—into special 3D versions, updated for modern times. New TV shows based on *Star Wars* are planned for upcoming seasons. And you now learn of parallels between this consequential film epic and one of the earliest religious traditions known to humankind. What's next? Only the Force is likely to know!

NOTES

1. From my unpublished manuscript, "The Jedi in the Lotus: Seeing *Star Wars* through a Hindu Lens" (© Steven Rosen, 2007).

— 22 —

Krishna's Divine Appearance*

In the Bhagavad Gita (4.9), Krishna, the Supreme Lord, says, "One who knows the transcendental nature of My appearance and activities does not, upon leaving the body, take birth again in this material world, but attains My eternal abode, O Arjuna."

While this verse alludes to God's birth, or "appearance," in the material world, we actually learn much more about this birth three verses earlier: "Although I am unborn and My transcendental body never deteriorates, and although I am the Lord of all living entities, I still appear in every millennium in My original transcendental form." And why does He take birth? Text 8 of the same chapter tells us that He comes "to deliver the pious and to annihilate the miscreants." He also comes to "reestablish the principles of religion," which often get lost as time goes on.

So we've learned much about Krishna here. First of all, He is never really "born"—He is "unborn." But He does appear in our world—He descends regularly, in fact. His body is not like ours. We have bodies that eventually fall apart, but Krishna comes in His original transcendental form. It is visible, but it is totally spiritual. The verse also tells us that He is the Supreme Lord, and it further implies that He has subsidiary forms, though His form as Krishna is His original one.

In these Gita verses Krishna talks about His birth and about our birth as well. He uses the Sanskrit word *janma*, which literally means "birth," for both events. However, He makes a clear distinction—we ordinary living beings are forced to take birth based on our desire and *karma*, or causal actions. Over the course of many births and deaths, we, the soul, take on numerous bodies to work out our wants and to receive our just deserts, until we become purified and return to the spiritual world. Krishna, on the other hand, is "born" according to His own sweet

*A lecture at the New York Public Library, Main Branch, New York City.

will. He comes to our world only to help us return to Him, to allure us with His beautiful *lila*, or spiritual activity. And He also comes to kill especially notorious demons—His devotees take pleasure in this.

One needs to understand Krishna's appearance in this way. It is not about understanding the historical phenomenon of just when He was born, or where, geographically, say, in India, or elsewhere. Along these lines, I've been noticing the accomplishments of Arun K. Bansal, the father of computer astrology in India, whose research has been in the news as of late.[1] He says that Krishna, the Supreme Lord, appeared in this world on July 21, 3228 BCE. This is not a "give or take" date, mind you—to him, this is the exact time of the Lord's appearance! Bansal's conclusion is calculated from two of his software packages: the Leo Gold and the Palm computer programs, both designed to simulate planetary configurations—those that have occurred, and those that will occur, in time.

According to scriptural tradition, Krishna was born in the Rohini Naksatra, in the month of Bhadrapada (August–September), on the eighth day of the waning moon at midnight. For those of us in the West, this tells us little. Bansal assures his readers that this date is accurate, however, and his evidence is based on the time of Krishna's departure, or His leaving the planet, which he says occurred at 2 P.M. on February 18, 3102 BCE. This date is crucial in his assessment of Krishna's birth—by working backwards, he arrives at Krishna's birth date.

Let me flesh this out a bit: Bansal quotes the *Srimad Bhagavatam* and the *Vishnu Purana* extensively, claiming that, according to these texts, Kali Yuga, the present age of quarrel and hypocrisy, started on the day that Krishna left the world. He adds to this another verse from the *Srimad Bhagavatam*, wherein Lord Brahma himself speaks of Krishna's chronological age: "Brahma says that 125 years have passed since Krishna's birth; this is just before Krishna plans his [departure]."

This information is augmented by the following: The advent of Kali Yuga is traditionally taken to be 3102 BCE, according to astrological experts and reliable Indian *panchangs*, or calendars. These same works say that 5,100 years of Kali Yuga had passed before 1999, a belief that is supported by the *Aryabhattiya*, an astronomical work prepared by one of India's famed mathematicians, Arya Bhatta. The same idea is expressed in the *Surya Siddhanta*, a respected text on astronomy dating back to 400 CE.

Deleting 125 years—the length of Krishna's manifest pastimes, or His "life" in this world—from the "disappearance" date, Bansal discerned that the Lord was born either in 3327 or 3228 BCE. Given this basic information, he then relied on his software to do the rest.

But even if Bansal is correct—and there's no reason to assume that he isn't—what does this really tell us about Krishna? As we learned from the Gita, Krishna is essentially a timeless entity—God—and His purpose in this world is served by giving pleasure to the devotees and by doing away with the demonic element. This is true whether He appeared 5,000 years ago or 50 years ago. The highest yoga process, or system of religion, is to assist Krishna in His mission of reminding this world's souls about their rightful place in the spiritual realm, about their mandate to develop love for Krishna. Great devotees throughout history have told us how to proceed. Briefly, Krishna comes to this world to show us His wondrous activities. So devotees can help Him accomplish this end by sharing those wondrous activities with others. We can talk to our family and friends about Krishna, write or read books about Him, and so on. Of course, before we can share Him with others, we have to know Him ourselves. That's why books like the Bhagavad Gita are so important.

The other thing Krishna seeks to accomplish, as I mentioned, is to do away with the demonic mentality. Again, we can assist Him by, first of all, doing away with our own materialistic disposition—we can purify ourselves by certain basic practices, like chanting His names. There are no sectarian considerations here: Allah, Jehovah, Krishna, and El—He has so many. It's really limitless. Just chant His names, whatever your religious tradition. We can also follow a certain religious regimen, such as vegetarianism, continence, honesty, sobriety, and so on. Just to situate ourselves in goodness. This way, once we're purified, we can help purify others. This will kill the demonic mentality so prevalent in our modern world. It will benefit us, and it will benefit all who come into contact with us. This is Krishna consciousness, and it is the secret of Lord Krishna's appearance in this world. Thank you very much.

NOTES

1. For more on Bansal's work, see Smita Mitra's analysis in the Indian periodical, *Outlook*, September 13, 2004, or see article online at http://www.dalsabzi.com/enlight_info/lord_krishna.htm.

— 23 —

From Ear to Eternity:
The Spiritual Dimensions of Sound

"Always chanting My glories," says Lord Krishna, in the Bhagavad Gita, "endeavoring with great determination, bowing down before Me, the great souls always worship Me with devotion" (9.14). Thus, the Gita teaches the importance of chanting—not sporadic chanting, but *always* chanting. This is the spiritual process employed by those who are serious about self-realization, at least according to the Gita.

The teaching brings to mind a recent interaction with my mother, in which sound vibration—which is at the heart of the chanting process—played a central part. My mom is now quite old, and hearing is not her strong point.

"What?" she asked. This has become something of a personal mantra for her—her hearing has been going for some time now, and "What?" is her frequent response to nearly every sound she hears. Or doesn't hear.

Her TV blaring because she doesn't hear it, and the neighbors banging on the walls—which she also doesn't hear—makes a visit to her home a bit like visiting an asylum. Still, she is alert and has a good sense of humor about her lack of hearing: "Ah, I've heard it all anyway. If there's something out there that I haven't heard yet, it probably isn't worth hearing!"

But my sister and I have been urging her to get a hearing aid for almost a decade. "The ear is an important organ," I tell her. "If it's not working right, it affects more than your ability to hear—it can also affect your equilibrium, your sense of balance."

"So I'll sit," she says.

Joking aside, she wanted me to ask her doctor about her loss of hearing, and what, if anything, should be done about it. So I did. The doctor explained to me that the ear is made of three parts. The outer ear captures and channels sound waves through the auditory canal to a tightly stretched membrane known as the eardrum. Beyond this is the inner ear, which contains three tiny bones. Sound waves on the eardrum cause these bones to vibrate. The vibration causes the bones to react in such a way that the sound message is conveyed to "the inner ear."

From "the middle ear" to the back of the nasal cavity is a tube that needs to drain properly—this helps equalize pressure on both sides of the eardrum. The fluid in these canals and the hairlike nerve cells at the end of each of these tubes allow us to hear and to keep our balance when we stand, run, walk, ride a bicycle, and, yes, even when we sit.

The doctor said my mom's inner ear was worn down—and that this happens to a good number of people over time.

As his barrage of technical words entered my own ears, my mind wandered to another kind of sound vibration, and another use of the auditory sense altogether.

The inner ear as referred to by this particular doctor, of course, is an entirely physical phenomenon. But I was more interested in an "inner meaning" to the inner ear—one that I learned from the Bhagavad Gita and the other texts of ancient India.

THE UNHEARD WORLD OF SOUND

Human beings are physically unable to perceive certain portions of the known vibratory spectrum. While extremely sensitive to sound waves of about 1,000 to 4,000 cycles per second (cps), man is all but deaf beyond 20,000 cps. Dogs and cats, on the other hand, can hear up to 60,000 cps, while mice, bats, whales, and dolphins can emit and receive sounds well over 100,000 cps.

In other words, there are definitely things we just don't hear. Vedic texts suggest that if this is true of hearing in the material sphere, how much more true must it be of sounds that exist beyond the material world—sounds that we must distinguish ourselves, through spiritual practice, to truly hear.

Despite our inability to hear certain frequencies—whether material or spiritual—we tend to hear better than we see. This was recognized by psychologist Katharine Le Mee:

> The sense of hearing . . . connects experientially with the heart, and music and sound touch us most directly. We do not resonate so deeply with the visual as with the auditory. This may be explained by the fact that our visual apparatus has a frequency range of slightly less than one octave, from infrared to ultraviolet, whereas our auditory system has a range of about eight octaves, approximately 60 to 16,000 hertz, or number of vibrations per second. We are sensitive to sound frequency as pitch and to light frequency as color. The frequencies of the visual field are much higher than those of the auditory field (by an order of 1010), and, as is well known, the higher the frequencies, the lesser the penetration of a given material. For instance, a piece of cardboard shields us easily from the light, but it takes a thick wall to block out sound, and the lower the pitch the deeper the penetration. We are very sensitive to sound, not just through the ear but through our whole skin, and all our organs are affected by it.[1]

Thus, science has shown that our human senses are imperfect and limited, and that there is a world of sensual experience beyond human perception. Vaishnava scriptures confirm these limitations in man's seeing and hearing and elucidate untold categories of spiritual sound.

SPIRITUAL SOUND IN THE VEDIC LITERATURE

Portions of the Vedic literature are almost like textbooks on auditory phenomena, informing us about an ancient art in which sound was used as a spiritual tool. The same concept is echoed in other cultures. Chronicles from lands as diverse as Egypt and Ireland tell us of a time when vibrations laying at the foundation of our universe were harnessed by spiritual adepts for the benefit of humankind. Like the Bible, which states, "In the beginning was the Word" (John 1.1), Vaishnava scriptures affirm that the entire cosmic creation began with sound: "By His utterance came the universe" (*Brihad Aranyaka Upanishad* I.2.4). The Vedas add that ultimate liberation comes from sound as well (*anavrittih shabdat*).

Primal sound is referred to as Shabda Brahman—God as word. Closely related to this is the concept of Nada Brahman—God as sound. *Nada*, a Sanskrit word literally meaning "sound," is related to the term *nadi*, denoting the stream of consciousness—a concept that goes back to the Rig Veda, the most ancient of the Vedas. Thus, the relationship between sound and consciousness has long been recorded in India's ancient literature. Vedic texts, again, describe sound as the preeminent means for attaining higher, spiritual consciousness.

Mantras, or sacred sounds, are used to pierce through sensual, mental, and intellectual levels of existence—all lower strata of consciousness—for the purpose of purification and spiritual enlightenment. The sounds of different letters, particularly Sanskrit letters, have been shown to affect the mind, intellect, and auditory nerves of those who chant and hear them. The seven energy centers (*chakras*) of the spinal column, as well as the *ida, pingala*, and *sushumna nadis*, or the three *pranic* channels of the subtle body, all respond to mantras, bringing practitioners to elevated levels of awareness.

A recently constructed device called a "tonoscope" graphically demonstrates the power of Sanskrit syllables to evoke forms in a physical medium. The tonoscope is a tube suspended over a thin membrane and covered by a layer of fine dust. When sounds are broadcast through the tube, corresponding designs form in the dust that can tell us something about the initial sound that went through the tube. While most sounds produce random, ill-defined images, the vibration of Sanskrit syllables produces quite a different result. When Sanskrit mantras are repeated at the proper pitch, for example, a perfect circle forms, and out of that a *yantra*, or a traditional geometric image used in worship. These experiments, which are still in their infancy, indicate that Sanskrit mantras embody objective vibratory energies that can act on the environment. If the sounds of mantras can activate a gross element like dust, one can only imagine the power such vibrations might have on human consciousness.

THE POWER OF GOD'S NAMES

The spiritual sounds most lauded in Vedic texts are the names of God. These sounds are said to have ultimate powers unlike any other sound vibration in or beyond the universe. Vaishnava texts state that in much the same way that one could awaken a person who is sleeping, by making a sound or calling out his name, man can awaken from his conditioned, materialistic slumber by calling out the name of God. In fact, the world's major religious traditions concur that it is by chanting the name of God that one attains enlightenment and freedom from the cycle of birth and death.

Mohammed counseled, "Glorify the name of your Lord, the most high' (Koran 87.2). Saint Paul said, "Everyone who calls upon the name of the Lord will be saved" (Romans 10.13). Buddha declared, "All who sincerely call upon my name will come to me after death, and I will take them to paradise" (*Vows of Amida Buddha* 18). King David preached, "From the rising of the sun to its setting, the name of the Lord is to be praised" (Psalms 113.3); and the Vaishnava scriptures, echoing the Bhagavad Gita, repeatedly assert: "Chant the holy name, chant the holy name, chant the holy name of the Lord. In this age of quarrel there is no other way, no other way, no other way to attain spiritual enlightenment" (*Brihad-naradiya Purana* 3.8.126).

Praise of the holy name of God is found throughout the literature of the Vaishnavas. Here are some examples:

"Oh, how glorious are they whose tongues are chanting Your holy name! Even if originally lowborn dog-eaters, they are to be considered worshipable. To have reached the point of chanting the Lord's name, they must have executed various austerities and Vedic sacrifices and achieved all the good qualities of true Aryans. If they are chanting Your holy name, they must have bathed in all holy rivers, studied the Vedas and fulfilled all prescribed duties" (*Bhagavata Purana* 3.33.7).

"The holy name of Krishna is the spiritually blissful giver of all benedictions, for it is Krishna Himself, the reservoir of pleasure. Krishna's name is complete in itself and is the essential form of all spiritual relationships. It is not a material name under any condition, and it is no less powerful than Krishna Himself. This name is not tinged by any aspect of material nature, because it is identical with Krishna" (*Padma Purana* 3.21).

And, finally, Lord Krishna says,

I dwell not in the spiritual kingdom,
nor in the hearts of yogis;
Where my devotees are chanting,
there, O Narada, stand I![2]

Because chanting the name of God is so much emphasized in Vaishnava texts, practitioners focus on chanting as a central devotional practice. Thus, deep meditation and great emotion accompany *japa* (the soft chanting), *kirtan* (the loud chanting), and *sankirtan* (the congregational chanting). When perfected, the chanting leads to awareness of God's absolute nature, that is, that there is no difference between the *nami* ("the named one") and *nama* ("the name"). Elucidation on the absolute nature of Krishna and His name is the heart of Vaishnava mysticism, leading to love of God.

CHANTING THE "HARE KRISHNA" MAHA-MANTRA

The Hare Krishna Maha-mantra, or "the great chant for deliverance," is considered by scripture to be the most powerful of incantations, for it includes the potency of all other mantras.

The Maha-mantra can be expressed in two distinct ways. The most significant and well-known version is: Hare Krishna, Hare Krishna, Krishna Krishna, Hare Hare/Hare Rama, Hare Rama, Rama Rama, Hare Hare. The medieval Bengali text, the *Chaitanya-charitamrita* (*Madhya* 25.64), a seminal scripture for the Hare Krishna movement, provides another version: *haraye nama krishna yadavaya namaha/ gopal govinda ram shri madhusudana*—"I offer my respectful obeisance unto the Supreme Personality of Godhead, Krishna. He is the descendant of the Yadu dynasty. Let me offer my respects unto Gopala, Govinda, Rama, and Shri Madhusudana, for these are all names of the same Supreme Lord." It is to such names that Krishna is referring in the Gita, when He says that great souls perpetually chant His glories.

Still, it is the chanting of "Hare Krishna, Hare Krishna, Krishna Krishna, Hare Hare/Hare Rama, Hare Rama, Rama Rama, Hare Hare" that is particularly recommended for the current age. Statements to this effect can be found in the *Brahmanda Purana* (*Uttara-khanda* 6.55), the *Kalisantarana Upanishad* (Chapter One), and in many other Vedic and post-Vedic texts.

Breaking down this sacred mantra into its component parts, the word "Hare" refers to Lord Hari—a name for Krishna that indicates His ability to remove obstacles from His devotees' path. In a more esoteric sense, the word "Hare" is a vocative form of "Hara," which refers to Mother Hara, or Shrimati Radharani, the divine feminine energy—Lord Krishna's eternal consort and transcendental counterpart.

"Krishna" means "the all-attractive one," referring to God in His original form. Etymologically, the word *krish* indicates the attractive feature of the Lord's existence, and *na* means spiritual pleasure. When the verb *krish* is added to the affix *na*, it becomes *krishna*, which means "the person who gives spiritual pleasure through His all-attractive qualities." According to Sanskrit semantic derivation (*nirukti*), it is also understood that *na* refers to the Lord's ability to stop the repetition of birth and death. And *krish* is a synonym for *sattartha* or "existential totality." Another way of understanding the word *krishna*, then, is "that Lord who embodies all of existence and who can help the living entities overcome the repeated suffering of birth and death."

"Rama" refers to both Balarama (Krishna's elder brother) and Lord Ramachandra, a prominent incarnation of the Lord, discussed at length in the epic known as the *Ramayana*. It is also said, however, that "Rama" refers to Radha Ramana Rama, which is another name for Krishna, meaning "one who brings pleasure to Shrimati Radharani." Thus the Maha-mantra, composed solely of the Lord's most confidential names, embodies the essence of the divine. As a prayer, the mantra is generally translated in the following way: "O Lord, O divine energy of the Lord! Please engage me in Your service." The selflessness of this mantra—asking to serve God rather than asking God to do something for us—situates it in a unique category, even among the best of prayers and the most powerful of incantations. But in its pure form, it can only be heard by the pure devotee—in his "inner ear," which is in his heart of hearts.

CONCLUSION

By the time I returned to my mom's home to tell her about my meeting with her ear doctor, she had already made up her mind: "I'm not getting a hearing aid." She just didn't want to be bothered. Truth is, her doctor said that a hearing aid would just add to her discomfort, and it probably wouldn't help her much anyway. I told her how my mind wandered to Vedic mantras and spiritual sound vibrations as I spoke to her doctor. But she couldn't hear what I was saying, literally or figuratively.

She asked me if I would get a hearing aid if I were in her shoes. "Probably not," I said.

"What?"

I spoke up: "No, I wouldn't get one." After some time, I added, very softly, that I had already accepted a hearing aid many years ago by studying the Bhagavad Gita. Amazingly, she heard me. And she knew what I meant, too. Letting out a loud guffaw, she made explicit my implication: "You mean that 'Hare Krishna' stuff, right?" She smiled. "Your hearing was definitely in trouble—but that chanting taught you to hear things properly."

She thought for a second, and added, "I should have such an effective hearing aid."

NOTES

1. Katharine Le Mee, *Chant* (New York: Bell Tower Publishing, 1994), pp. 28–29.
2. Cited in the *Padma Purana, Uttara-khanda* 92.

—24—

From the Transcendentalists to Transcendental Love of God

Many years ago, while living as a monk in a Hare Krishna ashram, I wrote the following words in one of my first essays on the Bhagavad Gita: "If from a purely historical perspective, the first English edition of the Gita appeared in 1785, translated by British Orientalist Charles Wilkins, the text had to wait until 1968 to manifest in English purely." What I meant was this: While Wilkins had rendered the ancient Sanskrit into English in the eighteenth century, it wasn't until Srila Prabhupada published his *Bhagavad Gita As It Is* that the English-speaking world received the text in its pure form, according to the knowledge and insights of the authorized teachers in traditional lineages. This is how the Gita is supposed to be studied, according to the Gita itself (4.3). Practitioners expect to penetrate the text under the guidance of a pure soul who lives its teachings. Thus, my original statement was coming from this orthodox concern, not from disrespect for Wilkins or his work.

Even still, the years in-between Wilkins' translation and the publication of Srila Prabhupada's Gita have a story to tell. Though the initial translation stirred some interest, leading to alternate editions over the next century, it took Sir Edwin Arnold's verse translation, released almost one hundred years later, to popularize the text. It was his version, in fact, which made its way into the hands of Mahatma Gandhi, leading the great Mahatma to praise the Gita again and again. He also enjoyed several versions of the text ushering forth from the Theosophical Society, who interpreted Lord Krishna's words in a metaphorical way. Notably, Gandhi did not read the Gita in its original language, nor was he privy to the insights of the traditional lineages.

It is from these origins, from the mid- to late-1800s, that the Western world witnessed the flowering of a unique intellectual movement. This was a movement that moved most particularly in Concord, Massachusetts, and was known—though it had no formal organization—as the Transcendental Club or Circle. Its members were Ralph Waldo Emerson and Henry David Thoreau, along with Unitarian Minister James Freeman Clark, teacher and philosopher Amos Bronson Alcott, journalist and women's rights activist Margaret Fuller, and some clergymen. Many consider their collective achievement for American literature, in terms of quality of style, to remain unsurpassed, even today. And their major influence, without exception, was the Bhagavad Gita.[1]

Historian Arthur Christy, thoroughly analyzing the literary works that most influenced the American Transcendentalists, wrote, "No one Oriental volume that ever came to Concord was more influential than the Bhagavad Gita."[2]

As Emerson (1803–1882) admitted, "I owed a magnificent day to the Bhagavat-Geeta. It was the first of books; it was as if an empire spake to us, nothing small or unworthy, but large, serene, consistent, the voice of an old intelligence which in another age and climate had pondered and thus disposed of the same questions that exercise us."[3] Emerson is the first great American literary figure to read deeply and fully the available literature on Hindu spirituality, which is evident in his own writings. In a letter to Max Mueller, he wrote: "All my interest is in Marsh's Manu, then Wilkins' Bhagavat Geeta, Burnouf's Bhagavat Purana and Wilson's Vishnu Purana, yes, and few other translations. I remember I owed my first taste for this fruit to Cousin's sketch, in his first lecture, of the dialogue between Krishna and Arjoona and I still prize the first chapters of the Bhagavat as wonderful."[4]

By 1856 Emerson had read the Kathopanishad and his ideas were increasingly reflecting influence from the East. His poems, such as *Hamatreya* (composed in 1845) showed his love for Hindu thought. Here he was concerned with the subject of illusion (*maya*), which he further wrote about in his essay, *Illusions*, where he said: "I find men victims of illusions in all parts of life. Children, youths, adults and old men, all are led by one bauble or another. Yogavindra, the goddess of illusion, is stronger than the Titans, stronger than Apollo."[5]

In his poem *Maya*, he wrote:

Illusion works impenetrable,
Weaving webs innumerable,
Her gay pictures never fail,
Crowds each other, veil on veil,
Charmer who will be believed,
By man who thirsts to be deceived.[6]

But the poem by which Emerson is best remembered—and the one often quoted for the influence the Bhagavad Gita had on him—is *Brahma*.

If the red slayer thinks he slays,
Or if the slain thinks that he is slain,
They know not well the subtle ways
I keep, and pass, and turn again.

Fear or forgot to me is near;
Shadow and sunlight are the same;
The vanished gods to me appear;
And one to me are shame and fame.

They reckon ill who leave me out;
When me they fly, I am the wings;
I am the doubter and the doubt;
And I the hymn the Brahmin sings.

The strong gods pine for my abode,
And pine in vain the sacred Seven;
But thou, meek over good!
Find me, and turn thy back on heaven.[7]

Some of his stanzas paraphrase the Bhagavad Gita:

He who thinks that the living entity is the slayer or that the entity is slain does not understand. One who is in knowledge knows that the self slays not nor is slain (Bhagavad Gita 2:19).

O son of Kunti, the nonpermanent appearance of heat and cold, happiness and distress, and their disappearance in due course, are like the appearance and disappearance of winter and summer seasons. They arise from sense perception, O scion of Bharata, and one must learn to tolerate them without being disturbed (Bhagavad Gita 2:14).

Emerson and Thoreau (1817–1862) are counted as the two leading Transcendentalists, the latter being the younger of the two. He was also the more exuberant and the more frankly admiring of the mystic East. There is no record of his reading any Vedic literature while at Harvard, but in Emerson's library, early on, he found and read Sir William Jones' translation of *The Laws of Manu*, which he found "fascinating."

Moving on to the *Dharma Shastra* in 1841, when he was twenty-four, and the Bhagavad Gita when he was twenty-eight, he gradually became a "devotee" of Hinduism's mystic literature. Regarding the Gita, he wrote: "The New Testament is remarkable for its pure morality, the best of the Vedic Scripture, for its pure intellectuality. The reader is nowhere raised into and sustained in a bigger, purer, or rarer region of thought than in the Bhagavat Geeta. The Geeta's "sanity and sublimity" have impressed the minds even of soldiers and merchants."[8] He had the Gita with him during his stay at Walden Pond.[9]

"What extracts from the Vedas I have read fall on me like the light of a higher and purer luminary, which describes a loftier course through a purer stratum," he remarked in 1850. "The religion and philosophy of the Hebrews are those of a wilder and ruder tribe, wanting the civility and intellectual refinements and subtlety of Vedic culture."[10] He writes in Chapter Sixteen of *Walden*: "In the morning I bathe my intellect in the stupendous and cosmogonal philosophy of the Bhagavat Geeta, since whose composition years of the gods have elapsed and in comparison with which our modern world and its literature seems puny and trivial."[11]

He sums up his reverence for the Gita:

> Beside the vast and cosmogonal philosophy of the Bhagavat-Geeta, even our Shakespeare seems sometimes youthfully green . . . *Ex oriente lux* may still be the motto of scholars, for the Western world has not yet derived from the East all the light which it is destined to derive thence.[12]

An American scholar, John T. Reid, commenting on *Walden* has said that if one read it, without screening its lines for possible foreign influences, the net impression will be that of a frugal, practical Yankee, greatly interested in the details of New England's flora and fauna, gloriously happy in the tranquil peace of unsullied Nature, an eccentric at odds with most of his neighbor's foibles. "He was not in any accurate sense a Yogi," adds Reid, "but he did pay devoted heed to those glimpses of light from the Orient which he saw."[13]

The relationship of Walt Whitman (1819–1892) to the Bhagavad Gita is considerably more complex. Emerson once described Whitman's *Leaves of Grass* as a blending of the Gita and the *New York Herald*. In his essay of reminiscence, "A Backward Glance O'er Travel'd Roads" (1889), Whitman claims to have read "the ancient Hindu poems" and mentions that in 1875 he had received a copy of the Gita as a Christmas present from an English friend, Thomas Dixon.

Whitman, from all available evidence, was vastly impressed by his readings, a fact that can be seen in such superb poems of the late 1850s and 1860s as, "Out of the Cradle Endlessly Rocking," "When Lilacs Last in the Dooryard Bloom'd," and "Passage to India"—a title, incidentally, which E. M. Forster picked up some time later.

In Whitman's "Passage to India" he writes of the soul, "that actual me," who must voyage beyond its material successes in order to amplify its love, its ideals, its "purity, perfection, strength." So "sail forth—steer for the deep waters only." This was written after his study of the Bhagavad Gita. Whitman's constantly phrased and rephrased conception of "the real me," along with, "I pass death with the dying," brings to mind the doctrines of the soul and reincarnation as it is specifically expressed in the Gita.

T. S. Eliot (1888–1965), who was born in St. Louis, Missouri, studied at Harvard, the Sorbonne, and Oxford and received the Nobel Prize for literature in 1948, was deeply influenced by Dante, Shakespeare, the Bible, St. John of the Cross, and other Christian mystics—and mostly, without doubt, the Bhagavad Gita.

Eliot was a twenty-three-year-old student at Harvard when he first came across Vedic philosophy and religion. What sparked his interest is lost to history, but, whatever it was, it ignited an abiding passion for Sanskrit and other languages of the East, along with the metaphysics found in Patanjali's *sutras* and the Vedic literature. He had also read the Upanishads, as is clear from the concluding lines of *The Waste Land*, a poem that ends with a salutation to the Three Cardinal Virtues originally found in the Brihadaranyaka Upanishad: *damyata* (restraint), *datta* (charity), and *dayadhvam* (compassion). Eliot then offers the blessing, *Shantih shantih shantih*, which he roughly translated as "the peace that passeth understanding."

But it is arguably the Gita that influenced him most. Its presence can be felt not only in *The Waste Land* but also in *Four Quartets, The Dry Salvages,* and *The Family Reunion.* As Professor Philip R. Headings remarked in his elaborate study of the poet, "No serious student of Eliot's poetry can afford to ignore his early and continued interest in the Bhagavad Gita."[14]

In *Four Quartets*, Eliot tells us, "Time the destroyer is time the preserver . . . "[15] that echoes the Gita. In that same work, he muses on the actual meaning behind Krishna's words:

> I sometimes wonder if that is what Krishna meant—
> Among other things—or one way of putting the same thing:
> That the future is a faded song, a Royal Rose or a lavender spray
> Of wistful regret for those who are not yet here to regret,
> Pressed between yellow leaves of a book that has never been opened.[16]

A little further along, Eliot directly refers to Krishna's instruction:

> O voyagers, O seamen,
> You who come to port, and you whose bodies
> Will suffer the trial and judgment of the sea,
> Or whatever event, this is your real destination.
> So Krishna, as when he admonished Arjuna
> On the field of battle.
> Not fare well,
> But fare forward, voyagers.[17]

In a sense, Eliot follows in the giant footsteps of Emerson and Thoreau and the early Transcendentalists, but only provisionally, and only where it had particular relevance. One of Eliot's virtues was that he glorified knowledge only when it had practical utility. And in this way, his message is much like that of the Gita, which is the proper utilization of all action. Of course, Eliot, like his forebears, could only hint at such utility. Without a spiritual master, he could understand the Gita's message only in rudimentary form. The next step, for those who came after Eliot, would not take place until the mid-1960s.

CONCLUSION

In modern times (since the death of T. S. Eliot in 1965) the influence of the Bhagavad Gita in America has become noteworthy. The turbulent peace-seeking days of the 1960s and 1970s opened the doors for alternative thinking, and "Spiritual India" was welcomed with open arms.

The Gita is so deeply embedded in Western thought that even the Beatles—arguably the most well-known icons of pop culture—were touched by it. George Harrison, in particular, took the Gita seriously and attempted to live according to its teachings. Certain editions of his autobiography, *I, Me, Mine* (New York: Simon and Schuster, 1980, reprint: San Francisco, CA: Chronicle Books, 2002), for example, proclaim this loudly with a frontispiece that quotes the Gita; his 1973 solo album, *Living in the Material World,* includes a separate insert for liner notes with a famous painting of Krishna and Arjuna from the cover of Prabhupada's text; and the liner notes to *Somewhere in England,* released in 1982, cites 2:12: "Never was there a time when I did not exist, nor you, nor all these kings. Nor in the future will any of us cease to be." Indeed, his numerous songs either quote the Gita directly or were heavily influenced by its teachings.[18]

But the Gita's involvement with the West goes miles beyond the Beatles. Words like *dharma* and *karma* have a place in our English dictionaries, and meditation (of one variety or another) is practiced, or at least attempted, by millions of Americans. This is largely the work of His Divine Grace A. C. Bhaktivedanta Swami Prabhupada, who, coincidentally, came West in the year of Eliot's demise. Prabhupada's release of his Gita in 1968, as mentioned earlier, accomplished something none of the other Gita translations could: it created devotees of Krishna.

While the earliest English translations gave people legitimate interest in the scripture, and even inspired poetry and philosophical elaboration, they couldn't change people's lives—at least not in a major way. They couldn't give people love for Krishna. This was accomplished by Prabhupada alone, for he carried in his translation a secret gem—the blessings of the disciplic succession. He was carrying in his text the one thing that can't be found in translations that are merely literal—Krishna Himself.

The list of prominent Western thinkers profoundly affected by the Gita—since Wilkins's translation, more than 200 years ago—is too long to mention. Especially noteworthy, perhaps, would be the likes of Aldous Huxley, Christopher Isherwood, Juan Mascaro, Allen Ginsberg, and Thomas Merton, the latter two contributing prefatory essays to Prabhupada's edition. But there were many others, and here we merely have a taste, a drop, of the story of the Gita's western sojourn.

Although the Western world experienced a slight shift away from Eastern spirituality in the 1980s and 1990s, it appears to have been only a momentary hesitation. The now materially exhausted Baby Boomers are again searching for deeper values, and New Age spiritualists, most of whom accept reincarnation, karma, meditation, chanting, and vegetarianism are filling the spiritual gap.

Of course, there are numerous materialistic entrepreneurs who seek to exploit the spiritual marketplace, and the New Age community is overrun with imitation and pseudo spiritualists. But the precious commodity of spiritual wealth found in the Vedic tradition—and in the Gita, in particular—continues to shine its light on sincere souls worldwide.

At the same time, modernity and technological progress, the virtues of the Western world, help more and more people gain access to that light. Thus, with the spiritual eyes of the East and the material legs of the West, the lame man and the blind man might cooperate for the sake of transcendence.

NOTES

1. For more on the subject the Transcendentalists and the Bhagavad Gita, along with other Western interest in this sacred text, see Eric J. Sharpe, *The Universal Gita* (La Salle, IL: Open Court Publishing Company, 1985) and also Catherine A. Robinson, *Interpretations of the Bhagavad Gita and Images of the Hindu Tradition* (London: Routledge, 2006).

2. Arthur Christy, *The Orient in American Transcendentalism* (New York: Columbia University Press, 1932), p. 25.

3. Ibid., p. 23.

4. Ralph L. Rusk, ed., *The Letters of Ralph Waldo Emerson* (New York: Columbia University Press, 1939), vol. 1, p. lix.

5. Quoted in Jan Patel, *Indian Thought in Emerson's Words* (New Delhi, India: Finethought Publishing, 1985), p. 16.

6. Ibid.

7. Bruce Atkinson, ed., *The Selected Writings of Ralph Waldo Emerson* (New York: Signet Classics, 1950), p. 809.

8. Bradford Torrey and Francis H. Allen, eds., *The Writings of Henry David Thoreau* (New York: AMS Press, 1968, reprint), vol. 7, p. 22. See also Benjamin Hart, *Thoreau and the Literature of the East* (New York: Penn Publishing, 1995), p. 10.

9. For more on this subject, see Barbara Stoler Miller's essay, "Why Did Henry David Thoreau Take the Bhagavad Gita to Walden Pond?" found as an Afterword in her edition of the text [*The Bhagavad Gita: Krishna's Counsel in Time of War* (New York: Bantam Books, 1986)].

10. See Torrey and Allen, op. cit., p. 66.

11. Ibid.

12. See Henry David Thoreau, *A Week on the Concord and Merrimac Rivers* (London: Walter Scott Limited, 1889), p. 110. See especially 1906 edition, p. 122f.

13. Quoted in Benjamin Hart, op. cit., p. 12.

14. Quoted in Thomas Cracknell, *The Many Sides of T. S. Eliot* (San Francisco, CA: Tanning Press, 1989), p. 7.

15. T. S. Eliot, *Four Quartets* (New York: Harcourt, Brace, 1943; London: Faber, 1944), p. 29.

16. Ibid, p. 29f.

17. Ibid., p. 31.

18. For more on Harrison's considerable involvement with the Gita, see Joshua M. Greene, *Here Comes the Sun: The Spiritual and Musical Journey of George Harrison* (New Jersey: John Wiley & Sons, 2006); Dale C. Allison, *The Love There That's Sleeping: The Art and Spirituality of George Harrison* (New York: Continuum International, 2006); and Michael J. Gilmour, "Brainwashed, By George Harrison and the Bhagavad Gita," *Journal of Religion and Popular Culture* 8 (2004), available online at http://www.usask.ca/relst/jrpc/art8-georgeharrison.html.

Afterword

The essays in this book should bring a few points to light: The Bhagavad Gita is not just another religious text; nor is it merely a Hindu scripture. Rather, it provides "applied spiritual technologies," or systematic procedures by which anyone, of any religious faith, can advance toward the ultimate goal of life. In other words, the Gita transcends its natural associations with India and with the sectarian boundaries within which most people would place it.

Historically, the devastating battle referred to in its pages centers around two kingly families and their dynastic concerns. In terms of its inner meaning, however, the battle is our own—it is the human spirits' ongoing struggle against lower desires and passions.

Theosophist T. Subba Rao observed certain resonances between the proverbial "dweller on the threshold," made famous in Edward B. Lytton's Rosicrucian novel, *Zanoni* (1842), and the plight of Arjuna, our hero in Krishna's song. Lytton's "Dweller" is a hideous creature with monstrous features, appearing before the book's protagonist just as he enters an unknown, mysterious land. The creature attempts to rattle him, to make him waver in his resolve, and our hero will succumb if he is not fully prepared.

The monster, of course, is merely figurative, and it lurks in each human heart. Like the temptations that came to both Buddha and Jesus, Lytton's monster attacks when we want it least—when we resolve to pursue higher reality.

The Gita addresses the discord that would obstruct our advancement—Lytton's monster—and systematically educates its readers in how to defeat the creature and to render him ineffectual.

But, more, the text guides us, in stepwise fashion, to live in that higher, magical realm of the spirit, where "dwellers of the threshold" no longer exist. It is this that the Gita bequeaths to its most sincere readers.

The present book, through Arjuna's example, uncovers five universal stages that all aspiring transcendentalists must one day go through, in one form or another:

1. Existential Agony
   As the Gita opens, we are introduced to the psychological and spiritual crisis of Arjuna, who represents all steadfast practitioners: Those who are spiritually evolved but also inexperienced on the spiritual path, reach a point of intense dismay—they realize that there must be something beyond the day-to-day, and feel overwhelming incompleteness in their lives. They gradually come to realize that this feeling will not go away without the presence of God in their lives. And so they embark on a spiritual journey. (As a side note, the Gita discloses that there are three other mindsets that can lead to the spiritual quest: those desirous of wealth, those seeking knowledge, and those who are wise might also embark on the path.)

2. Preliminary Surrender
   Such inner anguish leads to a rudimentary form of surrender. If one does not have preliminary faith—willing to make certain life changes and engaging in corresponding devotional practices—one cannot make further progress. At this point one would do well to find a spiritual master, or someone more experienced in the procedures of devotion. It is at this point, in fact, that Arjuna says: "Now I am confused about my duty and have lost all composure due to weakness. In this condition I am asking You to tell me clearly what is best for me. Now I am Your disciple, and a soul surrendered unto You. Please instruct me" (2.7). The first teaching, and all that follow, will make clear one's existence apart from the body—that the living being is a spirit-soul, encased in a material body, and that his or her main function is to serve the Supreme Lord, with love and devotion.

3. Passionate Search and Sincere Inquiry
   Such surrender is in itself liberating, and the spiritual aspirant begins to make substantial progress. He or she approaches the teacher with pertinent questions and renders service, developing love for God by developing love for His dedicated servant, the spiritual master. It is at this level that the science of spirituality begins to unfold. One learns how to read certain signs of advancement, as well as signs of faltering. Here, chanting the holy name—or prayer—becomes more meaningful, too, and one is now able to effectively utilize attendant practices that facilitate pure chanting.

4. The Dawn of True Knowledge
   The intricacies of God-consciousness and the nature of the Supreme gradually arise in the hearts of sincere practitioners. As Arjuna submits to Krishna on the battlefield of Kurukshetra, the Lord reveals transcendental knowledge to him that few will ever attain. Arjuna learns how to see God in natural phenomena, and how all things exist only because of His presence. Overall, such knowledge reveals that God manifests impersonally, as Brahman; He also pervades everything, from living beings to atoms, as Paramatma, or His localized Supersoul expansion; and He remains distinct as the Supreme Personality of Godhead, Krishna, who cherishes intimate relationships of love with His devotees.

5. Love for God
   The Gita finally promotes full surrender (18.66), for having pursued the science of transcendence; one finally is *able to fully surrender*—for one now knows what or who one is surrendering to. Krishna says, "I am the source of all spiritual and material worlds. Everything emanates from Me. The wise who know this perfectly engage in My devotional

service and worship Me with all their hearts. The thoughts of My pure devotees dwell in Me, their lives are surrendered to Me, and they derive great bliss and satisfaction enlightening one another and conversing about Me. To those who are constantly devoted and worship Me with love, I give the understanding by which they can come to Me. Out of compassion for them, I, dwelling in their hearts, destroy with the shining lamp of knowledge the darkness born of ignorance" (10.8–11).

This is the Gita's ultimate teaching, in which a new "dweller" emerges in the life of the spiritual practitioner—Lytton's monster, now gone, is replaced by Krishna, who we have since learned to love, and whose love for us knows no bounds.

Bibliography

Bryant, Edwin F. *Krishna: The Beautiful Legend of God* (London: Penguin, 2004).

Carter, Stephen L. *God's Name in Vain: The Wrongs and Rights of Religion in Politics* (New York: Basic Books, 2000).

Chandra, A. N. *The Date of the Kuruksetra War* (Calcutta, India: Ratna Prakashan, 1978).

Chanda, R. P. *Archeology and the Vaishnava Tradition* (Memoirs of the Archeological Survey of India, 5, 1920).

Chapple, Christopher Key. *Nonviolence to Animals, Earth, and Self in Asian Traditions* (Albany, NY: State University of New York Press, 1993).

Cornille, Catherine, ed. *Song Divine: Christian Commentaries on the Bhagavad Gita* (Leuven, Belgium: W. B. Eerdmans, 2006).

Dasa, Bhurijana. *"Surrender Unto Me": An Overview of the Bhagavad-Gita* (Vrindavan, India: VIHE Publications, 1997).

Dasa, Rohininandana. "Bhagavad Gita: A Book of Violence?" *Back to Godhead* 24(10) (October 1989): 20–33.

Dharma, Krishna. *Mahabharata: The Greatest Spiritual Epic of All Time* (Badger, CA: Torchlight Publishing, 1999).

De, S. K. "The Vedic and the Epic Krsna." *Indian Historical Quarterly* 18 (1942): 297–301.

Flood, Gavin. *An Introduction to Hinduism* (New York: Cambridge University Press, 1996).

———, ed. *The Blackwell Companion to Hinduism* (UK: Blackwell Publishing, 2003).

Gandhi, M. K. *M. K. Gandhi Interprets the Bhagavadgita* (New Delhi: Orient Paperbacks, n.d.).

Goswami, Srila Bhakti Raksaka Sridhara Deva. *Srimad Bhagavad-Gita: The Hidden Treasure of the Sweet Absolute* (Nadiya, West Bengal, India: Sri Chaitanya Saraswat Math, 1985).

Hawley, John Stratton. "Krishna's Cosmic Victories." *Journal of the American Academy of Religion* (1979): 210–221.

Herman, A. L. *A Brief Introduction to Hinduism* (Boulder, CO: Westview Press, 1991).

Hirst, Jacqueline. "Upholding the World: Dharma in the Bhagavadgita," in Julius Lipner, ed., *The Fruits of Our Desiring: An Enquiry into the Ethics of the Bhagavadgita for Our Times* (Calgary, Canada: Bayeux Arts, Inc., 1997).

Hudson, Dennis. "Arjuna's Sin: Thoughts on Bhagavad-Gita in its Epic Context." *The Journal of Vaishnava Studies* 4(3) (Summer 1996): 65–84.

Kapoor, Jagdish Chander. *Bhagavad-Gita: An International Bibliography of 1787–1979 Imprints* (New York: Garland Publishing Company, 1983).

Katz, Ruth. *Arjuna in the Mahabharata* (SC: University of South Carolina Press, 1989).

Kinsley, David. "Without Krsna There Is No Song." *History of Religions* 12(2) (1972): 149–180.

Klostermaier, Klaus. *In the Paradise of Krishna: Hindu and Christian Seekers* (Philadelphia, PA: Westminster, 1969).

———. Second edition. *A Survey of Hinduism* (Albany, New York: State University of New York Press, 1994).

Maharaja, Sri Srimad Bhaktivedanta Narayana, *Srimad Bhagavad-Gita* (Mathura, U.P., India: Gaudiya Vedanta Samiti, 2000).

———. *The Essence of Bhagavad-Gita* (Mathura, U.P., India: Gaudiya Vedanta Publications, 2000).

Majumdar, Bimanbehari. *Krsna in History and Legend* (Calcutta, India: University of Calcutta, 1969).

Masson, J. L. "The Childhood of Krsna: Some Psychoanalytic Observations." *Journal of the American Oriental Society* 94(4) (1974): 454–459.

Matchett, Freda. *Krsna: Lord or Avatara: The Relationship between Krsna and Visnu* (London: Curzon, 2001).

Miller, Barbara Stoler, trans. *The Bhagavad-Gita: Krishna's Counsel in Time of War* (New York: Bantam Books, 1986).

Minor, Robert. *Bhagavad-Gita: An Exegetical Commentary* (Columbia, MO: South Asia Books, 1982).

———. Ed. *Modern Indian Interpreters of the Bhagavad Gita* (Albany, NY: State University of New York Press, 1986).

Mitchell, Stephen. *Bhagavad Gita: A New Translation* (New York: Harmony Books, 2000).

Powell, Barbara. *Windows into the Infinite: A Guide to the Hindu Scriptures* (Fremont, CA: Asian Humanities Press, 1996).

Prabhavananda, Swami, and Isherwood, Christopher. *Bhagavad Gita: The Song of God* (Hollywood, CA: Vedanta Press, 1987, reprint).

Prabhupada, A. C. Bhaktivedanta Swami. *Bhagavad-Gita As It Is* (New York: Macmillan, 1972, reprint). See 1968 edition for Thomas Merton's Foreword, "The Significance of the Bhagavad-Gita."

———. *The Science of Self-Realization* (Los Angeles, CA: The Bhaktivedanta Book Trust, 1977).

———. *Krsna: The Supreme Personality of Godhead* (Los Angeles, CA: The Bhaktivedanta Book Trust, 2003, reprint).

Preciado-Solis, Benjamin. *The Krsna Cycle in the Puranas* (Delhi, India: Motilal Banarsidass, 1984).

Resnick, Howard. "The Supremacy of Vishnu/Krishna in the Mahabharata." *The Journal of Vaishnava Studies* 4(3) (Summer 1996): 5–21.

Robinson, Catherine A. *Interpretations of the Bhagavad-Gita and Images of the Hindu Tradition* (London: Routledge, 2006).

Rosen, Steven J. *Archeology and the Vaishnava Tradition: The Pre-Christian Roots of Krishna Worship* (Calcutta, India: Firma KLM Private, 1989).

———. *Vaisnavism: Contemporary Scholars Discuss the Gaudiya Tradition.* Ed., Foreword by Edward C. Dimock (New York: FOLK Books 1992; reprint, Delhi, India: Motilal Banarsidass, 1994).

———. *The Reincarnation Controversy: Uncovering the Truth in the World Religions* (Badger, CA: Torchlight Publishing, 1997).

———. *Gita on the Green: The Mystical Tradition Behind Bagger Vance* (New York: Continuum international, 2000).

———. Ed. *Holy War: Violence and the Bhagavad Gita* (Hampton, VA: Deepak Heritage Books, 2002).

———. *Holy Cow: The Hare Krishna Contribution to Vegetarianism and Animal Rights* (New York: Lantern Books, 2004).

———. *Essential Hinduism* (Westport, CT. Praeger Publishers, 2006).

———. *Black Lotus: The Spiritual Journey of an Urban Mystic* (Washington, DC: Hari-Nama Press, 2007).

Sargeant, Winthrop. *The Bhagavad Gita* (Albany, NY: State University of New York Press, 1984).

Schweig, Graham. *Bhagavad Gita: The Beloved Lord's Secret Love Song* (San Francisco, CA: Harper San Francisco, 2007).

Sharan, Mahesh Kumar. *The Bhagavad-Gita and Hindu Sociology* (Delhi, India: Bharat Bharati Bhandar, 1977).

Sharma, Arvind. *The Hindu Gita: Ancient and Classical Interpretations of the Bhagavadgita* (La Salle, IL: Open Court, 1986).

Sharpe, Eric J. *The Universal Gita* (La Salle, IL: Open Court, 1985).

Strohmeier, John, ed. *The Bhagavad Gita According to Gandhi* (Berkeley, CA: Berkeley Hills Books, 2000).

Tigunait, Pandit Rajmani. *Yoga on War and Peace* (Honesdale, PA: The Himalayan International Institute, 1991).

Tripurari, Swami. *The Bhagavad Gita: Its Feeling and Philosophy* (San Rafael, CA: Mandala Publishing Group, 2001).

Trivedi, Mark. *Mohandas Gandhi: The Man and His Vision* (Calcutta, India: Time Publications, 1968).

Upadhyaya, K.N. "The Bhagavad-Gita on War and Peace." *Philosophy East and West* 19 (April 2, 1969).

Van Buitenen, J. A. B. *The Bhagavadgita in the Mahabharata* (Chicago, IL: University of Chicago Press, 1981).

Wolpert, Stanley. *India* (Berkeley, CA: University of California Press, 1991).

Woodham, Carl E. *Bhagavad Gita: The Song Divine.* Badger, CA: Torchlight Publishing, 2000).

Zaehner, R. C. *Hinduism* (Oxford: Oxford University Press, 1966, reprint).

———. *The Bhagavad-Gita* (Oxford: Clarendon Press, 1969).

Index

About the Author

STEVEN J. ROSEN is the author of numerous books, including several volumes on the Bhagavad Gita, such as Gita on the Green: The Mystical Tradition Behind Bagger Vance (Continuum International, 2000) and Holy War: Violence and the Bhagavad Gita (Deepak Heritage Books, 2002). He is also the author of Essential Hinduism (Praeger, 2006) and the founding editor of the Journal of Vaishnava Studies.